M000087725

Have Laptop, Will Travel

HAVE LAPTOP, WILL TRAVEL

Memoirs of a Digital Nomad

Philip Nicozisis

Copyright © 2019 The Vegan Manifesto LLC
All rights reserved. No part of this book may be used or reproduced in any manner whatsoever without prior written consent of the authors, except as provided by the United States of America copyright law.

Published by Best Seller Publishing®, Pasadena, CA
Best Seller Publishing® is a registered trademark
Printed in the United States of America.
ISBN 978-1-090624-44-4

This publication is designed to provide accurate and authoritative information with regard to the subject matter covered. It is sold with the understanding that the publisher is not engaged in rendering legal, accounting, or other professional advice. If legal advice or other expert assistance is required, the services of a competent professional should be sought. The opinions expressed by the authors in this book are not endorsed by Best Seller Publishing® and are the sole responsibility of the author rendering the opinion.

For more information, please write:
Best Seller Publishing®
1346 Walnut Street, #205
Pasadena, CA 91106
or call 1(626) 765 9750
Toll Free: 1(844) 850-3500
Visit us online at: www.BestSellerPublishing.org

Dedication

This book is dedicated to my parents. Thank you, Mom and Dad, for believing in me ... most of the time. Dad, I'm so lucky that you were born before me ;)

Contents

A Life-Changing Decision

"Two roads diverged in a wood, and I — I took the one less traveled by, and that has made all the difference."

ROBERT FROST

With my 50th birthday around the corner, I had it all. Or, so I thought. As the saying goes, "If you're lucky enough to be born in America, you're lucky enough," and I was lucky that way. In the years leading up to this point, I had succeeded in creating a commercial real estate business, and I was involved in a rich portfolio of activities and travel. I lived in a beautiful waterfront condo in West Palm Beach, Florida. I wasn't married. I had no pets or children. It was me, myself, and I. I spent my time recording music, scuba diving, socializing, traveling, meditating, and practicing yoga and Pilates. For the previous eight years, I had also been a dedicated vegan and had begun to speak professionally about the topic in between business deals and galas.

Essentially, I was a bachelor living life on my terms. Every day was like Saturday night, and every Saturday night was like New Year's Eve. Yet, when I crawled into bed each night, I knew deep down there were frontiers that still needed exploring; namely, those of my own soul. I had a deep longing to get out of my comfort zone and reach for the next level of a life well lived.

In May 2017, I was sitting in my corner office on Clematis Street in downtown West Palm Beach completing a bit of paperwork. As usual, my desk looked like a bomb went off. My work style has always been organized chaos. My way has been successful, though, and it's the wash-rinse-repeat cycle of office chores that gives me a sense of satisfaction. On this particular day, I was weeding through the mundane work, when my attention was diverted by Facebook: the ultimate time-suck. Mindlessly scrolling through the newsfeed cluttered with strangers' birthdays, vegan food porn, pointless dog videos, and cheesy engagement photos, I came across an intriguing ad:

> Dreaming of work *and* travel? What if you could live in a new city every month for a year? Keep your job. See the world. Leave the planning to us. You don't have to choose between work and travel. You can do both.

That sounded cool! So, I clicked through to a website of a company called Remote Year to investigate further. On the homepage, I learned that the organization brings together independent professionals from across the globe to spend a year working and traveling: 12 months, 12 cities. I was floored by the idea! I could not imagine anything better to do with my 50th year on earth than to see the world this way. Even better, I would be traveling the world with equally adventurous professionals while connecting with local cultures and business ecosystems. I would be forming lifelong personal and professional relationships along the way.

And where, pray tell, did they want to send me? Just about everywhere! I scrolled through the proposed itinerary:

Split, Croatia – October 2017
Prague, Czech Republic – November 2017
Lisbon, Portugal – December 2017
Kyoto, Japan – January 2018

Chiang Mai, Thailand - February 2018
Kuala Lumpur, Malaysia - March 2018
Buenos Aires, Argentina - April 2018
Córdoba, Argentina - May 2018
Lima, Peru - June 2018
Medellín, Colombia - July 2018
Bogotá, Colombia - August 2018
Mexico City, Mexico - September 2018

WOWZERS! My mind went reeling, and I was blown away over and over again by the notion. I had never thought of doing anything like this, and now the universe was handing me exactly what I wanted on a silver platter.

Call me old-fashioned, or non-millennial, but this was the first time I had ever heard the term, "digital nomad." I had been balancing a lifestyle of traveling, building, and maintaining my business for most of my adult life, and now here was a term that accurately described me: I had, in fact, been digitally nomadic for the past 15 years. True, I ran 99 percent of my business obligations from a fixed location in downtown West Palm Beach, but the real estate was located here, there, and everywhere. For the next few days, I went through my mental checklist repeatedly, reasoning through the logistics on how to bring this opportunity to fruition.

I was lucky to have a father who dabbled in real estate over the years and incessantly urged his kids to invest in it. I had built my commercial real estate business to the point where I owned and managed a collection of 29 commercial properties across five states. After getting smacked down hard during the near-collapse of the economy in America in 2008, I had rebuilt my holdings over the last ten years and had once again reached a level of comfort and stability in my finances. Fortunately, most of my tenants were national companies with generous leases that favored the landlord—me. And helping me maintain a smooth enterprise, I had a team of trusted contractors, handymen, landscapers, property managers, realtors, attorneys, architects, and other third-party operators. I had also established my reputation as a good borrower and sponsor for loan transactions in connection with my properties. The business was operating well, and with online banking and electronic signature apps, I knew I could make this outside-the-box idea of working while traveling, work!

Of course, I still had some doubts. Would I have access to decent vegan food? Would I be able to practice my daily routine that usually included yoga, Pilates, or spinning? What if the living accommodations didn't meet my standards? What if I got sick or injured? What if I were to fall in love with someone on the other side of the world? Wasn't I too old to join a group of tech-savvy millennials? And what do you pack for an entire year of traveling the world? What the hell does that look like?

Who was I kidding? I was Philip Nicozisis! I wasn't going to doubt myself and talk myself out of this idea. I knew I wouldn't gain anything more by hanging around Palm Beach for another season of black-tie charity events and air kisses. When I really thought it through, I had nothing holding me back. On making the decision, I felt a flow of new-found energy pulsing through my body. This was my chance to get out of my comfort zone, scuba dive in new oceans, ski on foreign snow, and perhaps share my knowledge of veganism around the world ... and, all the while, continuing to care for my business.

The decision was made: I was going to apply to Remote Year. My main concern was announcing the news to my parents and sister. Coming from a tight-knit Greek clan, I already knew how they would react. Some decisions I had made in the past were initially frowned upon by my family, but, in time, my choices came to be celebrated, supported, and even adopted by them. For example, my family could not wrap their heads around my decision to enroll in the three-week Life Transformation Program (LTP) at the foremost healing center in the world, the Hippocrates Health Institute. It was there that I learned how to adopt a vibrant, vegan lifestyle. That was eight years ago, and by 2017, my parents had fully embraced the vegan lifestyle too, and following in my footsteps, they completed the Hippocrates LTP for optimal health. Being all too familiar with their standard operating procedure, though, I fully expected them to weigh in negatively on my decision to travel the world for a year.

I finally got the nerve to call my mom first. She was utterly blown away and kept repeating, "I don't know what to say. I don't know what to say. I don't know what to say." It took my dad about a week to hit me head-on about my travel plans. He asked me questions like, "What's bothering you so much that you have to leave for a year?" And, "What's wrong with you that you have to make a decision like this?" Within no time, I got a call from my sister asking me if I had lost my mind. I felt hurt at first, but I had expected things to play out this way. As George Bernard Shaw once said, "All progress depends on unreasonable people." I never thought of myself as unreasonable, but somehow my being *unreasonable* seemed to fit these particular circumstances. But still, I had no reason *not* to go! My family may not have agreed with my decision, but I knew it was the right one for me.

Before my year-long expedition, I threw a blowout party to celebrate the big Five-O and my departure. It was hard for me to fathom that I was half a century old, but overall, I had never felt more youthful. After days of being decorated, my condo's rooftop was transformed into the theme of *The Great Gatsby*; it was like stepping out of a time machine into the 1920s. Food and champagne flowed into the wee hours of the morning, and the karaoke tunes only paused when my dear friends took turns giving speeches. Oh, those speeches! Their heartfelt words reminded me of my deep roots and history with some very special and talented people who, like me, were trying to blaze their own meaningful trails during their short time on this earth. After all, we are here for just a short while.

That night we made memories to last a lifetime. Though I would miss them all, I knew that the world had great things in store for me beyond the Palm Beach bubble. I could hear the universe whispering secrets about what was to come, although I couldn't quite decipher all of it. My optimism was high. I was ready to throw myself into a year of unfamiliar places, food, experiences, and, hopefully, romance. I was ready for liftoff.

CHAPTER 1
Split, Croatia

"He who is outside the door has already a good part of his journey behind him."

DUTCH PROVERB

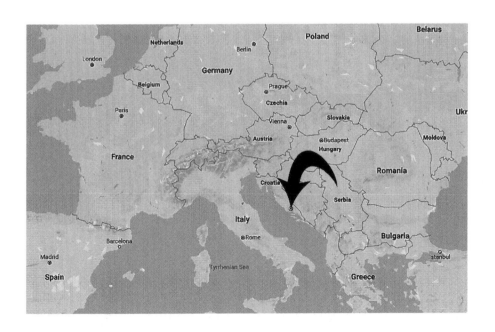

I woke up in a daze around 2:00 a.m. Where was I? It took me a minute to shake myself out of my stupor and remind myself that I was lying in the bed of my new studio apartment in Split, Croatia. A combination of flying for 15 sleepless hours (despite being in first class) and the unreasonably long layover in Germany meant that I entered month one of Remote Year (RY) in a state of exhaustion. Good old jet lag.

Realizing the time, I forced myself to catch a few more Z's. When I awoke again at 6:00 a.m., I was greeted by the sun's ritual rise over the sparkling Adriatic Sea. A few of Croatia's 2,000 islands dotted the horizon. There were incredible views from my waterfront condo back in Florida, but the view from my new home was like a dream.

> **Phil Phact:** The phenomenon of moonlight reflecting off a body of water in a road-like pattern is referred to as "mangata" in Swedish. It was a sight I enjoyed on many a night as I stood on the balcony of my West Palm Beach waterfront home. By a stroke of synchronicity, the name given by Remote Year to my merry group of travelers was *Mangata*—talk about foreshadowing!

I spent my first day in Split unpacking, napping, and settling in. It wasn't until the evening that I met the 48 other digital nomads of Mangata, or "Mangos" as we came to call ourselves. The plan was to meet at a waterfront bar called Plan B, located across the street from our workspace, named WIP (an acronym for "work in progress"). The high-energy evening was full of drinking, small talk, medium talk, and first impressions.

I enthusiastically introduced myself to everybody one after the other. More than once I came away thinking, *Wow, I really connect with this person. We're going to become great friends during this next year.* However, by traveling month after month with these fellow nomads, I would come to know their personalities in a very real way. The people who made the best first impressions did not always turn out to be the friendliest traveling companions for the long haul. Over time, I picked up on what brought certain people joy or what triggered them into anger, and I gained an intimate view of their quirky behaviors. I mean, you really get to *know* people when you travel with them! For some reason I am unable to hold grudges, but this gift was definitely put to the test as the journey rolled on. Traveling for 12 months with 48 people you don't know turned out to be a bizarre social experiment in many ways. I bet it would make for a hit reality TV show!

One of my Remote Year brothers confided in me that, at first, he was very focused on getting everyone to like him. I connected with him on that truthful front, realizing that I had taken the same approach. After all, it is human nature to crave that sense of belonging. I had to remind myself, though, that such validation-seeking behavior was not conducive to making meaningful and lasting relationships, especially while traveling the world in close quarters. I committed to just *being myself*, unapologetically, from that point forward.

> **No Philter:** There was not one female that I felt romantically attracted to in Mangata. What a relief... Hello, Tinder!

After the Mangata meet-and-greet at Plan B, about half of us walked over to Diocletian's Palace in Old Town Split and continued the kickoff celebration. The ancient palace was in ruins but still intact enough to house the many tourist shops, restaurants, and hotels that served Split's vibrant tourism industry. There was no clash of the old and the new; rather, Old Town was an intricately constructed maze that weaved both history and modernity into one. While Croatian people identify as Mediterranean Europeans, they also strongly identify as Slavic people who had to crawl out from under communism. What an amazing place to start our journey!

Phil Phact: Diocletian's Palace, a palace built for the Roman emperor of the same name, is now a commercial tourist hub that makes up half of the Old Town area in Split. It is half a mile in length and its highest point is almost 90 feet. Built mostly by slaves, it took more than 10 years to construct. In fact, the word "slave" comes from the people known as *Slavs*, such as the Croatians. Just as many Slavs were sold into slavery as people from Africa, maybe more.

The libertarian side of me couldn't help but notice the irony of my group's bold presence in Old Town that night. Most of the castles and palaces built throughout history were essentially income-redistribution schemes that enriched the rulers of the day. The fact that we were freely partying amongst hundreds of other people in the courtyard of a former Roman emperor's crib and ordering bottles of wine clearly exhibited a change in the human condition. Okay, I get it, not everyone gets to do this, but there was no denying that the post-communist era was seeing huge improvements for people here in Croatia and beyond. Shortly after posting a group shot in the palace's courtyard, my mom texted me that Diocletian was a savage ruler who crucified thousands of Christians. Thanks for the historic buzzkill, Mom! The past is the past, history has been made, and time marches on. My new friends and I were all facing new chapters in our lives. This gave us all the more reason to pop some more corks! It was the perfect way to usher in the future memories we would be making on this incredible year-long odyssey.

It didn't take long for me to balance my work life with my desire to explore this foreign country. I always made sure to knock out my business obligations before hopping into an Uber to discover new corners of Old Town or Croatia's beautiful coastline. Every day was perfectly sunny. We had about 30 days of sunshine out of 30. This was typical for Croatia, apparently.

My daily routine began with a five-minute walk from my studio apartment to our coworking space along the Split waterfront. It was the perfect way to start the day before getting down to business. Almost every week, Cindy, my secretary back at home, sent me both my business and personal mail via overnight delivery. Once received, I settled into a great spot at the WIP, steamed up an almond milk latté, and plowed through the stack of paperwork. I felt so high-tech when I scanned some signed documents to my phone and emailed them right back to her. I remember thinking, *Thank God! This is gonna work.* With whatever couldn't be scanned, like bills and government correspondence, I prepared a bundle that would be sent back via express mail. Lots of my workflow, however, could be facilitated through email, text, and phone (sometimes, there's nothing like a good old-fashioned phone call).

The paperwork part of my operation became a little joke with a few of the Mangos. They walked by with a little giggle in their throats, as I was tearing through the mail stack and sorting papers into smaller stacks. I realized that these "Young Turks" put the *digital* in digital nomads; it was as if they had never *seen* paperwork before! Though I had a few more years of experience on them, I had to admit that they did know their way around the technology world. I gleaned quite a bit of tech know-how and travel hacks from my fellow nomads over our year together.

Phil Pheelings: During my first job at a shop in my father's floor-covering chain, I had a fantastic but very tough boss named Bob Voris. Bob was a born salesman and fond of saying, "STPW!" which meant "Screw the Paperwork." I learned a lot from him in my formative years as a young adult. May he rest in peace.

The WIP coworking space was everyone's favorite of all that were to follow in the next 12 months. It was a stunning modern facility with floor-to-ceiling glass doors and windows that provided a glorious view of the beach. The WIP workspace was divided: one part was a silent work area, and the other part was where talking and socializing were allowed. In the noisy section was a classic Italian-made espresso coffee machine adorned with lots of chrome. The coffee was *redonkulously* delicious, so I couldn't stop myself from hopping on the coffee train. But my favorite detail inside this workspace was a quote scrawled across the wall that read: PUNCH TODAY IN THE FACE. Because I often used a voice-to-text method to write and send emails, I always worked in the noisy section. I grew to love working here. It allowed me to socialize with my new "tramily," the Remote Year term for "traveling family." From this point forth, for better and for worse, we would be a tramily!

Aside from facilitating a functional work environment for digital nomads, Remote Year provided us a wonderful program in each city that was hosted by up to five local staff members who were eager to show off their city. They organized numerous field trips and activities. They answered questions and helped with our issues—from recommending local hot spots, to assisting with apartment problems, to helping us plan weekend outings. Month after month, a new set of wonderful humans in the city team became part of the tramily, and new and lasting connections were made.

To kick off the year, Split's city team hosted a Remote Year orientation. It was like the first day of summer camp, only more profound. Travis King, from Remote Year HQ, led the orientation. One of the five original RY employees, Travis was now one of more than a hundred who were helping shepherd eight tramilies around the world simultaneously. Travis is one of those guys who is born to do his job, and his high energy and passion for bringing people together to promote self-exploration permeated the room. He tried to articulate what the year was going to look like, warning us about the potential highs and lows that we Mangos would experience, which turned out to be quite accurate. After all, we weren't just joyriding as tourists: as digital nomads we were holding down jobs via our laptops, and all the while pushing the envelope with city tours, side trips, and some hard partying. Lost phones and broken bones were bound to be in mix, for starters.

Travis warned the Mangos about FOMO (fear of missing out). I knew that everyone, including myself, would often feel we had to attend every event, see every attraction, and go out every night in order to avoid the dreaded FOMO. Doing it all, though, would have been impossible. Our bodies had not yet acclimated to so much change: new environments, new friends, new ways of conducting our businesses. Travis's warning was a pleasant reminder to treat my own mind and body with gentleness and rest when needed. And besides, I reminded myself that anyone who wasn't shadowing me was the one who should fear the FOMO!

In one orientation activity, we wrote a postcard to ourselves that would eventually be "mailed" to us after our final month in Mexico City. A fellow Mango, Chris, told me he wrote a small tribute of thanks to himself. Wow. I couldn't remember if I had ever stopped to thank myself for anything. This wasn't the first time that the young folk in the tramily would teach an old guy like me a new piece of wisdom. Two of Remote Year's core values are "empathy" and "being present." The Remote Year program strives to create an environment that not only expands our capacity to care for others but also encourages us to embrace awareness and gratitude in each moment. Remote Year further encouraged us to inspire one another and be open to new perspectives.

There were some spectacularly talented and skilled people in my program. Chadwick was a science fiction novelist with a growing monthly subscriber base of 15,000 people. Mitch was an electrical engineer who designed computer chips for well-known smartphone companies. Andrew was a Hollywood screenwriting agent who recently became independent. We had graphic designers, project managers, computer coders, photographers, videographers, and entrepreneurs. A few Mangos had recently quit their jobs in order to start their own businesses and to travel the world. Several others were granted permission by their companies to proceed with their work obligations while living and working remotely. The main idea of Remote Year is, essentially, that work and travel do not have to be mutually exclusive: they can be collaboratively inclusive. As the months went on, I gained so many friends in different time zones from around the world, that when I headed off to bed, I had to put my phone on a "do not disturb" setting so that it would not ping throughout the night. (Besides, it's a good habit to turn off our cellphones or put them on airplane mode in order to reduce the amount of radiation we're exposed to.)

For each of the 12 months of Remote Year, we Mangos were offered the chance to participate in activities called "tracks," consisting of activities curated by each city team. The tracks were a window into the heart and soul of a city and beyond anything a tourist would see or even know about. In week two of my month in Split, I was introduced to my first track experience. The city team arranged for Milena Šijan, a member of Mountain Rescuers, a highly respected Croatian non-governmental organization, to speak about her successful climb of Mt. Everest. In 2009, Milena fronted the first ever Croatian all-female expedition to the summit. She spoke to us as if we were her friends, regaling us with stories of endurance, struggles with nature, and of failures leading to success. I was proud just to be standing in the same room with her, knowing that 25 percent of the people who climb Everest never make it back alive. After hearing about Milena's mountaineering, suddenly my scuba diving adventures didn't seem so dangerous.

Milena said, "The most important part of the journey is to listen to your body. Eat well and drink lots of water as often as you can, and don't push yourself to impossible limits." Her simple words of wisdom resonated with me: It is important to know and honor your edge and respect your boundaries.

Phil Phact: More female than male Croatians have climbed Mount Everest.

For our second track later that month, some fellow Mangos and I closed our laptops at the WIP and headed across town to the port. The port was home to the renowned Brodosplit Shipyard, and we walked for what seemed like miles through the sprawling factory. Brodosplit is the largest shipyard in the country, covering an area of 560,000 square meters. The shipyard indirectly influences the daily lives of the people in Split, and its impact is felt even more in Croatia's relatively young free market.

The free market in Croatia began after the fall of communism in 1991, so it is still in its infancy. Nevertheless, many of the country's workers now live in an environment where their efforts must be tied to results. This shipyard, as a case in point, used to be owned by the state but was sold to private interests in 2013. Work relations between the union employees and the new, private management are still strained (no surprise), since the workers liked it better when the shipyard was state-owned. From my perspective, after a lifelong study of economic systems, it's not a stretch to assume that life under communism encouraged a mediocre work ethic.

Our guide at the shipyard pointed out that young people do not normally seek factory jobs in Croatia. Rather, they were leaving Croatia for economic opportunities elsewhere. Croatia was dealing with a population drain and losing its young people to other countries.

Phil Phact: Who knew Croatia punches above its weight in the production of mega sea vessels? Over the past 10 years, the Brodosplit Shipyard has delivered more than 450 ships, of which 80 percent were bought by foreign buyers. Recently, the largest luxury yacht ever built in the factory was launched. The shipyard's biggest competition comes from China, whom they accuse of charging artificially low prices.

On another day here in this waterfront paradise, the digital nomads boarded speed boats and went island-hopping around the coast of Split. You can't tour these islands without stopping at the magnificent Blue Cave. We entered the Blue Cave, or Grotto, between 11:00 a.m. and 12 noon—an ideal time when the sunlight reflects through the water that flows over the white sand floor of the cave, creating a surreal aquamarine light. The Blue Cave was formed by erosion from the consistent crashing of waves against the limestone rock. The cave itself is about 24 meters long. The man-made entrance is only 1.5 meters high ... in other words, you'd better duck!

Next stop was a private island and vineyard, where a wonderful couple curated a meal for us from their garden. But my favorite island stop was Hvar, where we climbed to the top of an old fortress and did some wine tasting. From that perch, I could see beyond the small town to the expansive Adriatic Sea. This perfect day was a blur of joy, but I knew I'd be returning to the charming island of Hvar again. Later, I jumped on Airbnb to see what was available by the month. I fantasize a lot about staying in a new place that I love.

One fine sunny day, which is every day in Split, I attended the Global Opportunities Beyond Borders conference for entrepreneurs, where six successful visiting entrepreneurs (based out of Chicago) led a series of three workshops: "Idea to Prototype," "Entering the Market," and "Scale and Growth."

The conference was interesting enough, but it was not in my wheelhouse of expertise. Even so, a fire in me was reignited that afternoon. As I watched the attendees interact with the panelists, I reminisced about the early stages of my path to becoming a vegan activist. I was taught the vegan lifestyle at the Hippocrates Health Institute, where I studied to become a health educator, and for the previous four years, my passion project was teaching people about the benefits of living a vegan lifestyle: in addition to the ethical, environmental, societal, and health benefits of this lifestyle, nothing tastes as good as vegan feels! This conference inspired me to reach new heights in sharing the vegan message. I had spent years building a strong foundation and reputation in the South Florida vegan community by delivering numerous lectures and speeches, and now it was time for me to upgrade from regional to international. I vowed in that moment that I would use Remote Year's platform to evangelize the tenets of veganism to as many people as I could reach, and this vow gave my trip an even greater purpose. Remote Year was no longer just about making me a better person: it was about making a better world.

I can recall a revelation I had during an Ayahuasca ceremony I attended just a few months prior to my year abroad. (I'll tell you more about Ayahuasca ceremonies when we get to my month in Peru). During that ceremony, the Mother Spirit lovingly commanded me to go out into the world and share the vegan message. I had the blessing from the Universe herself! And, yes, my Creator was revealed as a feminine spirit.

> **Phil Pheelings:** The Mother Spirit also blessed and encouraged me to forgive myself for past wrongs and to let go of some previously unsuccessful relationships. Emotionally metabolizing the past gave me a clean slate to go forward with on this incredible voyage of discovery.

Remaining true—and deepening my commitment—to veganism was important to me, and a close second was maintaining my yoga practice. Thankfully, several other people in my group shared my passion for yoga, and within the first week of arriving in Split, we found a yoga studio located within walking distance from the WIP. The classes were affordable, and the instructor, Elle, was outstanding. I got so much out of the first class with Elle that I hired her for private lessons (which still cost less than a group class in the States), and with her help that month, I maintained a steady practice of hatha (physical) yoga.

My relationship with Elle evolved into something much more meaningful than just yoga instructor and student: she became one of my dearest Croatian friends. She was strong-willed, exotic, and attractive, but our relationship stayed purely platonic. She was a long-time vegetarian, so she understood my vegan lifestyle. Because I couldn't get Hvar island off my mind, I chartered a speedboat to take Elle island-hopping. Once again, the day was heavenly. The temperature was perfect, the sun was glistening across the water, and the smell of sea salt in the air was intoxicating. I could feel a boost in my mental and physical health. My mind and body felt rejuvenated by both nature's salt therapy that emanated from crystal clear, shimmering waters, and the budding friendship with Elle.

Phil Phact: The benefits of salt therapy, known as halotherapy, have been known for thousands of years. Salt vapors boost the immune system, and since all health is reliant on the strength of the immune system, this is no small thing. The salt miners almost never got sick!

After a day on the Adriatic Sea, we headed back to the mainland of Split in time for dinner with a local vegan group called the Vegans of Dalmatia. I was back inside the imposing castle of Diocletian at the Wine House restaurant. Eating at the chef's table with fellow vegans topped off an incredible day! Everyone there was so friendly, and they all took interest in who I was, where I was from, and what brought me to Split. We exchanged stories about our lives, countries and cultures, in near-perfect English.

One thing we had in common was the political divide that seemed to be raging within our respective countries. Just like the divide between Democrats and Republicans in America, Croatians have their own political rivalries. Like zombies, the communists will not die, and they constantly agitate for state control of the economy. Transitioning from a centrally planned economy to free-market capitalism was a miracle in itself, but there was still so much work to be done. Fortunately, many of my new friends seemed to be doing well working in the tourism industry.

As if by kismet, I was scheduled to give my signature presentation, "The Case for Vegan," to the Mangos later that weekend, and now the Vegans of Dalmatia were invited too! I was well prepared, though slightly nervous about the attendance because my Google Calendar invite was somehow deleted. Fellow Mango Victor, who would end up being one of my closest friends of all time, saved me from my tech challenge and got it posted. In the end, I gave my talk to about 40 wellness seekers from the local vegan group and the tramily.

I pride myself on the fact that my presentations evolve to keep up with my constant quest to make the vegan message stronger and more accessible. And you can always count on me to throw in a little humor to break the ice. (I always have a cheesy joke or two up my sleeve, such as, "How do you know someone's a vegan? Don't worry they'll tell you!" or "How many people here are vegan? Please raise your hands. How many of you are pre-vegan? Please raise your hands. How many of you never raise your hands no matter *what?!*" For some reason, people laugh pretty hard at that second one.) I believe I delivered one of my best performances yet that night in Split. As if I were casting stones into the ocean, I sensed that the ripples of knowledge were sent and received. Forty-five minutes later, the WIP became the site of a fun after-party. During the party, my mom called to say hello, and before I knew what was happening, my phone was being passed from Mango to Mango. They said such nice things about their new friend Phil: it was all so sweet. Mangata as a cohesive unit was off to a good start. This event kicked off what would become my international vegan tour.

A week later, Animal Friends Croatia, a nonprofit animal rights organization, invited me to speak in the capital city of Zagreb. The organization was celebrating a recent legislative win that prohibited euthanasia for both cats and dogs. I rented a car and set out on a mountainous four-hour drive to Zagreb, with a fellow Mango named Shelly who needed to reach the U.S. consulate and have her home refinance papers signed and notarized.

We arrived at the Animal Friends office a little carsick but on time. The staff was overflowing with hospitality. We were served a full vegan spread, which included falafel, tempeh, tofu, and veggie burgers. It wasn't exactly a green and clean Hippocrates-style meal, but I would school them about that later! Essentially, the Hippocrates diet is vegan, raw, and whole-food based. It can be summed up in one word: nutritarian. Having said that, I am a vegan *human*, not a saint, so it's not always easy for me to resist eating cooked foods like veggie burgers and French fries when I'm feeling naughty.

> **Phil Phact:** The Hippocrates Health Institute's prescribed plant-based diet is all about properly fueling the body for optimal life force. Their dietary and lifestyle recommendations come from studying the healthiest humans throughout history and 65 years of their own research, leading to tried-and-true health transformation for hundreds of thousands of people who have gone through their programs.

At the Animal Friends event, I went a little over my 45-minute time limit, speaking for one full hour. I had so much that I wanted to convey, and my thoughts were flowing, so I just let them pour out. Afterward, many members of the audience, numbering over a hundred in total, told me how grateful they were for my talk. It did not surprise me that many of them had never heard some of the vegan technicalities that I shared; while a lot of people are vegan, not too many people know the Hippocrates version of being vegan. The well-known vegan activist and rapper IFEEL and the vegan bodybuilder Mislav Skrepnik were among those who attended my talk. Mislav is a true bodybuilding god who appears to be chiseled from brick, and Animal Friends had featured him in a billboard campaign around Zagreb with "Plant Power" as the tagline.

I called Mislav out in the middle of my talk and said that it looked like he ate furniture, not plants. The audience laughed heartily.

Shelly and I drove back to Split the next day, and I have to say it was one of my favorite road trips ever. The roadway coiled through the Croatian mountains. The views literally took our breath away, and our ears popped or clogged up with each ascent and descent. In Florida, road trips are quite boring; my State is flat as a table and the roads follow a grid. There's not much to look at.

Once I returned from Zagreb, I found myself back in a routine of regular work hours, yoga, and free time spent hanging out with Elle and the Remote Year tramily. One day following a yoga session, Elle drove us to Up Café, our usual vegan spot. On the way, she stopped to put gas in the car, and I stared in disbelief as she put only about $1.50 in the tank. When I questioned her about the small amount of gas, she abruptly retorted, "We laugh at you Americans who are so concerned over who is gay and who is white or black. Over here, we are just trying to make enough money to put gas in the car." I was taken aback by the dressing-down, but I could clearly see that her comment was an expression of pent-up frustration that everyday life is still a struggle for most Croatians. I never forgot that moment. After that, I kept my mouth shut and quietly thanked my lucky stars.

No Philter: Elle's perspective affirmed some of my own views about how the world works. I have a strong opinion against centrally planned economies, wherever they may exist, but especially as it relates to America. Our friends on the political left are often lusting for the same state-run, centralized, planned economies that are now on the ash heap of recent history. Croatia's former economy was a good example of what many people on the American Left are currently marching towards, whether they know it or not. Elle and the rest of her country want a better life that can only come from the free market system.

After our lunch, I grabbed an Uber ride back to my apartment. With Elle's comment about Americans still lingering in my mind, I was enticed to ask the Uber driver about his experience under the communist system. According to him, before 1991, the system wasn't pure communism, but rather a blend of the East and West socialist systems. He believed the old system was better, and I could tell that he sincerely missed the way things used to be. I confessed that I supported the idea of the free market and explained why it is the best economic environment for innovation and helping the common man attain a higher standard of living. Surprisingly, the Uber driver agreed with my free market speech, though maybe he was just kissing butt for a good rating on the Uber app. Nevertheless, we both ended our transaction with a hand shake and a five-star rating.

That night, the Mangos attended a soccer match between the country's two rival teams, Zagreb vs. Split. The soccer scene was intense. The match ended in a tie with a goal in the last three seconds, but that wasn't the only reason this event kept me on my toes during the entire match. The soccer match displayed some age-old prejudices between the two Croatian regions: according to a local, the people of Zagreb looked down upon the southern Dalmatians in Split, labeling them as lazy, while the people of Split think that the northern Croatians are robot-like.

The shenanigans of the sold-out crowd were probably more interesting than the game itself. The gang chants between opposing sides were thunderous and relentless. I couldn't believe that fans snuck fireworks into the venue and shot them off one after the other throughout the match. The match was stopped more than once due to extensive smoke on the field as the firefighters fervently tried to extinguish the smoldering explosives.

I thought that security had been pretty tight upon entry into the stadium. I saw lipstick and other personal effects being confiscated … but, as I was to find out, fireworks were no problem! There's no telling what kind of riot would have broken out if the Split team had lost. I've attended some crazy sporting events in my time (I'm a Philadelphia

Eagles fan, if you know what I'm saying), but I've never seen any event like this one!

You couldn't help but notice the giant American Confederate flag that was strung across one side of the stadium, that displayed the words "White Boys." To many Americans, this would be considered quite racist. However, considering the historical rivalry between these two teams, the Confederate flag in this context was, in fact, a symbol of rebellion by the southern Dalmatians. White Boys was a reference to the indigenous, spotted white-coat Dalmatian dogs found in southern Croatia. But they had to know what the Confederate flag means to many from across the Atlantic, so at best they were being insensitive. As the month went on, I saw the flag all over town. It was basically their team logo! But the point could be made that Croatians have bigger things to worry about in the here and now. Only 25 years earlier, fathers and uncles had died in the war to overthrow communism and to settle ethnic hatreds, and the effects were still being felt by many. Elle's father, for instance, suffered from PTSD and was disabled as a result of combat in the war.

All things considered, Split was a fantastic place to start the Remote Year craziness. While living there, I learned the finer points of running my business from abroad, living a healthy vegan lifestyle, and initiating some lifelong relationships with unforgettable people. The first steps in this journey of discovery were filled with high hopes and positive interactions all around. I learned so much about the Croatian culture and the nation's past. The sheer beauty of the place will stay with me also. I'll never forget the mountain-to-sea coastline, where the tramily set up our temporary home amid the ghosts of past civilizations, turbulent political systems, and rich history.

I promised myself I would return to Croatia again one day, but now it was time to go: the spirit of adventure was calling us to other foreign lands. If the journey of a thousand miles begins with a single step, in Croatia I took 50 and was ready for more.

Have laptop, will travel!

CHAPTER 2

Prague, Czech Republic

"People who prefer e-books… think that books merely take up space. This is true, but so do your children and Prague and the Sistine Chapel."

JOE QUEENAN

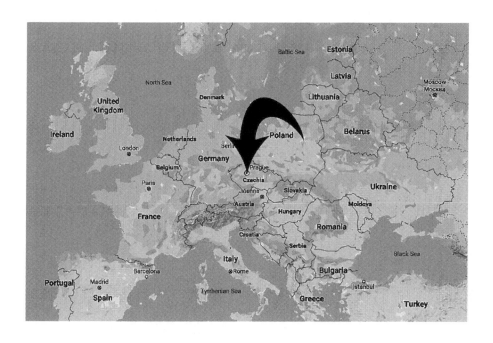

I arrived in Prague utterly exhausted. To fulfil a prior commitment, I had gone on a "side trip" (a term for any traveling outside the Remote Year schedule) to India. The term "side trip" sounds like a rather fun diversion, but this one was INTENSE. I was participating in a "vegangelism" (vegan evangelism) tour with the renowned vegan writer and speaker Dr. Will Tuttle, which involved 15 events in 12 days all over India. The entire trip could be a book in itself, so I won't go into the details here, but suffice it to say I experienced incredible highs, unbelievable lows and, of course, the inevitable Delhi belly. When I got to Prague, I couldn't wait to be among my tribe again and recuperate from all the craziness.

Buh-bye, India! Hel-lo, Prague!

I only slept for about three hours during the 20-hour flight from India, even while lying flat in business class. I barely touched the uninspired airplane food because after being spoiled by my hosts in India, airplane food seemed so unappetizing. Tired, hungry, and dazed, I grabbed my baggage and passed through customs and then, not thinking, headed straight to the taxi information booth to ask where I could find Uber. The man grabbed his crotch and shouted, "Uber is in my balls!" It wasn't a great first impression, but it was pretty dumb of me to ask the taxi people where to get Uber. It's no secret that ride-sharing services like Uber are game-changing competition for the local taxis around the world. It takes away quite a bit of business from the taxi drivers, and it's great for foreign travelers especially. All I have to do is enter an address and that eliminates the difficulty of explaining a destination to a driver. Also, an Uber ride is often cheaper than a taxi, and it has even been proven to be safer (unfortunately, some unscrupulous taxi drivers scam patrons and run rackets with local thieves). There are laws in some countries and cities banning ride-sharing services simply because the taxi cab industry is powerful: crony capitalism at its worst.

When I arrived on November 9, the Mangos had been there for a week and had already settled into their new apartments in three separate neighborhoods across Prague. I felt like I had missed so much. During our orientation in Croatia, Travis King mentioned that one week starts to feel like two months when you're traveling in Remote Year. This was certainly accurate as the rest of the month played out.

For my month in Prague, I had two roommates, Max and Ron. Ron was on a programming team for Microsoft Windows, and Max was a documentary filmmaker who used each city location as a springboard to different locations around the world. For this month, he made a side trip to Dubai for a short film assignment (digital nomads in Remote Year come and go as they please). Remote Year guarantees a private bedroom for all the nomads, but I hadn't lived with roommates since college. That might not have been as much of a problem had the apartment been more accommodating. Three grown men had to share one bathroom. Worse yet, the toilet was basically in the kitchen, behind a door. In another small space across the hall was the shower and sink. Communist-era layout for sure! I was grateful that Max and Ron were two very clean and low-maintenance dudes, and they agreed to allow me to hire a cleaning service that came every Friday to tend to our apartment.

I could already tell that I had a great month ahead of me, but I was still somewhat sluggish from the India trip, and it took me quite a bit of time to settle in. Four blocks from my apartment, I found a great hot yoga studio and a cute organic grocery store. I was eager to get back into my healthy routine, and nourish my mind, body, and soul. India sure did take a toll on me, and the culture that gave the world yoga had, in fact, no yoga studios. I Google-mapped "yoga" in every city we visited in India and always came up empty.

The weather in Prague was perpetually cold with a misty drizzle. Nevertheless, the Mangos agreed that Prague offered more history and architectural beauty than we could have imagined. The Czech culture was shaped by a complex mix of World War II consequences and communism, which resulted in a healthy dose of skepticism and, somehow, warmth that counteracted the cold weather.

Prague's architecture was simply spellbinding. Gothic, Renaissance, and Baroque styles gave the city an otherworldliness.

Throughout the city, many of the multi-colored architectural gems remained intact because the city was not rebuilt like most European capital cities during the 18th or 19th centuries. It's also one of the few cities that was not completely destroyed during the Second World War. Now, in this era of urban redevelopment, there's no way you would want to knock these beauties down: they were already gentrified! Observing my surroundings, it felt like I had traveled back in time. If you take a closer look, though, you'll see that communism left some scars in the architecture where everyday people lived—my own apartment, for example, was directly next to the iconic "TV Tower." It was probably the ugliest structure I had ever seen, a symbol and reminder of the communist era. The Czech people considered it so ugly that its very existence was largely resented. At around 700 feet tall, the television tower had small pods protruding out and an enclosure on the top. The pods and apex looked like GE construction trailers. The entire structure was coated in a dingy grey popcorn finish. Before cable and high-speed internet, the tower was used to transmit antenna signals for televisions. Now it is a tourist attraction with a restaurant at the top.

The buildings and some streets whisper incredible stories, like the Cathedral Church of Saints Cyril and Methodius, known by locals as the "Parachutists Church." It's easy to miss the memorial at the church's front entrance that commemorates a priest and a parachutist who sacrificed their lives in Operation Anthropoid against the Nazi Regime.

If you observe closely while walking through certain neighborhoods of Prague, you will see brick-size plaques embedded into sidewalks that are engraved with names of real people and the dates they were forcibly removed from their homes by the Nazis. They serve as poignant public markers of these former homes of men, women, and children who perished. The idea was conceived and designed by the German artist Gunter Demnig, calling them *Stolpersteine*, meaning "stumbling blocks."

Phil Pheelings: These copper plaques are Holocaust memorials. As I walked these streets, I could feel the spirits of the innocent people who were yanked from their homes, imprisoned, and perhaps sent to an early death. Walking the streets of Prague gives the pedestrian a reminder of some dark history. Never Again. Never Forget.

The coworking space was no less impressive than the city itself. To get there, it was a 25-minute walk past Baroque-style apartment buildings, quaint cafes, and busy public transportation. Just when I thought our coworking space couldn't be any cooler than the WIP in Split, our new workspace proved me wrong—it definitely held its own. Known as K10, the property was formerly the Danish Embassy, and it boasted a classy, antique appearance with old-world embellishments scattered throughout the architecture. The Mangos now shared space with some local small businesses and startups, and I made it a goal to spend a lot of time there during my month in Prague. Just being there made me *want* to be productive.

All work and no play make Phil a dull boy, but with my Tinder dating app, it wasn't long before I was able to make a date with a Czech girl, Jenny. She invited me to visit her city for the weekend, so I took the three-hour train ride and met her in Brno. The train was outdated, but it was a big improvement on the hellish trains I rode in India. As Jenny would later explain, the trains in the Czech Republic are hand-me-downs from Germany. I kept quiet about the fact that it cost just $2.60 to take an Uber to the train station (across town) and $8.00 for the train to Brno. The RY city team leaders in Prague warned us not to speak to locals about how inexpensive things were in the Czech Republic because prices had actually jumped 30 percent within the last year. This inflation was economically challenging for many citizens.

The view on the way to Brno was a moving picture of rolling hills and farms. It reminded me so much of the drive through Lancaster County in Pennsylvania where I was raised. I dozed off for a few minutes, and when I awoke, I could clearly make out the elaborate Spilberk Castle in the distance with its Gothic features and two beautiful chapels. The town scenery during the train's approach was majestic to say the least. There's nowhere like old-world Europe.

When I arrived at the station, Jenny was waiting for me in brown high-heeled boots and a long red petticoat dress. She was tall, lean, and in-shape in an Eastern European way, which means she was *hot*! I could tell that she was shy and excited all at once, or maybe that was me. She had a sort of nervous bounce about her. She didn't talk a lot, and her accent was thick, but she was extremely eager to show me her world. We had plans to tour a winery, explore the famous caves, hit up some cool restaurants, and perhaps go clubbing. This was going to be one long date!

The first stop was the winery on the outskirts of Brno. We were greeted by a jovial, burly man named Zdenek. Zdenek's winery was decked out in red, white, and blue accents, and was festooned from top to bottom with American flags. Because his birthday was July 4, he had an *extreme* love for America. He couldn't speak a lick of English and had never visited the U.S., but he was beyond proud to be affiliated with America, its history, and its principles. Framed letters, addressed to him, graced the walls of the winery from elected American officials and dignitaries, such as the late George H. W. Bush. There was even a sign in front of his winery that read, "United States Embassy." What a hoot! The underground wine cellar was adorned with medieval knickknacks and picnic tables with checkered tablecloths draped over them.

> **Phil Pheelings**: I was amazed by how a grown man could feel so strongly about a country he had never even visited. I felt very proud to be holding an American passport.

That evening, Jenny and I attended "Super Panda Circus," a French-inspired cabaret show and nightclub boasting a very unique tapas menu and a drinks menu featuring 400+ cocktails. They sure did put on a spectacle of a show for us.

The next day, Jenny drove us to the Macocha Abyss in the Moravian Karst caves area. The cave system is more than 138 meters deep, with the biggest ravine of its kind in all of Central and Eastern Europe. The abyss was formed when a cave ceiling collapsed, thus creating a deep hole with debris at the bottom. We took lots of pictures including some selfies as we filed along the path with the other tourists.

After exploring this cave and river system, we shared a vegan dinner at a quaint restaurant and then called it an early night. I'll keep our nights together private, but I will say that Jenny was a great girl with a unique personality, a wonderful heart, and exceptional looks. In the morning, she returned me to the train station, and I made my way back to my home in Prague. I set a personal record for the longest date ever. I didn't expect the longest date ever to be a fling, but that's what it turned out to be. I kept faith that there was someone else out there for me. I loved getting out of the gloomy weather of Prague and into the sunnier countryside. The sunshine I had been craving didn't grace Prague often enough. The cold, windy, and damp weather of Prague coupled with perpetually grey skies was mood-challenging.

The next few days were very low key. I caught up with my digital-nomad roommates, who always seemed to be busy with their own agendas. We hosted some happy hours with other Mangos in the building, and they graciously reciprocated. I served up some vegan "Parmesan cheese" with flax crackers that I found at the health food store close by. I also took advantage of those few slower days to continue my yoga practice and relax a bit.

Phil Phact: They call it a "yoga practice" not a "yoga perfect." This means, if you fall out of a pose ten times, you get right back into the posture for the 11th. Take this sage wisdom outside of the yoga studio and apply it to life. Persistence pays!

Part way through the month, I was invited to be on a speaker's panel entitled "Entrepalooza." I was thrilled because the invite came from none other than the U.S. State Department, which wanted three Mangos to talk to an audience of Czechs about American business. On the panel with me was Gil (a.k.a. Gillionaire) and Tommy. We spent the afternoon sharing our experiences as entrepreneurs in the United States, specifically about overcoming business hardships. A few of the Mangos were in the audience to cheer us on. My respect and admiration for Gillionaire and Tommy grew even more after hearing their stories.

Erin Kotheimer, a career diplomat with the U.S. State Department, met with us in a back room prior to the panel for a short briefing. By way of background, she explained that the Czech people are generally averse to taking risks and easily accept the word "no" when it comes to business ideas and sales. They are used to keeping their heads down, and not sticking their necks out. They even think that we Americans possess "irrational optimism" when it comes to business difficulties. I thought to myself, *Guilty as charged. We always find a way to succeed very often against impossible odds. After all, we are Americans.* Even though decades of communism had reinforced this ethos in the Czech people, things were changing and their future was looking brighter. Erin wanted us there to help support her efforts in encouraging those hesitant Czechs that they were headed down the right path with free-market capitalism. To me, this small example clearly showed how America can be a force for good in the world.

Tommy spoke about how he took a leap of faith when he went from working as an "intrapreneur" in a large corporation (being innovative for an employer), to becoming an entrepreneur (being innovative for himself) through selling technology to Expedia and other Fortune 500 companies. He said that everyone on the team is so focused on succeeding with the project at hand that failure is simply not an option and a solution can always be found. It was such a cool moment. What seemed to be common sense to us was not necessarily known to the good people in attendance, as evidenced by the number of times their mouths hung open in wonderment. Gillionaire, on the other hand, discussed how his ambition to teach himself computer coding and technology resulted in so much business that he couldn't handle it all. He got in way over his head but eventually figured out how to scale up his services, which resulted in more revenue. It was classic "fake it till you make it."

I began my story by talking about the importance of our ancestors, who traveled to America in search of the "American Dream." I spoke specifically about my grandparents and father who immigrated from Greece as war refugees. They were the pioneers who made it all possible for our family's successive generations. America gave them the opportunity to work hard and to live a much better life, all the while assimilating into a different culture, with a new language and new ways. Despite assimilating, we still held strong to our culture and maintained our family traditions. Sharing about my family's awesome journey to America gave me chills, but I was quick to point out that my family's story was not unique. People from all five continents who call the United States their home have their own, special immigration stories. Then I shifted gears. I shared how specific mentors had played an important role in my career, and I got the audience involved by asking how many of them had mentors in their lives. More than half the people in the room raised their hands. "I am standing on the shoulders of giants," I declared. I was referring to my parents, grandparents, and all the people who took enough interest to mentor me along my journey to success. It wasn't always a smooth road: People were tough on me and sometimes even belligerent, but by pushing me to my limits, those challenging experiences and tough people made me more successful than I otherwise would have been. Once the panel adjourned, the happy hour in the next room was a good place to make new connections, new Facebook friends and Twitter followers. That event was a great evening, a real highlight of my time in Prague.

Another highlight of the month did not, in fact, take place in Prague. For my second side trip, I headed to London where my friends Paula and Andersen live. Paula and I met a few years back in Palm Beach, Florida. She met her husband, Andersen, in England while visiting her sister. I stayed in touch with Paula and made several trips to visit them whenever I was on that side of the pond. London over the years had become my favorite city, and a big part of that was having friends who were such fantastic hosts. I could not wait to reunite with them.

As I waited in the airport for the flight, I sent my mom an email asking her to pick up a bunch of items from the Hippocrates Health Institute. Since she and my sister were coming to visit next month in Portugal, she was going to be my pack mule! Here's what I asked for:

> GIA Wellness earbuds/headphones that bring the sound to your ears via an air tube, thereby eliminating unwanted radiation. Plus, the sound quality is incredible!

> 2 tubes of Periopaste toothpaste—a fluoride-free toothpaste that fights the spirochete bugs (bad bacteria) that infest our mouth.

> 2 bottles of nitro drops—a plant-based liquid concoction that promotes cardiovascular circulation, dilation, and overall wellness.

> 1 bottle of magnesium drops, which help facilitate the uptake of calcium.

> 1 bottle of H Zyme PLUS—a plant enzyme pill that essentially substitutes the benefits of eating raw, uncooked food. When we cook food, without exception, we lose H.O.P.E. (hormones, oxygen, phytonutrients, and enzymes).

Phil Phact: Out of over eight million known life-forms on earth, we are the only one that cooks food. How bizarre!

Soon after takeoff, I leaned over to the stewardess as she passed by with the beverage cart. I showed her what I had typed in the notepad section of my phone. It read: "It's terribly refreshing to be treated with English ways and manners." She smiled politely, served me my drink, and moved on to the next passenger. It was true. I love that about the English: everyone is just so damn polite. It was such a contrast to my encounters with the people of Prague. It isn't that the Czechs were not polite, but they had a somewhat cold manner. Smiling didn't seem to come easily for them.

No Philter: I'm positive that the condition known as "Resting Bitch Face" (RBF) was invented and perfected in Prague.

Being back in London is always a good experience. (Just watch out for traffic, since they drive on the wrong side.) I met Paula and Andersen for dinner near their flat, and we spent the evening catching up and exchanging stories. They were so intrigued with Remote Year and life as a digital nomad. I realized once again that the future of work, this digital nomad lifestyle, was truly something unique. It was a little hard for people to grasp.

So, does Remote Year pay you to travel the world?

What do you do all day?

How many people are you traveling with?

Are you allowed to go home at all?

Where do you live in each city?

How did you pack for a whole year?

The questions were endless, but I did my best to explain everything. I made sure they understood that I still had my business and the freedom to work, explore, and return home whenever I wished. I set my own schedule. That was the beauty of Remote Year! As long as I paid my monthly fee, I could attend everything or nothing at all. It was a free and open platform.

> **Phil Phact:** Paula and Andersen live very close to Hyde Park. This is truly one of the greatest parks in the world. It covers about 350 acres, has over 4,000 trees, a large lake, a meadow, and ornamental flower gardens. It was originally used by King Henry VIII as a hunting ground.

> **Phil Phact:** People in the Remote Year community often use the term "glowtrotter" to reference one another, which is a play on the word "globetrotter." A glowtrotter is a person who traverses the world often and with ease. I was fast becoming a full member of the glowtrotter club.

Thank you, London. A couple of days of fine accommodations, top of the line meals, rejuvenating city walks, and a few massages had me feeling like a king. I was pumped to return to Prague and fully immerse myself in the city's history, customs, and bone-chilling winter. I returned just in time for the country's anniversary of the Velvet Revolution, marking the Czech people's overthrow of the communist system.

It was a tracks weekend, so naturally I picked the Velvet Revolution track. Our tour guide, Marcus, walked us through Prague's main avenues on a chilly but clear Saturday afternoon. We were walking in awe, surrounded by the captivating architecture. As we strolled, Marcus told us about the Velvet Revolution, which occurred in 1989. Decades prior, the communists were democratically elected, but then the country fell into the sham of one-party rule and a bureaucratic dictatorship. This brought four decades of lies, deceit, poverty, and misery—Marcus's words, not mine. Citizens were full-on subjects of the State and could not leave the country without special connections and permission. People were trapped! From 1948, communist-controlled television projected a false prosperity, showing farmers on tractors and laborers in factories often appearing on the screen with contented smiles on their faces. During this period, lots of magazines and newspapers were shut down, and many books were confiscated from homes and libraries. Finally, in the 1980s, the Czech government lifted their censorship of the newspapers, as well as the infamous travel bans. Soon after these liberalizations, the Czech and Slavic people got to see what life was like in much wealthier parts of Western Europe. Finally, their dissatisfaction reached boiling point, which resulted in a massive, countrywide workers' strike.

As we walked along the wide pedestrian avenues, Marcus pointed at some regal buildings that played a pivotal role in the rebellion. One was a newspaper building where journalists had helped to plan and communicate the subversion. Another important institution of the revolution was the theater; venues were meeting places during the strike and the rebellion, which took place before the internet made organizing super easy. The communists realized they had no more authority and that their jig was up, so they voluntarily stepped down in 1989. The Velvet Revolution was planned and won in these public venues and private houses, and we Mangos were seeing them up close and personal. This was no history book—this was real. What a thrill!

The Velvet Revolution is so-called because it was largely nonviolent, except for one pivotal and dramatic event. Pointing to the ground, Marcus indicated we were standing on the very street where a fateful student protest had occurred. The students coordinated a march to protest the communists, and because they were heading home for the weekend to see family, they had brought bags of laundry with them. Good ol' Mom! During the march, thousands of them became trapped by the police. The police beat them with billy clubs, and in the melee the laundry was strewn everywhere. The blood-spattered linen made it appear like a massacre: it looked much worse than it actually was. In the news media, as you know, "If it bleeds it leads," and these images were "a shot heard around the world." This incident is considered the tipping point of the revolution, and it spelled the end for the communists. You could say, then, that dirty laundry defeated communism in Czechoslovakia!

Marcus continued with his story. With the communist now defeated, the country had no plan for what to do next. So, like many places that experienced the fall of communism, the nation essentially became the Wild West for a short period of time. I learned early in life to be careful what you ask for; the newly freed Czechs learned this the hard way.

Given what I knew of the country's struggles, it was amazing to see how commercialized everything had become in just three decades. Along the wide, clean, prosperous streets of downtown Prague were department stores, fashion boutiques, and all kinds of upscale shops. Many of the tenants were multinational corporations. While some bemoan this, I call it a sign of progress. Why? Because multinationals are careful with their money, so their presence was a signal that the country had made it. Indeed, the Czech Republic has the lowest unemployment rate in Europe, at only 3.5 percent. In my dealings with the Czechs, they may not be the most upbeat people I have ever encountered, but they are a no-nonsense, industrious people. Once you get to know them, they are as warm and optimistic as their renowned springtime.

Phil Phact: Remarkably, a communist party lives on in the Czech Republic and in many surrounding European nations, like a zombie that will not die. If, like me, you have a curiosity about the subject, a great book to read is *The Black Book of Communism*, which is written by six authors who scholastically document the atrocities in the former Soviet Union, China, Cuba, and elsewhere. It reveals the actual consequences of communism, including terror, torture, famine, unjust incarceration, mass deportations, and massacres. The book is the first comprehensive attempt to catalogue and analyze the crimes of communism that has killed over 100 million people in the last 70 years.

Being a warm-weather wuss, it was tough to live for a month in the Czech winter, but there was no way the bitter cold was going to bring my spirits down. I loved this gorgeous, walkable city. There was a wide variety of vegan food options, as well. I was constantly checking my HappyCow app on my phone to find another great vegan restaurant nearby, or across town.

Phil Phact: HappyCow was founded in 1999 as an application to assist people around the world find healthy vegan food options. It's like "Yelp" for vegans. Users can review restaurants and post pictures. It's an indispensable travel tool. I used it everywhere I went.

No description of Prague would be complete without a mention of Prague's fantastic transportation system. In less than 20 minutes on foot and the metro, I could be in Old Town, on the Charles Bridge, or at the graffitied Lennon Wall. By the end of the month, I was an expert metro rider and could get anywhere in the city with just a little help from Google Maps.

In addition to being an affordable and gorgeous city, Prague had me smitten by its nightlife. Walking around Old Town at night was just dreamy, like something out of a fairy tale. Year round, this area is buzzing with bars, restaurants, high-end stores, and opera houses. The famous astronomical clock in the large pedestrian square, for example, was just the beginning of nonstop eye candy. On top of the usual city buzz, Christmas was around the corner, so Christmas markets were popping up all over. Vendors selling hot wine and cinnamon twists called *trdelnik*, lined the streets. Intoxicating hints of burning wood and holiday spices drifted through the air. I spent many evenings walking through the main square with a cup of hot wine in my hands while listening to street performers playing Christmas music. We had one fine night out on the town at a local jazz bar called Rock Bar & Café where the musicians blew us Mangos away. One of the performers vocalized a beatbox like I've never heard before. Seriously impressive.

The next RY track activity took us to "Little Hanoi" on the outskirts of Prague—a ten-acre area selling all kinds of things: Vietnamese food, clothes, toys, and souvenirs. There were beauty parlors, travel agencies, and financial services. The food was spectacular, and so was hearing about their history. The Vietnamese started immigrating to the Slavic lands during the communist era through cultural exchange programs. You could call it a commie-to-commie exchange program. Today, there are approximately 60,000 Vietnamese people residing in and around Prague, and they play a big part in Prague's culture and economy.

Phil Phact: There were 11 million Vietnamese who became refugees and sought a new home in the United States. Vietnamese communities now seem so entrenched in the fabric of America that it's easy to forget that opposition to them in the 1970s was strong. My hometown church in Lancaster, PA, the Greek Orthodox Church of The Annunciation, sponsored one refugee family of 26. Yes, that's right, a family of 26: aunts uncles, husbands, wives, nephews, nieces, etc. Each and every one of them went on to be productive members of our Lancaster community. As a boy, with this experience and others, I began to understand that people who were different were okay. America is truly the land of the five continents.

In my final week in Prague, I met Susan, a local vegan activist with a similar passion for the plant-based lifestyle. We had corresponded through email prior to meeting about an idea I had brewing since my trip to India. Susan and I were working together to assemble a team to translate the book *The World Peace Diet* from English to Czech. Upon completion in 2019, this will become the 18th translation of this best seller. This was only the beginning of my effort to help get this essential book translated and available to more people around the world.

Phil Pheelings: With the translation project underway, I felt like I was making a real contribution in this world. My life was always about building something for myself in business; now, advocacy was giving me a higher purpose.

I enjoyed my time in Prague very much, and I knew that I wanted to return some day. However, many of my fellow Mangos fell into a funk because of the bone-chilling, depressing weather. The weather stood in sharp contrast to the dreamy, sun-kissed coastline of Split. But we would come to learn this was a marathon and not a sprint. Overall, our digital nomad lifestyle was still fresh and full of possibilities. We knew that change would be a constant for the ten months that lay ahead.

As would be the case time and time again, just as I got to know and love a city, I was ripped away from it and placed in another. I had to start all over from scratch: new yoga studio, new office, new apartment, new neighborhoods, new Wi-Fi passwords, new money, new restaurants, new grocery stores, new Tinder searches … I think you get the picture! This was supposed to be (and was) the fun of it all, but at my stage in life, I also enjoyed routines. I knew I would miss the stunning Gothic-influenced architecture, the convenient transportation systems, and the wide varieties of vegan food. Lisbon, Portugal, had a lot to live up to in order to reach the high bar that Prague had set for us.

Until next time, Prague. I will miss you. My bags are packed, and I am ready for the next frontier.

Have laptop, will travel!

CHAPTER 3

Lisbon, Portugal

"The tourist sees what he has come to see.
The traveler sees what he sees."

G K   C H E S T E R T O N

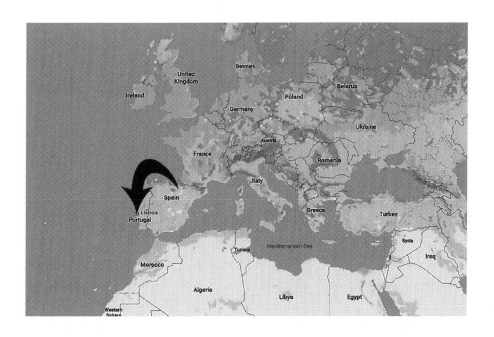

On December 1, Portugal welcomed the digital nomads of Mangata with open arms. We had all heard many great things about Lisbon, so our spirits and expectations were high. With the holidays right around the corner, Mangos would be heading back home to visit their families or spending the holiday season away for the first time.

> **Phil Pheelings:** By now I was definitely homesick. The last time I felt homesick was when I first went to sleep-away camp as an 8-year-old child. Thank God that Lisbon was a direct flight away from the Miami airport. I made plans to return home in West Palm Beach to spend the holidays with my family.

Lisbon is a magnificent, up-and-coming city settled on the west coast of Europe and next door to Spain. The sun was always present, emitting a special light that reminded me of San Diego's sunshine.

I was assigned to my own flat for the month, and it was nice to regain some privacy. I was only one block from the workspace in a very charming historical part of Lisbon called Sao Bento. In fact, I was walking distance to just about everything: the waterfront, to the downtown area, to the main square, to numerous restaurants, and even to my paperwork lifeline at DHL Express. I definitely got my daily quota of steps in. The weather wasn't as warm as I would have liked, but it sure wasn't the damp, freezing air that challenged us in Prague. It was a sunny December that sometimes ensured we broke a sweat walking up and down the cobblestoned hills throughout the city. The city streets and sidewalks were steep for sure!

I was fascinated by Lisbon from the start. The week prior to our arrival, our Remote Year program leaders (PLs) gave us a brief preview of what to expect. Lidia and Jenna were our travel moms for the year on Remote Year staff. Lidia was actually from Lisbon, so she was our proud expert on the city. One detail that she stressed was the "Lisbon light." She encouraged us to take note of the ways the sun shined on the city at different times of the day. She was right! This was one of the brightest, most sun-soaked cities I had ever experienced. The sun's rays bounced off the glossy blue, yellow, green, and magenta tiles. Tiles covered just about every building and made the cityscape an eye-candy paradise. Even the slick cobblestone that covered every sidewalk reflected this special light. The sunsets were absolutely unforgettable. Walking along the waterfront at dusk, I caught moments of the fiery sun setting beyond the huge bridge that resembled the Golden Gate Bridge in California. For the month, this magic carpet ride of mine would be exquisitely solar powered!

> **Phil Phact:** Lisbon is well known for the mosaic tiles that decorate its buildings. These elaborately painted tiles are called "azulejos," and they are often arranged in tessellated patterns or in massive murals that depict battle scenes and religious stories. Individual tiles might also bear images of game animals, flowers, or birds. The name "azulejos" isn't derived from the Portuguese word for "blue," but from the Arabic word "az-zulayj," roughly translated as "polished stone."

Lisbon was filled with a sense of optimism, which stood in contrast to Prague. People walked around with smiles on their faces, and they would even greet you as they passed by. Signs of the booming economy were evidenced by numerous construction projects. It didn't take long to notice that renovations were being performed on many of the old buildings, while many abandoned structures were awaiting their turn at gentrification. By the middle of the month, the city workers had even dug up my street, Rua Fresca (Fresh Street), and had begun repaving it. For two beautifully sunny weeks, I had to hop and skip my way around the Rua Fresca construction zone to my little green door, which was just five feet in height.

It was a whole new vibe compared to the Czech Republic. Lisbon was now a secret that had been discovered by me and everyone else. Outsiders were clearly moving in. A Russian lady owned our neighborhood bistro and had bought the business only four months beforehand. I also befriended a delightful Italian-Canadian couple, who did not speak a lick of Portuguese, but who nonetheless moved to Lisbon to open a chiropractic office. Foreigners were coming in to swoop up properties and take advantage of business opportunities.

Portugal, like the Czech Republic and Croatia, had emerged from a challenging past. After being granted its independence from Spain in the 1600s, Lisbon was destroyed by one of the largest earthquakes in history. A modern reconstruction of the country led by Marques de Pombal was set in motion, and it was then followed by several centuries of unstable monarchies and revolutions. In 1926, António de Oliveira Salazar seized power in Portugal and led the country through a dismal period of dictatorship that lasted until 1974. Portuguese locals could argue that industry and public roads improved under the leadership of Salazar. Poverty, however, was pervasive and individual liberty suffered. But after about 45 years of authoritarianism, a rebel group named MFA, staged a coup on the government, which led to the Carnation Revolution and Portugal's introduction to democracy in 1975.

Phil Phact: They called it the Carnation Revolution because almost no shots were fired. The soldiers and citizens wore red and white carnations on their lapels as a sign of support for the revolution and transition to democracy.

Okay, I won't pile on any more history. But from the beginning, I viewed my year-long journey with RemoteYear as a voyage of discovery to see what the world was really like. This platform provided an opportunity to learn about other cultures and to experience living like a local. In America, we are taught that we are exceptional as a nation. I am a proud American, but I had to ask myself if we were truly exceptional, or if that was just jingoistic poppycock. After a while, I began viewing my travel experiences through a more objective lens. Remote Year really fostered this type of mentality by organizing events and tracks that introduced us to more than just what a tourist might see. I believe that is what makes this particular travel program so unique.

If you can't tell by now, economic and political systems have always been of interest to me. These first three countries had all undergone tumultuous transformations of some sort within the last few decades. They were all still experiencing a significant season of change and progress while I was living there. So far as I could tell, the countries I lived in were striving for positive growth with market-based systems, each following their own paths and methods for facing the past and looking to the future.

> **Phil Pheelings:** In many ways, this idea of change applied to each of us in Mangata. We were all on a journey. We all had a past, maybe even some skeletons, but we all wanted to make a better future for ourselves.

I quickly grew accustomed to the European sensibilities of Lisbon, and I was ready to show off my latest home to a dear friend. I had enjoyed meeting new people, but I was ready to reconnect with some familiar faces … and to stop overusing Tinder. It just wasn't natural, and it seemed too random. So, I invited my friend from Boston, Callie, with whom I have a romantic history, to come visit. She was delighted to come see me, and we spent a beautiful five days together walking miles around the colorful neighborhoods of Lisbon. We both loved the street art that decorated the city. Locals used public art to visually display Portugal's history and express political statements and worldly controversies. I may not be much of a graphic artist myself, but I bought a black paint marker and made my own contributions. Next time you're in Lisbon, look for "Phil Nico" or "PN" scrawled on the buildings as you stroll the tiled sidewalks.

> **Phil Pheelings:** Callie and I enjoyed moments of intimacy, but we parted ways when she left for her hometown in Sweden. "The One" was still out there somewhere in this big, wide world, but I knew I wouldn't find her unless I kept putting myself out there. In the back of my mind, I am always wondering, *Is there really The One, or am I just chasing butterflies?*

I continued to play host when my mother and sister, Jeannie, arrived in the city of light for a visit. The tramily of digital nomads was cool, but there's nothing like *family*. I was beyond thrilled to see them. Pangs of homesickness were still lodged in my gut. Unfortunately, my father didn't make the trip. He was now getting to an age where long distance travel is not something he wants to do very often. But, he was there in spirit and sent his love and best wishes through the video phone.

With the holidays around the corner, it really was special to have my mom and sister with me. Plus, it may have been one of the last times in a while that we would be traveling together because my mother had a knee surgery coming up. I had planned so much for them to see, and Greek hospitality was in full force.

On the first day of their visit, I took them to one of my favorite spots in my neighborhood called the TimeOut Market, just across from the waterfront. The TimeOut restaurant group came up with the idea to fill large, vacant areas with some of the top gourmet restaurants and bars from the local scene. There are several TimeOut Markets running successfully across international cities, including New York, Miami, and Montreal.

The TimeOut Market location in Lisbon was once a local market hall used for bartering and selling goods. It was eventually bought, gutted, and transformed into a booming hotspot. These vendor stalls surrounded the perimeter of the building, while, in the middle people could sit, eat, and mingle. It was like a fancy food court. Every time I went, it was packed with locals and tourists alike. My family loved it.

After filling our stomachs with some delicious eats, I took my family to the neighborhood of Alfama. We took the 28 trolley to the hill-top heart of Lisbon, feeling the rush of the wind on our faces. The cute cafés and markets that passed us by in a blur gave us an authentic sense of this grand city. We hopped off the trolley at the National Pantheon and joined a walking tour that took us through the winding facades of the Alfama neighborhood and the Sao Jorge Castle. Some of the old streets were so narrow that cars couldn't fit through. We walked and walked and walked through many pedestrian passages which suddenly ended in dazzling vistas of the city, the bay, and bridge. As we were taking it all in, our guide recounted stories of earthquake tragedies and the rebuilding that followed.

All the while, that Lisbon luminosity never let up. It was always there to provide a good feeling. Watching the sun go down and listening to the faint tunes of Fado music gave me a blissful connection with my mom and sister that I don't think I had ever felt before. Having them there to experience that magic was such a blessing. I wasn't homesick anymore.

Next stop: Fatima to visit the holy Fatima Shrine where the Miracle of the Sun occurred. The story goes that in the early 1900s, three children were visited by the Virgin Mary on their walk home from school. Word spread throughout the town, and many people visited the spot of the said apparition, hoping to have a sighting of their own. As it turned out, the Madonna only appeared for those children. In 1917, one of the children predicted that Mary's final appearance would occur, and over 70,000 people gathered in Fatima in anticipation of her arrival. Most of the pilgrims claimed to have seen the sun dance or emit some variety of colors, coining the name "Sun Miracle," and they believed that the event was Mary's prediction that World War I would soon end. Today, approximately five million Catholics and other curious people from around the world make the pilgrimage to this holy site each year.

I watched many hundreds of people crawl on their knees to the Virgin Mary shrine with offerings, notes, and trinkets, all hoping for something in their lives. As a whole, people all want the same things: peace, health, and mercy. Coming from a Greek Orthodox Christian background, similar to Catholicism, I could understand why this visit was important to my mother and sister. I identified with their spiritual aspirations but had recently begun to question certain aspects of established religion, especially in relation to veganism. I began to wonder, somewhat obsessively, why is it that the leaders of these major faiths do not follow and espouse the original teachings? I'm talking about the principles of nonviolence and kindness toward other beings— all beings.

Phil Pheelings: As I watched thousands of people struggle to the altar on their knees, I was struck by the irony that people ask for peace but are unwilling to give peace. How can we pray for peace at the dinner table and moments later dine on animals that were violently slaughtered after living lives of unimaginable pain and cruelty? It seems to me that our efforts are hypocritical and fruitless if we cannot give that which we ask for. I do my best not to judge people, since we are all wounded by a world organized essentially around eating animals. I believe that the deeper meaning of veganism is to have compassion for those who are not yet "woke."

On the final day of my family's visit, I hired a driver and tour guide named Frank to take us to Sintra, a gorgeous resort town located in the foothills of the Sintra Mountains, and just along the coast. Its hilly terrain gives way to steep cliffs and intriguing rock formations that line the sandy shores of the Atlantic. There's nothing like mountain-to-sea views! In the center of town, a grand, brightly colored palace of Moorish design acts as the main tourist attraction. After exploring the palace, our guide drove us to the lighthouse of Cabo da Roca, where we got to stand on the westernmost point of mainland Europe with nothing between us and our beloved United States but the great Atlantic Ocean.

No Philter: Frank complained a lot about the Spanish tourists and their "condescending attitude." He passionately hated that they talked down to him as he drove them around. I thought back to the White Boys in Croatia and their feelings about their countrymen to the north. Throughout my travels, I would discover these ethnic rivalries everywhere. Incredibly, in many places, people still hold fast to deep-seated ethnic stereotypes, although they basically look the same. When it comes to race relations in America, forget about what you see on the news, because *an ounce of experience is worth more than a ton of theories.* In the United States, most people from all five continents get along just fine on a daily basis.

That evening, I helped my mother and sister pack for their return to the States. Well, I hung out and watched them do it. They were so impressed with Lisbon and the surrounding areas. I could feel their appreciation and gratefulness, and I couldn't have felt prouder to be related to two such incredible women. It was always difficult to part ways with them, but I knew it wouldn't be long before I saw them again. I had plans to return to West Palm Beach for Christmas, which was now only a few weeks away. Until then, I would spend my days catching up on work, checking out more vegan restaurants, walking the hilly cobblestone sidewalks for miles on end, and participating in Remote Year track events, one of which was a visit to a scenic vineyard in Evora.

Portugal is full of these hidden-gem places. Evora was another adorable little town with ample character and history. It is known for the ancient Roman temple, the Chapel of Bones, and for its wine, of course. On the way to the winery, we stopped at the chapel, which is very interesting. By the 16th century, the cemeteries were taking up valuable land in and around the town of Evora, so the monks decided to build a church where the bones of the deceased could be relocated. The monks decided to put their bodies on display as part of the building materials of the new church. Written on the chapel's front door is, "Nós ossos que aqui estamos, pelos vossos esperamos," meaning, "Our bones are waiting for yours."

> **Phil Phact:** The bones of over 5,000 human beings are clearly seen in the bricks of the Evora Chapel of Bones. Very creepy!

The trip continued with the wine tour. The air and the sky were clear. Our van whizzed by the rolling hills filled with rows and rows of grape vines as far as the eye could see. I am a wine enthusiast and (self-proclaimed) connoisseur, so I was eager to get coiffing. It turns out that Portugal is the 11th largest wine producer in the world—news to me.

The bus pulled up to the large white estate house of the João Portugal Ramos Vinhos winery. The house was adorned with Spanish tiled floors, handmade oriental rugs, large windows, and gorgeous French doors that opened up to an outdoor terrace. I wanted to move in. Our guide began the tour by explaining that creating wine is an art, and that the winery had been perfecting the art for centuries to ensure the highest and most unique quality of wine. We learned that many of the grape varietals are solely native to the land, climate, and environment in Portugal, including Tinta Barroca, Rabigato, Touriga Nacional, Baga, Alvarinho, and Maria Gomes. Each wine has a story worth hearing. There is a lot of technical information related to each type, such as acidity, tannin, age, and so on. I don't get too tangled up in all of that. Ask me about guitars and I can speak with passion about the technicalities, but with wine, I just care that it tastes good. (Does the wine have a cool label, and is it expensive? If yes to both, then it *must* be good!) When the tour guide said, "And now we can taste the wine," I knew it was time for fun. The Mangos took turns making blends of the different vintages. We passed around lab beakers, certain that we had concocted the next commercial success.

Before I knew it, it was now time to "glowtrot" back to Florida for Christmas. It had been nearly three months since I had been home, and I wanted to personally check in on my house, work, family, and friends, and I was excited to share some holiday cheer. I was able to take care of some condo maintenance and business matters with my secretary, Cindy. There's nothing like taking a meeting in person. It was the right thing to hop across the pond back to the U.S. before spending three months in Asia, living in some of the farthest points away from home. Christmas with my family is a long-standing tradition, so it felt wonderful to keep the tradition alive and spend it with them. But it went too quickly, and by December 28, I was back at the WIP office in Lisbon finishing up some last-minute leasing deals for one of my properties.

I would miss that quaint little workspace along our hilly, cobblestoned street. I would miss the trolleys whizzing by every few minutes, and the colorful tiles, tiny doors, and corner markets of the Sao Bento hamlet. On New Year's Eve, I would be on a plane again with my fellow Mangos, heading for Japan—a country that seemed the most foreign to me. I couldn't believe it. Three months abroad had passed so quickly; time has a funny way of disappearing like that. I made a New Year's resolution that I would strive to be more mindful of my day-to-day experiences and to show more gratitude and appreciation toward what the universe was giving me. After all, not everyone is afforded a journey like this … for an entire year! Even though I wasn't flying privately and didn't have a crewed yacht on hand (which were once actual goals of mine), I was living large.

On the way to airport, where I would embark upon 26 hours of air travel, I savored the romantic memories I had of basking in God's special sun zone here on Europe's western edge.

Until we meet again, Portugal! It's time to see if Asia's Wi-Fi is worthy of us digital nomads.

Have laptop, will travel!

CHAPTER 4

Kyoto, Japan

"I told him there was one city that they could not bomb without my permission and that was Kyoto."

HENRY L. STIMSON,
UNITED STATES SECRETARY OF WAR

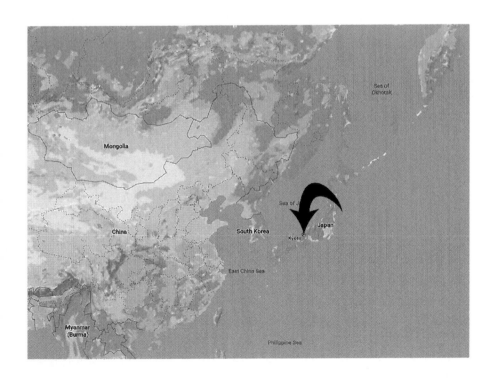

10 ...9 ... 8 ... 7 ... 6 ... 5 ... 4 ... 3 ... 2 ... ONE! HAPPY NEW YEARRRRRR!

The noise from the party poppers, horns, and shouts of celebration kept ringing in my ears long after I left the Irish bar where the Mangos ushered in 2018. We had gone straight from the airport to our new homes, dropped off our bags, and arrived at the bar just in time for the countdown that would put 2017 behind us and welcome 2018. My first impression was that the Japanese really know how to party! Choruses of karaoke tunes spilled out of multiple venues while tinsel, bright lipstick, and wild outfits sparkled in a sea of giddy revelers that filled the streets. I felt like I was dreaming, in an Ambien-induced kind of way. After the long, exhausting flights across Europe to Asia, here I was celebrating New Year's Eve in our new home city of Kyoto, Japan.

Flying first class on Emirates Airlines was heavenly, but once we landed in the Osaka Airport, going through customs was less than heavenly. Remember all those supplements and vitamins that my mother brought me from Hippocrates? Well, all of that, plus my ski boots and scuba gear, were unfurled and strewn about for close inspection by the Japanese authorities.

Customs patrol had a field day going through my luggage, pulling out all my mysterious cargo and closely inspecting everything as they interrogated me. They wanted an explanation for everything. What was a scuba regulator? If these are ski boots, where are the skis? What are these vitamins all about? They took a few pills to the back office for contraband testing. After 26 hours of travel, I definitely wasn't in the mood. I was mostly worried about the CBD oil in my toiletry bag because of its main ingredient: Cannabis. I knew how strict Japan was about drugs and unapproved medicines. My heart rate increased as they dug through my big bag, because I could vaguely smell the pungent CBD oil coming from a small opening in the zip of my toiletry bag. The luggage smelled like pot!

No Philter: Travelers to Japan are limited by law to a 30-day supply of medications and vitamins. Let's just say I had way more than that! The customs lady held up one of my giant bags of plant enzyme pills, gave me the stink eye and in almost-incoherent English, asked me, "Hah manee munts?" Being the smart ass that I am, a Japanese accent almost slipped out when I replied, "Only one month." I shut my mouth and stared back at her with my poker face. She took my word for it. Maturity is knowing when to keep your mouth shut, though I would have drawn the line had they demanded a cavity search!

Kyoto was spared the bombings of World War II because it was, and still is, considered the cultural heart of Japan. The city was the capital of Imperial Japan for 1000 years, and—as we quickly learned—it was now on the cutting edge of modernity. It didn't take me long to gain a strong appreciation for the Japanese and their ways, rituals, and values. For starters, it was customary on New Year's Day to visit a Shinto shrine or Buddhist temple. So, sure enough, our local city team escorted us and our hangovers to the nearest temple where we participated in Japan's tradition of *hatsumode*. Upon entering the gate of the temple, I bowed toward the *sanmon* ("mountain gate"). Next, I was to purify myself before prayer. Taking the wooden ladle (or *hishaku*), I rinsed my left hand, then my right, then my mouth, then my left hand again. Finally, I lifted the ladle so that the water came trickling down the handle to cleanse it for the next person. I stood at the altar for a moment of prayer. I clapped my hands and rang the bell so that heaven could hear me. Finally, I clasped my hands together and bowed in prayer. Of course, I didn't know any of the Buddhist chants, so I internally prayed (to Jesus, of course) for a new year filled with love, prosperity, and inner peace. I couldn't have imagined a better place than Kyoto, Japan, to foster the seeds of these prayers. I had never thought about my ancestors before, but a reverence for those who have been before us was stressed by our city team. This made a lot of sense to me; somehow, this recognition opened me up to a fuller understanding of myself. Of course, no visit to a place of worship is complete without a money offering. So, I gave.

As I bowed one final time toward the *sanmon* on my way out of the temple, a brief feeling of déjà vu flickered through me. It was almost like a chill. I'm not a superstitious person, per se, but I can't resist looking for an underlying meaning for such occurrences. Maybe I had seen this place before in my dreams. Maybe I had had a vision of it while meditating one morning. Whatever it was, I truly felt like I was in the right place at the right time. I wouldn't have had the opportunity if I hadn't agreed to go on this year-long odyssey. I knew I was headed down the right path.

Phil Pheelings: Shinto and Buddhism are the main religions of Japan, and many Japanese fluidly practice both. Earlier in my adult life, I would have feared that participating in that Buddhist ceremony on New Year's Day was blasphemy against my Christian faith. I would have no fears like this anymore, especially after living in Asia for three months. After all, God is God.

Everyone in the Remote Year tramily had their own apartments that month in Kyoto, although calling them apartments was a stretch. The studio flats assigned to us were hardly larger than shoeboxes. However, I came to love that tiny closet, as it taught me a lot about minimalism and reducing the desire for material possessions. At only 18 square meters, which is less than 200 square feet, that apartment was by far the smallest place I have ever lived. There was just enough room for the essentials: one bed, a one-burner stove, a sink, a mini fridge, an eco-washer, a tiny desk, and a bathroom the size of an airplane lavatory. My tiny home for the month was no wider than the length of the single bed they provided. Before Remote Year, I was used to living in luxurious homes with maximum amenities, but I quickly became accustomed to my mini-digs. My Kyoto apartment was exceptionally clean, and I picked up the habit of removing my shoes upon entering my home. All of the Mangos quickly adopted this. I praise the Japanese highly for that custom. I soon found out that it was practiced throughout most Asian cultures, even in many public places such as restaurants, spas, hostels, and workspaces. Everyone takes off their shoes. If a workman came to the apartment to fix a leak or make a repair, he always took off his shoes.

Kyoto has to be the cleanest, most efficient city in the world. Even though it is sprawling and dense, not a single piece of trash or even grime could be found on the streets. How is that even possible? They were even very particular about their trash and how recyclables and other waste was sorted. Trash pickups and procedures were very specific as well. For example, city residents were required to sort their glass, wood, plastic, and compostables in separately colored bags, to be taken out for pickup on certain days. Mindfulness was practiced even in the way they took care of the trash.

Even though there was no Uber in Japan, the cabbies were top-notch and reasonably priced. One cabbie, one of the few who spoke English, was proud to say that the Japanese children are taught at a young age that cleaning is important not only in the home but also in classrooms.

Phil Phact: There are no janitors in the Japanese schools. For the first half hour of the school day, the children work hard deep cleaning the bathrooms, hallways, and classrooms. This got me thinking: try that in America, and kids would be hurting themselves on the job and the lawsuits would fly. The parents would clamor for restrictions on physical exertion and Lord knows what else! It was about this time I began to realize there was more wrong with my home country than I had previously thought. Where did we go wrong?

Soon after that cab ride, I was riding the Kyoto subway with my fellow nomad Chris, who accidentally spilled his Coke. We, along with the fellow passengers, initially ignored the spill, until an elderly man got on at one of the stops. Two adolescent boys noticed the man take a little detour around the puddle, and within seconds they were on their hands and knees wiping up the mess with their winter gloves. Chris and I then lurched forward to help, but they were too damn efficient at cleaning up the mess that we made, and it was already gone. Can you believe it? Toto, we are not in Kansas anymore! It often felt like I had landed on a completely different planet that was way ahead of its time. This was especially evident in the men's room. I had never taken care of my business on a fancier toilet. Talk about making me feel like a king sitting on his throne! On those magic toilets, I could listen to music while washing and drying my butt, and most of them even had a built-in sink.

Walking through some of the pedestrian markets, I encountered those notorious Japanese gaming arcades. Out of curiosity, I entered one through a set of automatic double doors: it was like getting sucked into an alternate dimension. Aisles and aisles of Pachinko machines and a few claw-machine games filled the first floor. I was instantly overstimulated by the bright lights, cartoon memorabilia, pinging sounds, and robotic children (and even some adults) who were fixed in a trance as they played. The basement floor was just as over-the-top. Top-notch video games, virtual reality simulators, arcade games, and slot machines were lined up like soldiers. There was even an area to dress up in costumes and take photos. By the time you added filters and enhanced your eyes in the post-edit, you looked like a movie star. This is Japanese youth culture.

Pachinko parlors were all over Kyoto. Invented in the 1920s, a Pachinko is a vertical pinball machine. You shoot the little steel pellets into the vertical maze, and hope that you can score more and more points based on where the balls hit, as they travel downward. These colorful, cacophonous parlors were everywhere, and when you walked into a large parlor, the decibel level was through the roof as the rows and rows machines sounded off at the players.

Despite these parlors, being Japanese is all about hard work. The fun they have in an arcade is highly compartmentalized. When they walk out of those arcade doors, it's back to work in one way or another. Another thing that captivated me was the feeling of security I had in Kyoto and throughout Japan. There's an unspoken sense of honesty that defines the Japanese ethos. It's impossible to rid a place of *all* crime, of course, but Kyoto and all of Japan has the lowest crime rate this side of heaven. At a café, you could leave your computer and belongings at your seat for a bathroom break with no worries, and I saw unlocked bicycles outside stores and apartment buildings just asking to be taken. But it seems that the Japanese don't need a religious or legal commandment not to steal; they have cultural capital that's been accumulating for thousands of years to guide their conduct. I admired this so much.

Phil Phact: Japan is an honor-based society. If you leave even two yen (fractions of a penny) behind from your restaurant bill, they will chase you down the street to return your change. This actually happened to me a few times. They are not a tipping society but instead they view it as overcharging. Their sense of honor would never allow them to overcharge no matter how small.

There was so much to see and do in Japan. The city plan of flat, sprawling Kyoto was grid-based, making it very easy to find my way with just a glance at Google Maps. My walking route to yoga and the office would lead me through buzzing pedestrian markets with a plethora of shops selling all kinds of things like pickled vegetables, steel knives, candy, and souvenirs. This was a land of abundance, yet Japan has no natural resources and has to import everything it uses for the manufacturing process.

That month, we had two workspaces at our disposal: Andwork and Space Kante. I didn't necessarily favor one over the other, but I found myself knocking out my paperwork and business calls mainly at the Andwork coworking space. The 13-hour time difference meant that I was calling people at odd hours, at least for me. If I called a banker on the Eastern seaboard at 6:00 a.m. Kyoto time, I greeted them with, "Hello from the future!" (it was still 5:00 p.m. the previous day).

The coworking area was on the eighth floor of a sleep-pod hostel called millennials, where we enjoyed some awesome views of downtown Kyoto through floor-to-ceiling windows. The coworking space also doubled as the hostel lobby, where other passing travelers came and went. In the lobby, happy hour began every day at 5:00 p.m., and that assured me fun and fellowship with fellow Mangos and other nomads on a daily basis.

> **Phil Phact:** The word "hostel" to me always meant a low-budget, backpacker-type lodging with bunks and common quarters. But in Asia, hostels were different. On that side of the planet, a hostel was clean and modern like a regular hotel, but without all the amenities of a full-service resort.

No Remote Year immersion is complete without tracks, and Kyoto was no different. For the field trips that month, I chose a tea ceremony and a Japanese dessert class. The tea ceremony exceeded my expectations. The Japanese winter rain made me crave a warm cup of tea, so I chose the right track. At the doorway of a small Japanese home in the heart of Kyoto, the digital nomads were pleasantly greeted with a bow and *kon'nichiwa* (hello). By now, taking off our shoes was habit; we didn't give it a second thought. On the opposite side of the stark room was a glass window that stretched from floor to ceiling, offering a peek into a classic

Japanese garden with tiny waterfalls trickling into a long pond where I could see coy fish mingling. Each of us quietly found a pillow to sit on. The tranquility in the room placed some sort of spell on each of our tongues, and no one dared disturb the silence … except maybe for me. Just as I was about to crack an unnecessary joke, the tea master walked into the room wearing an elegant kimono. She gave us a brief history of the ceremony's tradition and origins. She emphasized that warriors or aristocrats, for example, would leave their societal roles behind once they crossed the doorway's threshold. Most importantly, they checked their troubles at the door so that they could imbibe the tea with a clear mind.

Phil Phact: Tea and the ceremonial rituals around drinking it actually originated in China. Japanese monks and priests who traveled to China brought tea back home to Japan where they helped spread the tradition of the tea ceremony. The ceremonies then evolved to be distinctly Japanese.

The tea ceremony is an aesthetic ritual with two main components: preparing the tea, then enjoying the tea. The ceremony is just as much about appreciating the entire experience through one's senses. So much detail was evident as we observed her every move: There was the timing of when the tea is served, which is always after the desserts. There was the perfect temperature: not too hot, not too cold. There was protocol on how to receive and hold the bowl of tea, and then how to take a sip. The final sip was to be slurped, with an emphasis on making noise, which indicates to the host that the cup was finished.

I became infatuated with the green powdered tea, called matcha, which became my new best friend for the month. It had a different effect than brewed coffee. My order at the local Kyoto Starbucks was "Tall soy matcha tea. Half with hot water, and half with hot soy milk, no foam.

Extra matcha powder please. Thank you!" Of course, this was only made possible via the Google Translate app, which came in handy everywhere I went in the world. The Japanese, for the most part, do not speak a lick of English, and have no desire to learn. This is emblematic of their resistance to outside cultures. They do not bring in immigrants like other countries do. The standardized English section on the national exam is simply the gateway for higher learning and job placement. It is well known that students memorize voluminous passages of English words and spit them back out during the test, without really knowing what they're writing.

> **Phil Phact:** The monks of Japan drink matcha tea because of the combined effect of caffeine, phytochemicals, and antioxidants it contains. As I was to learn by direct experience, the combined effect of the ingredients produces an alert yet relaxed feeling. Best of all, there is no caffeine crash, which I often experience with coffee. The effect of matcha on the body and mind allows the monks to sit in meditation for longer periods of time and to have an enhanced experience. I had found the perfect elixir.

Next up was our dessert track. During this track, the Mangos were passionately guided through making three types of mochi desserts. Mochi is essentially a rice-based substance pounded into a ball that can easily be molded into decorative shapes, and it is often filled with sweet bean paste, matcha, or even ice cream. Our instructor, the chef, who also didn't know any English, showed us how to smoosh, fold, pinch, and mold our clay-like edible substance into beautiful designs. Each of our desserts depicted a flower that represented symbols of the new year. Just like the tea ceremony and other Japanese arts (origami, for example), these mochi desserts were made with intention. Each one is unique, and because they are meant to be eaten, they contain a deeper meaning: impermanence.

Phil Pheelings: Not everything is meant to last forever, so let's appreciate what we have and be mindful during each moment. For the moment, that means take a bite and enjoy life!

When I wasn't working, practicing yoga, or on an RY track, I was strolling through the markets and visiting the nearby sights. I'm pretty sure I walked at least five miles every day. The winter was cold, so I was wrapped in layers while blending in with the locals by wearing a white surgical mask. I thought it looked cool, but it had an important utility. The mask is worn with respect to others so that germs are not spread. Two cool places I visited were the Fushimi Inari-taisha Shrine and the sacred Arashiyama Bamboo Grove. Of course, I blended in with the sea of tourists, but I didn't feel like one. I felt a connection to these places; I could truly feel this city's history and essence engulfing me. It wasn't heavy or ominous, but rather protective and encouraging. Fushimi Inari is the most important of the many shrines dedicated to Inari, the Shinto God of Rice (the rice plant has nourished many civilizations for thousands of years). It's famous for its thousands of bright red-orange "torri gates" that create a semi-covered walkway through the mountain's trails. The famous bamboo forest gave me great photos for Instagram. Thousands of bamboo trees had a multi-prism effect on the sun's rays, and there I was in the middle of it all.

By now it was high time for a side trip. It was the height of ski season in Japan, so we set our sights on the outskirts of Sapporo, located on Hokkaido, the northernmost island of Japan. Wow … Sapporo was actually a place and not just a beer? I was accompanied by four of my Mango brothers: Gillionaire, Alvin, Victor, and Martin. We called our team

"Shred the Pow Pow" because, in case you don't know, "pow" is lingo for freshly fallen snow powder. Fresh pow is a skier's and snowboarder's dream. And to our delight, we had a lot of it. At the airport, a man holding a "Shred the Pow Pow" sign was quickly spotted. He drove us through the winter wonderland to the Kiroro ski village, located in the middle of mountainous nowhere.

The resort's service was phenomenal in a quintessential Japanese way. They didn't need The Golden Rule to guide them; their own version of it had been passed down for thousands of years. This was especially true for our meals. Via email ahead of time, I requested vegan meals during our stay, and the resort chef was thrilled to accommodate (the chef and his brother were originally from India, so they knew vegan cuisine well). The spread was so generous that my four friends decided to become vegan that week. All this special attention for only $15 per meal—for lunch or dinner. An entree on the regular menu could cost $60 and up. This was one of my all-time, menu-cheating conquests; I guess the millennials would call it a "menu hack."

The next day, we woke up early, very eager to hit the slopes. Some of us went snowboarding while the rest of us went skiing. Without a doubt, I had one of the most spectacular skiing days of my life. Having my own boots set me up for greatness, and if you are a skier, you can appreciate this. Every day we were gifted with fresh champagne powder. There was so much pow that I had to keep exchanging my skis for fatter and fatter ones. As a pack, we sped down the mountain over and over again in near-synchronous zigzag formations, showing off, howling, and laughing with each other. But there was one tiny mishap …

Back in Kyoto at a convenience store, I had purchased body-heat activated hand and toe warmers in anticipation of the cold temperatures. This is standard issue gear for a lot of skiers, especially for a warm-weather wuss like me! On the first day of skiing, I cracked open my warmers and placed them in my boots as I got all geared up. As we were ascending in the ski lift I felt a hot tingling sensation in my right boot, but I was too excited about skiing to pay it any attention. A few hours later, however, I noticed that the tingling had turned into a more intense pain. I figured that I had a small blister, since I hadn't worn my boots in a while. No big deal. After a full day of blazing trails on the slopes, we headed back to the resort, where I was finally able to inspect the damage. As I pulled off my ridiculously expensive compression socks, I discovered that the "tiny blister" was much more serious than I had anticipated. The foot warmer that I had placed in my shoe that morning had, in fact, given me a third-degree burn on the first two toes of my right foot. The two blisters, one on each toe, were the size of teacup saucers! Well, not quite *that* big, but I never let the truth get in the way of a good story. This is the tale of the *rogue toe warmer!*

The staff at the front desk mobilized fast, Japanese style, and summoned a taxi to take me to the nearest hospital. Unfortunately, the closest was an hour away, and it was snowing hard. I was hesitant to go, but I knew that my burn required medical attention. My taxi driver was a kind old soul who, thankfully, knew some English. He sped off into the cloud of precipitation and didn't seem to break a sweat as his large Toyota fishtailed all over the road. I white-knuckled it in the back seat for the entire drive, making a mental checklist of all my affairs and making sure they were in order. Yes, the drive was *that* bad for the entire hour.

My anxiety subsided when I entered the hospital. It took no time at all to be admitted, seen by an English-speaking doctor, have my burn cleaned and wrapped, sign some paperwork, and pay a reasonable fee in cash. Before I knew it, I was back at the resort. During my hospital visit, I watched in awe as the nurses scurried purposefully back and forth through the hallways on their tiptoes, carrying documents and release forms on my behalf. This was Japanese culture in action. They were in a hurry to serve their patients and to save them time. At that moment, I was the beneficiary of their excellence. Whether I was being treated at the hospital or shopping at Family Mart (buying bottled water or my fateful toe warmers), I noticed that the Japanese were always in mode of excellence, and it was always done right ... as in *perfectly!* Being in Japan was heaven for a guy like me who values things done right and on time. I am not entitled; after all, I do the same for others.

With the exhausting day behind me, plus some mild painkillers, I slept like a three-toed sloth on a branch. I didn't even get up in the middle of the night to take an old-man piss. When I awoke the next morning, I felt as good as new and didn't think twice about hitting the slopes again. Of course, I went skiing. I still had two blisters that were now (truthfully) the size of golf balls. Later that evening, my friends couldn't stop gushing about my perseverance, endurance, and skills on the slopes. They assumed that my vigor was due to my plant-based diet. I was happy to give my healthy vegan lifestyle the credit, but when I reflected on this later, I realized there was no way I would have been able to take on so many adventurous activities at my age if I didn't eat a plant-based diet and practice meditation and yoga regularly.

Phil Pheelings: I felt total freedom while skiing down those Japanese slopes. With the chilling wind pelting my warm cheeks, and the flakes of snow powder dotting my ski goggles, I forgot about the stresses of everyday life for a time. I was in the moment, and it felt amazing. The magic carpet ride that was Remote Year was taking me to new heights!

After a week of ski bliss, we "Shred the Pow Pows" packed up and headed back to Kyoto. Once back at home base, I barely had a moment to settle in before I had to pack my bags once again for a trip to Tokyo. I was booked to give my signature presentation to the Vegans of Tokyo Meetup group. After waking to sounds of nearby construction, I met my fellow Mango, Felix, at the Kyoto Station for a glorious two-hour and twenty-minute bullet train ride to Tokyo. I am so thankful for Felix's skills as a videographer. He stepped up to film my presentation, and it turned out beautifully. It's up on YouTube, and it is my favorite of them all.

Since the introduction of the bullet train, it has been a dream of mine to ride one, especially to Tokyo. Riding in first class made the moments even more precious. We were the only passengers in our train car, so we felt extra awesome in our super-plush, reclining seats. Within seconds, we reached speeds of over 320 km/h (200 mph). If we hadn't looked out the window, we would have no idea we were going that fast. The ride was smooth as glass. But when we did look out the window, it was one big blur. Town after town went whizzing by. What a thrill! From afar, we could see the sweetest of eye candy: Fuji Mountain. The formation was so massive that it appeared much, much closer than it actually was. Spellbinding.

We arrived in Tokyo perfectly on time, of course. From the station, Felix and I went briefly to our accommodations, then on to the venue where we met Susan, my translator for the event. She was a young, bright-eyed, and intelligent Japanese woman. She had long, pin-straight, black hair with bangs that hung just above her exotic Asian eyes. We had an immediate camaraderie, which made for a successful and organized presentation the following day. Unfortunately, the hall they originally rented fell through, and now there was a waiting list of 50 attendees who couldn't fit into the small restaurant hall that was our venue. We had to turn some people away. Nevertheless, it was a success.

To top off this experience, Susan even agreed to work with me on my passion project to translate Will Tuttle's book, *The World Peace Diet*, into Japanese. What a blessing.

Phil Pheelings: Even though it was my first time using a translator, I was relaxed because I was prepared. Moreover, I had spent two hours meditating with the NUCALM app. Curious? Check out www.nucalm.com.

The Tokyo talk was the first full vegan presentation I had ever given without using any PowerPoint slides. I spoke directly from knowledge, memory, and my heart. Of course, I had some butterflies in my stomach speaking in front of 50+ people without my PowerPoint safety net, but as soon as the first words left my mouth, it was smooth sailing from there. Speaking through a translator is so fun! I loved the back and forth parlaying between languages. The gap between my spoken thoughts gave me time to gather my next thought. Speaking at the Tokyo meetup marked a milestone for me. Speaking without slides encouraged me to break things down and organize the message in a way that served me well going forward. It would become the basis for my upcoming book on veganism. The presentation in Tokyo would also serve as a template for my talks throughout the rest of Asia and beyond.

After the longest Q&A session ever, we left the small venue and took a stroll on cloud nine. It was such a thrill to hear my words become Japanese words. I'll never forget it. On the walk home, I noticed groups of girls walking very pigeon-toed. I had seen it in Kyoto, too. Sorry if it seems like I was trolling these girls, but I posted some videos on Facebook. The ignorant comments came rolling in that bowleggedness was a feature of the Japanese skeleton. Not true. After speaking with a local and completing a simple Google search, I learned that this form of walking is 100 percent *cultural*. It is a remnant of a past cultural practice of breaking a girl's feet so that she would walk daintily. Yikes!

Phil Phact: Pigeon-toed walking by females in Japan is considered *kawaii*, which means "cute."

After the event, it was time to party in Tokyo! Felix and I met our fellow Mango, Monica, at the famous Robot Evening Cabaret Show in the entertainment district of Tokyo. Imagine a supper club on steroids: super-trendy dining meets Mr. Toad's Wild Ride in Disney World. Just when I thought Japan could not get any weirder, we were transported to some other dimension where robots, giant pandas, dinosaurs, and glitzy performers in outlandish costumes acted out their trippy dream show. I sat there with my friends laughing as the show unfolded only a few feet in front of us. Just over an hour later, we stepped out of the venue and onto the sidewalk.

The streets that had been bustling with people were now nearly empty. However, scattered about were more than a few drunkards in suits and ties. They were laid out on park benches and even on the sidewalk itself. A culture of contradictions. The grown men that I had seen during the day with their game faces on, all suited up for work, were now passed out drunk on this very chilly night. I mean they were knocked *out*!

Phil Phact: A *nomikai* is the term used to refer to a kind of drinking party particular to Japanese culture. They are essentially business parties held in restaurants and bars to foster coworker bonds outside of the office. Attending these *nomikai* gatherings is considered a social aspect of work, and they are compulsory if you want to please your boss. Alcohol consumption is the central theme. The Japanese are generally small-framed, so I'm guessing it doesn't take much to get smashed. Oh, what fun!

The month in Japan was drawing to a close so fast. This country taught me a lot about human excellence, and it set a high bar for the countries, cultures, and experiences that were to come. I can never overstate that Japan is the most efficient and organized country I have visited. In fact, I came to believe that they have a near-perfect society. I say "near" perfect because there is something missing. When you think about it, it does sound ideal to have an orderly society where there's no crime and everybody treats each other with respect. But where is the passion? The *drama*? Some of us thrive on the spiciness of life.

There were times during my month in Japan when I found myself feeling terrible that we Americans had bombed what seemed like wonderful, peaceful people. I could not hide, detached, behind the spine of a history book: being here with them, eye to eye, shit got real for me. As a nation, we Americans are definitely not perfect. That's the beauty of us, though. America is an idea experiment, based foremost on principles of political and economic freedom. Japan, on the other hand, is steeped in a long-standing culture replete with social morals and rich history. America has much to gain from the ways of the Japanese. I could never live in Japan, but I will always remember her lessons in excellence. Removing footwear indoors and cheerfully sorting garbage had become second nature to me. Bowing rather than shaking hands seemed like the better way. Chopsticks were no longer odd, but the fork and the knife now were. Those habits alone were worth the transcontinental plane ride.

If this was Asia, then I loved it! As before, the moment I had learned my way around a city, it was time to move on. The digital nomad lifestyle beckoned the Mangata tramily to our next destination: Thailand.

Have laptop, will travel!

CHAPTER 5

Chiang Mai, Thailand

"Same, Same, But Different."

THE PEOPLE OF THAILAND

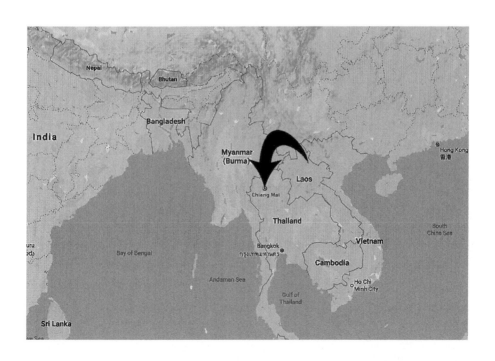

I stepped off the curb onto Siri Mangkalajarn Road, and out of nowhere, seven motor scooters, four tuk-tuks, and two Isuzu trucks came whizzing past. I jumped backward onto the broken-up concrete sidewalk with sweat dripping down my temples. Where were the signalized pedestrian crosswalks? Why were there so many red trucks in this new city of mine? I definitely wasn't in Japan anymore. I felt a strong urge to turn around go back.

As I walked to my new workspace, The Brick, to join my fellow Mangos for Chiang Mai's city preview, I took in the organized chaos around me. The city grid containing people and small funky buildings seemed endless. The tinkles of street vendors' bells chimed in with the cacophony of traffic. The smells of ripe mangos and pineapples blended with stinking clouds of car fumes. There was beauty too, though. So much lush greenery everywhere: flowers in every shape, color, and size decorated the fences and walls of tiny boutiques, hostels, and cafés. My senses were overloaded. My eyes burned from sleep deprivation and smoky air, but my body was full of energy. I couldn't wait to take a nap in my deluxe California King bed. I was heading to my jaw-dropping modern apartment that I had rented instead of staying in the accommodation that Remote Year had arranged.

RY had rented studio apartments across three buildings at the newly built Palm Springs apartment complex, situated in the Nimman neighborhood. Although those apartments were comfortable and modern, I found something else that was too good of a deal to pass up. My new home was situated on the top floor of a 14-story apartment building. What sold me was the private rooftop deck, which reminded me of my roof deck in Florida, with dazzling 360-degrees views of the city and lush mountains. Both the apartment and rooftop were about 5000 square feet each! The gourmet kitchen was larger than my entire Kyoto apartment, replete with a full complement of modern appliances and cooking gadgets. The floors were laid with freshly polished caramel-colored wood, and the walls were lined with large windows displaying inviting views of the city. And, don't get me started on the master bedroom, where there was room to roam.

Phil Phact: My rooftops in Florida and Thailand were "same-same-but-different"! Because Asian cultures emphasize the avoidance of face-to-face confrontations, the phrase "same, same, but different" is the Thai version of this Asian principle: it's a catch-all phrase that allows people to find common ground even if their views are completely at odds. "Same, same, but different" can be found on t-shirts and caps, and it is widespread in popular culture. Many Asians, I noticed, often avoid saying the word "no." Instead, they will look down to the ground and say, "I'm sorry." This happened to me many times in conversation. They just don't know how to say "No!"

You might be thinking, what happened to minimalist Phil and his love for the tiny shoebox apartment? Well, some things will never change. Even though Japan taught me a lot about the principles of minimalism, I will always prefer an upscale crib. I appreciate Japan for showing me how to lessen my desire to obtain more and more things just for the sake of accumulation and for teaching me to appreciate what I already have. That being said, there was no way I could pass up the chance to live in style at such an unbelievable price.

While I was in Japan, I not only researched apartments, but I got a jump start on researching the women in Thailand, as well. I had come to realize that many females use Tinder to make themselves feel good by getting attention from suiters, without actually intending to physically meet their matches. Luckily, I hit the Tinder jackpot and began a meaningful conversation with a beautiful Thai woman named Fong. She was very responsive to my messages, which wasn't behavior typical of a Tinder girl, at least not for me. We chatted daily, and she agreed to meet me as soon as I arrived in Chiang Mai.

When I finally met her, for once in my online dating experience, her pictures *didn't* do her justice. In person, Fong had what I consider to be "elite" physical features. Lookswise, she was quite the package … but by no means do I mean to objectify the female form. My mother always told me to treat every woman with the same respect that I would give to any woman in our family, and I do. At the same time, I won't apologize that I appreciate a fine figure. Who would argue that having a physical connection is not just as important as having a mental connection with a significant other? Fong and I had all of that and more.

Fong and I hit the ground running and dove right into a relationship. She said she picked me because I was vegan. Her plant-based lifestyle was based on her Buddhism, and I thought once again, *Why can't the Christians make the same connection?* She was direct about what she wanted: a better life, a loving husband, and to be a mother. She had life goals that many Western girls in their upper twenties are conditioned to be against, but her clear goals did not scare me. In fact, I admired her for them. Why couldn't American females come out and say what they really wanted? What was with all the game-playing? I'm not saying a woman shouldn't be out there trying to achieve her career goals if that is what she's called to do. I support that wholeheartedly. However, I am not in favor of a woman completely suppressing her desire to be a mother in exchange for career success. We need mothers to be mothers! How do you think we all got here? And how do you think the good ones got so good? A woman who is not ashamed to say out loud that she wants her main responsibilities to be raising a child, maintaining a home, and supporting the mission of her family, is my kind of woman. Meanwhile, she had earned her master's degree in economics from Chiang Mai University, on full scholarship, and her thesis was written in English. As the saying goes, "All that, and brains too!"

Fong spent nearly every day with me that month in Thailand. We got to know each very well and very fast. Our chemistry was electric. Together, we hosted several dinner parties in my fancy-schmancy rooftop apartment, where she prepared some mind-blowing vegan Thai dishes. Of course, I always put myself in charge of the kitchen and had no problem getting in the way. Still, Fong didn't hesitate to put me in my place. Fong opened the door to so many new vegan-cooking hacks, and my spice collection grew, as did my love for tempeh.

Phil Phood: Tempeh is a traditional Indonesian staple made by fermenting soybeans in banana leaves until they meld into a firm savory patty. Similar to tofu, tempeh is used as a meat substitute. Because the soy is fermented, it digests more effectively than unfermented tofu. Whether tofu or tempeh, soybeans are a benign phytoestrogen with proven power for protecting our cells. Conversely, when we ingest animal estrogen, it is often linked to invasive breast and prostate cancers. Tempeh is jammed with protein and contains more protein and dietary fiber than tofu. Its mild, nutty flavor contributes well to a plethora of recipes.

In no time, I discovered Thailand had so much vegan cuisine. In fact, many of my fellow remotes decided to "go vegan for a month" while we were in Thailand. Both Victor and Krystal attended my last talk in Kyoto, the night before we boarded the plane to Chiang Mai. Following my talk, they both declared they were going vegan in Thailand. Others followed suit. I was beyond pleased about this micro-movement within Mangata. I was ready to share my knowledge and advice with my Mango mates, and through a group chat on WhatsApp, we were able to communicate and support one another. There, we posted photos of our favorite vegan meals at restaurants, texted invitations to eat together, and sent fun facts about health and nutrition.

HappyCow would strike again and send me to a local vegan grocery store. I thought the Uber driver had dropped me off at the wrong location, because I didn't see the food at first. A blast of cool air conditioning hit me as I entered the store and browsed the tall shelves stocked with Buddhist icons, statues, trinkets, religious DVDs, and much more. But then I smelled the comforting hints of curry and coconut. Drawn to the other side of the store, I stopped suddenly in my tracks with my mouth gaping. I was in vegan heaven! Tofu, whole food, mock meat, spices, sauces, drinks, veggies … Oh my! I filled my shopping cart to the brim during my first trip there.

> **No Philter:** There it was again in my mind: why don't the leaders and followers of Christianity adhere to the original teachings of their religion? Where were the Christian food stores? I don't recall seeing an asterisk next to the "thou shalt not kill" commandment. I think it's sad that I must go to a store branded as Buddhist to find exclusively plant-based options.

My spirits were sky high after paying for my goods. I just hit the vegan grocery store jackpot! Instead of calling an Uber, I decided to catch one of the ubiquitous red trucks to take me back to my place. This Thai method of transportation is called a *songthaew*. I saw the *songthaew* as the lovechild of a trolley and a taxi. You wave down the driver like you would a taxi and tell him (all men, as far I could tell) your destination. From there, he mentally calculates whether your destination is in the area he is headed toward, how many people you have in your party, how long the distance is, and how many people he already has in the back of his truck. After assessing that information, he will either decline you a ride, or quote you a very cheap fare. If both parties are in accord, you jump in the back of the enclosed payload with your new travel friends, and away you go.

I got lucky on the first truck I waved down. He was already headed toward the Nimman neighborhood with two passengers in the back of his truck. For only 30 baht (just 90 cents), I made it back to my apartment with my six bags of groceries with only one stop to pick up three more passengers. There was no extra charge for all my freight. In fact, they helped me load the groceries before we sped off. The red truck rocked!

> **Phil Phact:** A *songthaew* is basically a converted pickup truck named after the two rows of benches in the truck bed. The red songthaew is usually only found in Chiang Mai city. Besides red, there are also yellow, white, green, and blue *songthaews*. The different colors indicate different routes to the nearby towns.

The next morning, I watched American Football history go down in a bar 8,000 miles away from the stadium: Super Bowl 52. My beloved Philadelphia Eagles were making their third trip to the Super Bowl. At 6:00 a.m. Chiang Mai time, I was joined by several Mangos at a sports bar catering to expats. It was another hello-from-the-future moment as I texted predictions of victory back home. After all, I was 13 hours ahead, and I assured everyone that there was an Eagles victory in the hours to follow. I've been a diehard Eagles fan since I was in diapers, and I had waited my whole life for this day. As it turned out, victory would be ours for the first time in Philadelphia football history. I couldn't sit still during the entire 4-hour game. It was nonstop standing, jumping, knocking my chair over, yelling, dancing, and yelling some more as I intensely watched the smash-mouth championship game. My Mango brothers cheered me on and fueled my lunacy. With nine minutes left, the Patriots were leading 33 to 32. If I had ripped off my shirt, you would have seen my heart pulsating at 140 beats per second. We were *so* close.

With five minutes left, the Eagles scored! And, if that wasn't exciting enough, they scored three more points in the last two minutes of the game. It was unbelievable! "Phil! Phil! Phil! Phil!" chanted my fellow Mangos, who knew what this win meant for me. Despite my distance from home, I never felt so close to it. One by one, I called friends and family. We exchanged the primal chant through the telephone lines: "E-A-G-L-E-S ... EAGLES!" I never could have predicted that I would be watching my team make history in a country other than America, let alone Thailand. Last but not least, I called the Philly sports radio station, 97.5 The Fanatic, and gave them my take on the game. The call screener put me right through because I had called in frequently from all over as *Traveling Phil*. Even though they were ecstatic, they were just as interested in learning about Thailand. They were always so fascinated with the digital nomad lifestyle. This call was no exception. I tried to explain to Fong what it all meant, but sadly most of it was lost on her. Nothing is perfect. That night a quorum of Mangos celebrated the Super Bowl win at my place with various versions of wok-fried veggies served under the rooftop stars. The Chiang Mai nights were always the perfect temperature for al fresco dining.

Following the Eagles' win, I was basking in the afterglow for days, weeks, and even months. All the while, I was rocking my own business from the other side of the world, glowtrotting like a boss, taking in all of Thailand's glory, and building a strong relationship with an incredible woman. Life was too good to be true ... and yet the skeptic in me was just waiting for the flip side to show its face. Nothing could be that good without a catch, could it?

Despite my doubts, all these positive feelings reminded me to count my blessings. As a result, a seed of giving sprouted deep inside me while I was in Thailand. I have always been one who strives to give back to charities and other organizations, in my own small way. It feels good to give! Fortunately, Remote Year is proactive about making a positive impact in our resident cities. Every month, in each city, Remote Year partners with local nonprofits. In Split, the charity of choice was a dog shelter. In Lisbon, the program was to spend time with underprivileged kids, helping them make cameras from old food cans. In Thailand, they were affiliated with a women's shelter called the Wildflower Home. After a listening to a presentation, the Wildflower Home tugged on my heartstrings in a way I had never felt before, and I was eager to help.

Located 30 minutes outside of Chiang Mai, the Wildflower Home is a place of refuge for women who have very young children, or who are fleeing crisis situations such as pregnancy out of wedlock, domestic abuse, and/or severe poverty. The women stay for as long as they need. They learn skills that can provide a way to support their babies. The home thrives on volunteers, with people coming and going all the time. There are several areas of the operation to get involved in, including childcare, organic farming, vocational skills, cooking, and really anything that could help the mothers prepare themselves for self-sufficiency. The Wildflower Home is affiliated with the Catholic Church. Unfortunately, the mission of the shelter and those of other similar institutions largely go unreported, because as you know, the sex scandals of the church sell more newspapers.

Phil Phact: Some of the women at Wildflower Home weren't necessarily kicked out of their homes and villages because of embarrassment, but rather due to superstition. In rural tribes to the north, near the border with Myanmar (formerly Burma), it is considered bad luck for the village if an unwed female becomes with child. The village elders will shun her and force her to leave. Once the baby is born and some time has passed, the young mother will receive forgiveness and is often allowed to return to her tribal village. Meanwhile, the Wildflower Home provides a safe and nurturing home for the unwed women and their newborn children, where they learn skills that afford them economic empowerment.

On the first visit, I joined six other Mangos early one Monday morning to volunteer our time with a few manual labor projects around the Wildflower property. Our red truck took us there quicker than I thought because there was no traffic. At 8 a.m. and beyond, many folks are still sleeping or relaxing at home. This means there is no morning rush hour! One project entailed moving a huge gazebo from one side of the yard to the other. This was necessary in order to make room for a new wing that was being constructed. Another day, I shoveled small stones from the ground into large holding bins. This was staging for the hydroponic growing system that was to be installed. After that, I gave fellow Mango Lola moral support as she painted a large mural in the small daycare hut. Art is not my strong suit, but I kept her company and kept her teacup filled. It had been a while since I got my fingernails dirty in that way, so just chilling with her was what I needed.

One of the staffers, an American named Tanya, gave me a tour of a hydroponic growing system that was still in the development phase. They had perfected it but needed money to scale it up. By the end of day, I wired $5,000 into their U.S. PayPal account. Problem solved.

Before I left that last time, I spoke with Tanya about leading a seed-sprouting workshop for the mothers in residence. Before I could even finish my offer to hold a workshop, Tanya said, "Hell yeah!" That gave me two days to scout out all the supplies needed to teach these young women the basics of sprouting.

Phil Phact: For 62 years and counting, Hippocrates Health Institute has been putting sprouted foods on the map. Humankind can solve world hunger overnight with these edible sprouted seeds because they are cheap and incredibly nutritious. Each seed contains the intelligence of the larger tree or plant; they are, essentially, baby trees. This is why a sprout's nutrient concentration is many times more than a regular whole vegetable. For example, broccoli sprouts contain 100 times more sulforaphane than regular broccoli. Broccoli sprouts were, in fact, patented in 1998 by Johns Hopkins University because they are so effective in fighting cancer. A judge threw out their claim to intellectual property a few years after the patent was issued because, as he explained, trying to patent a plant is like trying to patent air. Therefore, since it was not considered a patent chemical, i.e., a prescription medicine, it was dropped from the wellness conversation by the medical industry. Sadly, and all too often, the money is in the treatment and not the cure.

The next day, I sped off in an Uber to Old Town Chiang Mai in search of hand-held sprouting containers and sprouting seeds. Old town is crowded, dusty, and chaotic, but the buildings and the people have soul. I hit a couple of dead ends in my search, and the tropical heat of the day took some of the fun out of it. But lo and behold, I found just what I was looking for in a plastics superstore somewhere in the labyrinth of the ancient city. I bought as many sprouting container pitchers as I could fit into two large plastic bags. Soon after, I found seeds for sprouting at a large covered market. After several conversations made possible by Google Translate, I was able to score some mung bean seeds and raw almonds. Almonds will sprout just like sprout seeds if they are not pasteurized first like they are in California. One lady pointed down the hall to another lady who then sent me to the next building, where I finally found the sprout lady. I was so happy to find her. She enthusiastically joined me in a selfie as I held up the large bags of the seeds.

Mung beans are a good introduction to sprouting since they sprout so quickly and easily. It's really hard to mess up sprouting with mung beans. I also bought some colorful fresh veggies from street vendors who laid their produce on the tarp-covered sidewalk.

> **Phil Phood:** Soak the mung beans in water for eight hours. After eight hours, drain the water, rinse the seeds, and sit back to watch them grow little tails. The tails indicate the sprouting process has begun. You can eat them right away. Add your favorite dressing, and you are eating the most nutritious food known to humankind. Sprouts keep fresh for up to a month in the fridge, and cost only pennies per serving. Besides mung bean sprouts, try sprouting lentils, fenugreek, pea, sunflower, buckwheat, onion, garlic or beet, just to name a few.

Workshop day arrived, and I was excited to share the simple techniques of sprouting, but I was a bit nervous that they wouldn't understand what I was showing them. I used a lot of body language and repetition as I kept telling them, "Low cost! High nutrition for the children! Low cost! High nutrition for the children!" They seemed to pick up on everything I showed them. What impressed me even further, though, was that the mothers were holding, feeding, soothing, and entertaining their children throughout the workshop. Talk about multitasking!

The following day I returned to the Wildflower Home for a feast where we made fresh sauces to eat with the sprouts. The cutest three-year-old boy seemed to be starved for a male figure in his life and became somewhat attached to me. He was always running up and wrapping himself around my leg. I learned to walk with him affixed to my leg as the nuns eventually intervened. Once they had peeled him off, he would grab my hand to play outside. It still hurts to think about the moment I left him for the final time.

> **Phil Pheelings:** After hearing some of these mothers' stories, I was reminded of how much pain there is in the human condition. It struck me hard that I might write a check to a charity like this one, spend a few afternoons onsite sharing my knowledge and volunteering, but then return home to my "pleather" couches and flat-screen TVs and continue living my charmed life. They, on the other hand, will probably have few opportunities and somewhat limited horizons.

I found Thailand's history to be an interesting contrast to other places I had lived or visited. Thailand never had colonial rulers because through the ages their strong monarchy kept foreign imperialists at bay. Thai kings of the past made it a point to have good relations with the British Kings. A local explained to me that the Thai King, in so many words, had firmly relayed to the British Crown: "Don't worry about us. We can take care of ourselves. We can be kind to one another. You don't need to take us over."

To this day, Thailand is governed by a strong constitutional monarchy. Even the parliament was fully dissolved in 2014. This seemingly heavy-handed monarchy would offend most Westerners, especially a Greek-American like me who is proud to be a descendant of the creators of democracy itself. Yet something else became apparent to me while living in this South Asian nation: cultural capital. As in Japan, Thailand has a cultural capital that consists of knowledge passed down from one generation to the next, which consolidates the culture's deep roots. Patterns of behaviors, social norms, and morals are guided by the sensibilities developed over time through cultural capital. So, I thought, *why the hell do you need representative democracy when you have thousands of years of cultural capital guiding the people?*

I was taught that the founding fathers of the U.S. Constitution made it a point to do away with monarchy because of the persecution that the American colonists suffered at the hands of the British. It's been engraved in my mind that monarchies are oppressive and outdated and do not possess the virtues of a democracy. And now, here I was on the other side of the world, living in a society which was successful and peaceful precisely *because* of monarchy. Part of me is still too proud to accept this. I believe in the first principles of the American Constitution: The right to speak your mind, the right to defend yourself, the right to be protected from searches and seizures, to be protected from the confiscation of property, and so on. Yet, I found myself living contentedly in a land where I could be imprisoned for casually speaking out against the king or crumpling up Thai money because some dude named Maha Vajiralongkorn Bodindradebayavarangkun has his portrait printed on the front. A typical Thai household proudly displays a framed photo of the royal family, much like we would hang a picture of Jesus on the wall. The monarchy is ubiquitous, and royalty is universally loved in Thailand.

One weekend while visiting Bangkok, Fong and I were on our way back to the hotel after dinner. Police, at a checkpoint, pulled over our tuk-tuk. They ordered me to get out of the open-air vehicle, and then they proceeded to aggressively pat me down and search every nook and cranny of my wallet. They were certainly looking for drugs which, if found, could mean years of incarceration. I almost resisted when the pat down began, but it happened so fast. I had to remind myself not to play hero. As much as I despised their laws and disagree with statist tendencies, I had to accept their policies on their turf. It works for *them*.

No Philter: Thailand had just completed its official period of mourning, following the death of their king in 2016. The new king, his son, is dubbed the "Playboy Prince." He is a somewhat of a tragic figure who lives mostly outside of Thailand, mainly in Britain, Germany, and Austria. He has been divorced three times and has disowned four of his seven children. Five of his children were born out of wedlock. The Playboy Prince is heir to a 30-billion-dollar empire that has been siphoned off from the Thai people over the years. The royal family even owns most of the shopping centers in Thailand. No wonder the framers of the American Constitution were so adamant about prohibiting an American monarchy. The money is better in the hands of the people, which gives them power and rights over the government.

Most of our host countries gave travelers 30 or 90 days to stay as tourists. Yes, we were technically working, but we digital nomads pass ourselves off as tourists. Thailand's tourist visa was for 30 days, but our stay in Chiang Mai was for 35 days. There were a few ways to solve this. I could have applied for a visa extension and paid a few extra bucks to legally stay in Thailand for five more days. That would have required going to a government office, filling out paperwork, sourcing new passport photos from a third party, and so on. But, like most Mangos, I took a little side trip to a nearby country to execute what travelers call a "border hop" and took Fong on a three-day jaunt to Singapore.

Boy, was it worth it! We stayed at the famous five-star Marina Bay Sands Resort. You may have seen its crazy sci-fi design comprising three towers of 55 floors each, and what appears to be a giant ship resting across all of them. Well, that "ship" is the longest elevated swimming pool in the world, standing at 200 meters above ground level. The giant infinity pool with the Singapore skyline as a backdrop made for a great photo op. Top of the world!

From our master suite high in the sky, Fong and I had the ultimate vantage point for the impressive laser show. Our eyes wide, we watched the choreographed lasers dance across the bay waters and clinked our champagne glasses to celebrate our romance that kept rolling along splendidly.

The next morning it was time to explore. We had one full day to see this enchanting island nation located at the southern tip of the Malaysian peninsula. By noon, we were fully immersed in Singapore's Chinatown. Having visited so many Chinatowns around the world, I thought they were all alike, but this one was special—even more so on our visit because the Chinese New Year was still in full swing. The streets were festooned with colorful decorations, and I loved seeing everyone celebrating with their families, practicing traditions, praying in temples and remembering their ancestors. I even began to feel a bit homesick. I had seen my folks not too long ago, but it already felt eons.

No Philter: The Chinese New Year festivities sparked my curiosity. So I googled the calendars of different civilizations. I discovered that the Chinese calendar began around 2637 B.C. In the same search, I saw that the Jewish calendar had started over a thousand years earlier. And that got me wondering: What did the Jews do for a thousand years without Chinese food?

> **Phil Pheelings:** Would I ever have a family of my own to pass on my old traditions and create new ones? Did I see a future with Fong? Would little Greek-Thai babies be running around a big house in Florida one day?

I had lots of questions about my relationship with Fong on that enchanting trip to Singapore, but I was able to get out of that spiral thought tunnel because my dear friend Teddy would be visiting me from home in just a few days' time. I yearned for fellowship that can only come from the home front. Teddy is a retired marine who had become a home builder. We met during our scuba diving training several years ago, and our relationship had morphed into something more like siblings. Every year for the last five, we had traveled to a different bucket-list location for scuba diving. We've been to the Red Sea, Fiji, Cocos Island, the Maldives, and now we were off to the Andaman Islands in Thailand.

> **Phil Phact:** Cocos Island is uninhabited and lies 400 miles off the coast of Costa Rica and is the location of the film *Jurassic Park*. I mention Cocos because our dives there had set the bar very high for Thailand. Cocos Island is well known for large aggregations of hammerhead sharks and other large aquatic species. We spent nine days on a liveaboard yacht and were not disappointed. We were surrounded by so many sharks of all kinds, we called it "shark wallpaper." Sharks are, perhaps, the most maligned animals. Contrary to popular belief, humans are not on their daily menu, and shark attacks are nearly always a case of "mis-steak-en" identity, if you will. The sharks prefer sea lions or seals. The moment the shark takes a bite of

a human, it gets freaked out and flees the scene. The biggest challenge we faced on the Costa Rica dive trip was figuring out how *not* to scare the awesome sharks away. Each year, more people die from falling in the bathtub than by sharks. Having said that, sharks are not our friends and are to be respected as such.

I bade Fong goodbye for a few days, and Teddy and I embarked on our annual "big dive." We flew from Chiang Mai to Phuket, where we were picked up by the dive shop. We spent the afternoon waiting to board the scuba yacht that would be our home for the next five days. While we waited to board, we found a restaurant on the main drag of the tiny harbor town outside of Phuket. We were greeted by a tall, thin, middle-aged white guy with salt and pepper hair, originally from California. He turned out to be the owner of this American-style sports bar, and he immediately befriended us. After some small talk over some tasty bean tacos, he shared stories about his life with his Thai wife and son, and what it was like to live in Thailand. We covered a lot of ground, but one particular thing stuck out when I asked him about his opinion on the Thai monarchy system. He said that the Thai people "need to be told what to do," and that "the system is good for them." This seemed to reinforce what I was picking up about Thailand, which is called "The Land of Smiles." Actually, the word "Thailand" translates to "land of the free."

Teddy and I boarded the yacht and gave each other high-fives as we pulled out of the marina. The vessel headed west to the islands as the sun glistened on the water in front of us. Before we knew it, we were 20 meters deep in the Andaman Sea on our first dive, exploring a colorful reef of hard and soft corals buzzing with small tropical fish. It felt great to be back in the water with Teddy as my dive buddy. The routine for the next five days was eat, sleep, dive, and then repeat. We did five dives per day, including some night dives, which is a skill all its own. During a night dive, a new set of creatures often comes out to play.

The scuba gear I had brought from home served me well. There's nothing like diving with your own gear. After completing almost 700 logged dives in 18 water columns around the world, scuba diving was like riding a bike for me. The style of diving in Thailand was pretty easy, though. There was no current, the water was calm, and the visibility was a consistent 20 meters. In Florida, we have what is technically known as "drift diving," whereby we dive along the brisk Northern current, often in rough seas, with spotty visibility. Typically, we are between one and three miles from land. Because of the current, it is easy to get separated from your buddy and the group. At the end of the dive, I often need to deploy a safety marker buoy (SMB) so that the boat can find me. If the seas get really rough, it's easy to not be seen by the boat. For those rare situations, I have a GPS beacon that can be deployed in an emergency—the GPS signal is picked up by all the boats in the area and the Coast Guard. Thank God I've never needed to be rescued, but there have been some close calls. Florida diving can be dicey, and it requires skills not practiced by many divers. As the saying goes, "If you learn how to dive in Florida, you can dive anywhere."

On our second day at sea, I took a tumble down a flight of stairs and smashed into the corner of a bench. It was a mean spill, and I immediately knew that it was pretty bad. My right shin started bleeding profusely. The crew mobilized to help me, along with a sweet man named Ernie, a retired EMT from California. My fall resulted in two severe gashes, which the guys cleaned and dressed, but there wasn't much they could do for the pain. My shin felt as if someone had hit me hard with a hammer over and over again. Needless to say, I took the rest of that day off from diving. However, the next morning, I decided to keep diving. This was risky, given the possibility of infection—the vicious pathologies of the ocean are not kind to humans—fortunately, though, Ernie had a supply of iodine solution that he selflessly gave up. This granted me the peace of mind I needed to get back in the water. I thought, *What if it had been me who had the iodine? Would I have been so generous with my own supply?*

Although it was great, I mean *really* great, to get back into the water with Teddy, this big annual dive did not make it to the top our all-time greatest dives list. Thailand, like many places around world, suffered from overfishing. We didn't see one shark, not one, and this is one sign of overfishing.

Phil Phact: Marine ecosystems around the world are suffering, and we are heading swiftly towards fishless oceans because of the human demand for fish flesh. A documentary called *Cowspiracy*, (www.cowspiracy. com), makes the case very soundly, but there are many other sources that also document this sad reality. They say that all science is observation: I don't have to be a credentialed scientist to validate what I see happening in the oceans. I have seen what is happening. We can solve many environmental problems all at once, especially concerns for the ocean's fish population, simply by eliminating the animal products on our plates. When consumers make the connection with the consequences of their food choices on their plates, I believe the free market will once again bring us quality products at reasonable prices and serve up some amazing mock-meat substitutes. It will have to come from the grassroots.

Teddy and I returned to Chiang Mai with enough time for me to show him around the city. One afternoon we went temple-hopping, and I thought, *Wow, my life had evolved from bar-hopping to temple-hopping!* The Buddhist temples are a joy to visit for the views both outside and in. The interiors are colorful and highly ornate, and the peaceful mood is set by the monotonous chants of the many monks there. I *love* the chanting! The monks repeat unintelligible phrases, which engender a trance state. A few of the monks are posted at stations where you can give them slips of paper bearing names of your loved ones, and they will sing a song of prayer on their behalf right then and there.

My time with Teddy was great, and reconnecting with him was good for my soul. As soon as he left, I went right back to the digital nomad lifestyle, which included indulging in daily two-hour massages for about $15. In addition, I kept up my hour-long meditation, which was a combination of Transcendental Meditation and the NUCALM app. Following yoga, the workspace, and the massage, I returned home to my exotic girlfriend. Food, wine, and friends on the rooftop under the stars capped off a perfect day, day after day.

Only one week remained before I was to depart for Malaysia. A wave of sadness swept through me every time I thought about leaving Chiang Mai; but, like a drug, traveling to new cities had become somewhat of an addiction.

My five-week stint in Thailand reached a dramatic crescendo on the last night: let me tell you about the time I saved Victor's life... On that night, some club promoters held an outdoor music festival right next door to my apartment building. The theme of this rave was water, which meant they shot fire hoses into the crowd of over a thousand. Fong and I watched from the sidelines of the wet-and-wild pit, but a few other Mangos, including Victor, joined in. Victor, a big partier wherever he is in the world, scored some ketamine, a recreational drug also known as Special-K—essentially, horse tranquilizer—that can be very dangerous if the wrong quantity is taken. He confided in me that he had taken it, so I kept an eye on him.

A few of us noticed Victor starting to walk very erratically as he came out of a bathroom stall. The next thing I knew, he was squirming on the ground right in front of several Thai policemen. They dispassionately looked down at him and didn't seem to care. Gil and I tried to pick him up, but weighing in at around 300 pounds, he was impossible to lift. He wasn't passed out, but he was lost in his own world, laughing, and smiling: he was, as they called it in the drug scene, in a "K-hole."

Fellow Mangos, Krystal and Charlotte, a nearby stranger, and I were eventually able to drag him into a tuk-tuk. We piled in with Victor, who was like the dead guy in *Weekend at Bernie's* except for some occasional laughing, slobbering, and mumbling. I don't know why the tuk-tuk accepted him and our motley crew (a tuk-tuk normally carries only three people plus the driver). Maybe he was avoiding saying no. I'll never forget how Charlotte repeatedly slapped him across the face, yelling and screaming at him to "wake the fuck up." Besides that, she was calling him every other dirty word in the book, but her anger was lost on him. Once we made it to his apartment, we dragged Victor through the lobby, up the elevator, down the hall, and finally into his studio apartment.

We dumped him onto the bed, but he somehow landed face up and on his back, which is when it got interesting. The others were tired of dealing with him, as was I, and they were in a hurry to get out of there. However, knowing better, I said, "Hold up a minute. Let's just watch him." I noticed that his breathing was pretty shallow, and it occurred to me that if he were to pass out on his back, he could potentially be in danger. Too many of my favorite rock stars had died by asphyxiating on their own vomit. So, I whacked him in the shoulder a couple of times and ordered him to turn on his side. He was still lifeless except for a few gurgles. I then gave him my hardest shove and managed to roll him over on his side as the bed squeaked in agony. Just as I was pushing him over to his side, out it came. Like a live fire hydrant, a torrent of vegetable pad thai vomit shot out all over the place. Needless to say, the sight and smell were vile. Oddly, the noodles and vegetables were intact, so I made a mental note to lecture him about chewing his food better when he sobered up.

When the vomiting session was over, I kept him on his side. After a quick Google search, we learned that Special-K wears off after about an hour, so I knew it wouldn't be long before we were in the clear. After about 20 minutes of observing him, we decided it was safe to leave. But before we left, Fong sprang into action and cleaned him head to toe like a nurse.

After cleaning the vomit off him, she took the bed comforter and used it to mop up the rest of the hurl. When she finished the task, she folded up the comforter to minimize the smelly mess and placed it outside on the balcony. She knew just what to do. It was quite a display of her character, and I loved her even more for that. It showed me who she was.

Phil Pheelings: "When things are easy, a person really doesn't learn about himself ... It's what a person does at the moment of struggle that shows who he really is ... Some people never get that moment ... What I do now is who I am." Robert Kurson, Author, *Shadow Divers*

Next morning, I received texts from the Mangos who took part in the Special-K incident. They thanked me for essentially saving Victor's life. Victor didn't remember a thing, but once he heard about what happened, he also thanked me, and apologized. None of us ever brought it up again. I felt so good having had a hand in saving my friend from the very real possibility of catastrophe. As the months went on, I got to know Victor on a deeper level. I got to know his heart, and I came to love him like a brother. If I hadn't been there to help him that night, who knows how things would have turned out?

Phil Phact: At Hippocrates Health Institute, we are taught to have mindfulness with every bite. Every bite should be chewed 30 times before the next bite. This is because the teeth act as a blender. You may love your smoothies, but without exception, the best blender is your teeth because the enzyme-enriched saliva secreted from the glands mixes with your food, initiating a jump-start for optimized digestion. As they say at HHI, "Chew your water, drink your food."

That last night was a dramatic and somehow fitting send-off to an incredible five weeks in our second Asian country. We were all hungover the next morning, our departure day. Bleary-eyed, I stared out of the coach window on the way to the airport, and the strangest thing caught my eye: a billboard was advertising cosmetic products, and in English at the bottom, they promised to make facial skin whiter. Fair skin was a clear desire throughout Asia and India: a tan from the sun was avoided at all costs.

Thailand was nothing short of exquisite. The potential future with Fong presented the opportunity for a return to this magnificent land. Until then though, we made plans for her to visit me in the cities to follow. I will never forget our parting moments at the airport when Fong held me close and almost wouldn't let me go. As I ascended the escalator to meet the others at the gate, we stayed locked in a lover's gaze until she fell from view.

For the first time in a while, I had found love. Of course, there was a woman, but I had now been enchanted with yet another country. I fell hard for Thailand's exotic food, vibrant cities, and remarkable natural surroundings. From the constant sunlight radiating off the golden temples, to the cool evenings hosting dinner parties on my rooftop, to the chaos of buzzing traffic jams, Thailand had truly captured my heart. A place that was once so foreign had become so familiar. Once again, just as I had learned my way around a city, it was time to move on and start it all over again. Okay, no problem.

Have laptop, will travel!

CHAPTER 6

Kuala Lumpur, Malaysia

"Travel is the only thing you buy that makes you richer."

ANONYMOUS

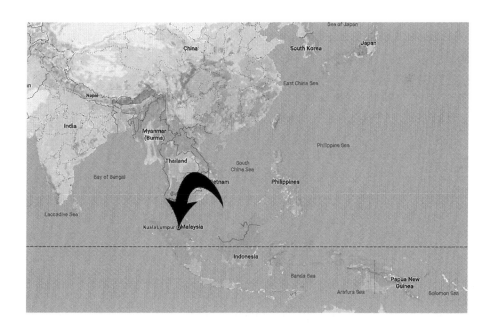

It was almost midnight when I stepped off the bus into the blistering heat of a brightly lit concrete jungle of giant skyscrapers and LED billboards all screaming for attention. The air was so thick with humidity that I had to tell my lungs it was only a quick swim. I was used to a humid climate in South Florida, but this place was a whole new level of humid. You couldn't walk more than a hundred meters without getting drenched with sweat. My regular long walks that month would be put on hold in my new Oriental city. In Kuala Lumpur, it was going to be Uber all the way, which introduced me to the world's worst traffic. At least Uber was very cheap, like everything else in Asia.

I was skeptical of my new home in a Muslim nation. In fact, I had a chip on my shoulder. After the tragic incident of 9/11, my library filled up with books on Islam and biographies of Muhammad. I spent years educating myself on the faith's history and beliefs, and I admit that I entered month six of Remote Year holding on to a lot of negative preconceived notions, but I made the effort to keep an open mind—after all, Malaysia is known to be a melting pot of Malay, Chinese, Indian, and European cultural influences. The interactions between these cultures seemed to play out harmoniously in everyday living, at least from a street-level point of view. Malaysia is a geographically small country made up of similarly sized parts: the Malay Peninsula, a landmass separated by the South China Sea, and the island of Borneo. It's on the same peninsular land mass as Singapore, and you can drive from Kuala Lumpur to Singapore in about six hours.

This month, we were all residing in the Maple Suites, a hotel-turned-apartment complex. Everyone had roommates, except me. As the elder statesman of the tramily, I was grateful to the program leaders who gave me a single apartment when possible. On my first morning, I woke up with the sun shining through the sheer curtains, lying in the king-sized bed of the three-bedroom apartment assigned to me, myself, and I. Maple Suites was located in the Golden Triangle district of Kuala Lumpur. My apartment was on the 12th floor, with awesome balcony views. There were four elevator banks that served the building, but it seemed like only two ever worked. And, we were still in Asia, so of course the construction noise was constant, even *right* next door on both sides.

> **No Philter:** There would never be malfunctioning elevators in Japan!

After getting up and out of my apartment at Maple Suites by 9:00 a.m., I broke my own Uber-only declaration, and walked the 15-minute route in the scorching heat to our new workspace. I traversed through the bar and restaurant district, which was all buttoned-up from the night before. I thought, *Gosh, I was in the hustle and bustle of Chiang Mai just yesterday, watching millennials in a mosh pit getting hosed down with water.* Google Maps led me through the bustling downtown area, which was filled with souvenir shops, pungent durian stands, and numerous commercial shopping plazas. There were also many ultra-high-end luxury malls and tall, class-A trophy skyscrapers. Kuala Lumpur was indeed a first-world megatropolis.

Our workspace was located on the 14th floor of the Fahrenheit 88 mall and office building. It was a very modern space with a kitchen area, common room, and separate workspace room. There were couches, pool tables, and Remote Year themed murals and graffiti all over the walls. I spent only the first week going to the workspace. It was too far, too hot, and not conducive for my type of work. At my apartment, I was able to use the large dining room table to spread out and organize stacks of paperwork. Besides, Fong was arriving sometime during the second week, and it would be easier for us to hang out, eat, and work inside the apartment. It rained nearly every day. Those Malaysian thunderstorms were loud and unpredictable. After all, we were living in a tropical rainforest turned mega-city.

Hosting Fong for most of March felt like we were "living together." When we were together, we got along great. She treated me like a king as no woman ever had. The meals she cooked were better than any restaurant food (whole food, plant-based Thai dishes, with little to no oil), so we ate at home most of the time. Our meals were basically sautéed vegetables with savory sauces of different varieties. I never went hungry with her around. Even though I ate like a horse, my clothes were fitting better. Fong's father owned ten farms, and her mother served prepared food at a stand in the province of Phrae. Fong had clearly learned from the best. (Incidentally, I met her parents when they stayed for a few days in Chiang Mai. They didn't speak a word of English, and when Fong wasn't readily available to translate, we just smiled and bowed to each other. The feelings were warm and deep, but I couldn't begin to fathom just how they would fit into my Palm Beach world, let alone meet my parents. There was still so much to figure out about our relationship.)

Phil Phact: "A whole food, plant-based diet, with little or no added salt, oil or sugar, solves more health problems than all the pills and procedures combined." Dr. Colin Campbell, 2015 Freedom Fest Conference, bestselling author of *The China Study.*

There was much to see and experience in Kuala Lumpur. The mix of old colonial buildings, busy shopping districts, and skyscrapers could never be fully explored. Our single neighborhood, Bukit Bintang, had all of this and more, including the iconic, 451-meter-tall Petronas Twin Towers. At first glance, Malaysia seemed to be a booming, fast-paced, high-tech, and efficient city like Kyoto or Tokyo. On the flip side, though, Malaysia's capital city suffered from water and air pollution, acute infrastructure problems, and the world's worst traffic. There were many high-end luxury condos ready for people to move in to but so little room on the city's roads and freeways to handle any more traffic. To create more public transportation, the government built metros and monorails, but these modes of transportation very often didn't take us where we needed to go. When it came to public transportation, Google Maps basically said, "Can't get there from here." The government was trying to keep up with the rapid growth but was failing. In just a few decades, the population of Kuala Lumpur went from one million to ten million. Kuala Lumpur's dizzying development was made possible due to an almost 60-year rule of a one-party government. There was little or none of the stakeholder input that exists in the messy democracies of the West—just autocratic vision and a healthy dose of corruption to grease the wheels.

Kuala Lumpur's skyline, however, had to be one of the world's best. As in New York City, when I walked the streets of Kuala Lumpur, surrounded by architectural wonders towering to infinity, I felt an extra bounce in my step. That is until hijab-wearing Muslim women came my way; it's a sight I'll never feel comfortable about. To me they looked like Halloween goblins. They probably think that we Westerners are pretty strange too. It's obvious to any free thinker that this traditional dress is oppressive and goes against a woman's individual identity. I learned that Islamic culture dominated the society. According to Malay law, a Muslim man can have up to four wives, which many had, and most restaurants didn't serve alcohol. A Remote Year experience manager shared with me that some Muslims patrol the streets in the restaurant and bar districts of Kuala Lumpur. They look for other Muslims that they know personally to see if they are actually drinking the alcohol. Sounds farfetched, I know, but this is what he told me. No matter the culture or religion, people love to gossip!

Phil Phact: Traffic in KL has a "1 to 1 ratio." In the car we traveled 1 kilometer per 1 hour. Two hours to go 2 kilometers. Really? Can I get those two hours of my life back please?

The lack of alcohol in Malaysia turned out to be a blessing. Sure, I loved a fine wine, but it was about time that I cut my alcohol intake, so this was the month I jumped on the wagon. Since Fong hardly ever drank alcohol, and I was living in the heart of a Muslim country, I said, "Sayonara" to the booze!

> **Phil Phact:** One of the Arabic contributions to the world was the discovery of alcohol. The linguistic origins are "al" and "goul," meaning "the take away," thus referring to the mind-altering effects of inebriation. Arabic contributions to the world are often revealed by the root letters "al," such as in the word "algebra."

Month six, in the unlikely country of Malaysia, was also the month that I became a vegan celebrity—a "vegebrity," if you will. My Indian friend Shankar, whom I had met on my side trip to India with Dr. Will Tuttle, connected me with a wonderful medical doctor living in Kuala Lumpur. Enter Dr. Vythi, the pioneer of the local vegan movement in Malaysia and beyond. Following our epic experience in India, Shankar had promised to refer me for speaking opportunities, and he followed through on his word. As I learned later, I was vetted through my YouTube lecture videos. Soon after my arrival in KL, Dr. Vythi planned a sumptuous dinner and meet-and-greet in my honor. He wasted no time booking me for talks and presentations for the month.

I spoke at five prominent events, including one in Kathmandu, Nepal, where I was to be the keynote speaker at the Annual Vegetarian Asian Pacific Congress. It was the thrill of a lifetime. On March 9, I took a four-and-a-half-hour flight to Kathmandu, Nepal. The flight itself was tolerable, but once we landed, getting out of the airport was less than fun. It took 90 minutes to get through immigration. Upon entering the immigration area, a cattle shoot led me to a computer system that was to replace the hand written customs paper that's normally handed out on the airplane. I suffered through the glitchy computer system for 20 minutes, just to generate a piece of paper with a crude facial image: if you joined the dots, you might have figured out it was me. Then I had to wait in a ridiculously long line to pay $25 for a tourist visa. Once that was taken care of, I was led through a labyrinth of misleading signs, ending in another line to get my passport stamped. The immigration officer decided to put my documents aside and started working on his administrative paperwork. By now I definitely wasn't in the mood. I displayed my annoyance and motioned to grab my passport and papers because the agents next to him were twiddling their thumbs. His sleepy eyes looked up at me as he put his hand over my documents. This guy was messing with me. Nepal was not giving me a good first impression. I was finally allowed to enter the country.

I headed straight to the nearest ATM for some "sparkies." I like to give things and people nicknames, and a sparky is any currency other than the dollar. With all the glowtrotting, a digital nomad can forget the name of the currency du jour, so I thought sparky was a good catch-all name ... and more polite than "funny money." Many Mangos also adopted the term. Of course, a few virtue-signaling, easily triggered millennials in the tramily were offended by the term. I still loved them, though. It's not as if I was perfect.

I walked back toward the exit and found a short man holding up a piece of white paper with my name scribbled on it. The driver helped me with my bags and hastily, yet politely, loaded me into a tiny green car with bald tires and dents all over it. We made a pit stop for some bottled water and bananas at my request. Bananas had become my go-to travel snack, and bottled water was mandatory wherever I traveled.

Nepal is said to be the birthplace of Buddha, who lived about 500 years before Christ. This fact of history is a big tourism draw. But the main draw is that Nepal is the gateway to Mount Everest and the Himalayas (kind of like the Acropolis to the Greeks). Close to a thousand people visit Nepal each year and attempt to climb Mount Everest. Beyond the exclusive club of Everest climbers, many more adventurers come to hike and climb less ambitious heights. As I learned in Croatia during my first Remote Year track, 25 percent of the people who climb Mount Everest die trying to climb it or perish making the descent.

After happily checking in at the upgraded section of the Radisson Hotel, I did a face-plant into the white comforter of my king-sized bed. I had two hours before meeting Dr. Vythi and the conference organizers for dinner. I had just enough time to meditate and freshen up. At dinner, I was somehow observing myself as if there were a camera looking down at the scene. My imaginary video feed included a large round table with sharing plates of savory Indian food and a slew of new friends. Four activists from China had flown in with a Thai man who was living in Hong Kong. My WhatsApp contact list continued to grow. The following day, it was showtime. There's always that adrenaline rush right before giving a presentation to a large crowd. I found my flow of words without the slideshow, which came so easily by now. I love a big stage because it allows me to create a rhythm by striding from one side of it to the other, and people like to watch an animated speaker. As I recall, I was the only non-doctor (PhD or MD) who spoke at that conference.

On the final day in Nepal, I toured the local scene in Kathmandu, exploring forgotten side streets and haggling with scarf peddlers. That evening, I attended the conference farewell party. The people of Nepal sure do know how to have a good time! There was music, dancing, speeches, flowers, traditional costumes, and a little body odor but lots of love. The farewell celebration was an energetic party sans alcohol, just like Malaysia. It was a great send off for a short stay, but I was ready to head back "home" to Kuala Lumpur.

In the morning, the driver arrived 45 minutes late to take me to the airport. No surprise there. He was definitely running on Nepali time. We weaved in and out of traffic, dodging cows and potholes, and made it to the airport just in time. I sank into my seat, exhaled some gratitude, and stuffed my zero-radiation headphones snugly inside my ears.

The airplane jerked and began to head toward the runway for takeoff. All seemed as it should … but nothing prepared me for what happened next.

I was about to doze off into Phil-land when I heard and felt a loud explosion. It sounded like a bomb. I knew something was very wrong. Was it coming from our plane? Did one of our engines combust? The passengers and I began to look out of the windows for answers, while asking a hundred questions. No announcements came from the cockpit for what felt like an eternity.

A stewardess fixed her stressed-out gaze outside her window and pointed. "There's a plane crash," she said. I couldn't see it from my side of the plane, so I got up to view what she saw. There it was: smoldering, twisted steel, and continuous plumes of flames and smoke. Several of us jumped on our one bar of mobile phone reception and learned that a turboprop commuter plane had just crash-landed.

I felt nauseous. A split-second glance was all I needed to feel the weight of the devastating crash. We later learned that 49 people died out of 71 and many of the bodies were completely incinerated. Swarms of military personnel and rescue teams were running and race-driving towards the crash scene. Fire trucks had their hoses on full blast, but no amount of water could undo the carnage. It quickly became a recovery operation instead of a rescue mission.

Traffic control ordered us to remain inside the plane and on the runway. With my one bar of cell reception, I called my mom and dad, and then my sister. It was one of those moments when you needed your *real* family. Voice shaking, I informed them that everything was fine, but my flight was delayed by the crashed plane. It was a bad idea to tell them; my parents reacted in their usual worried way and begged me to get off the plane. It was time for me to come home—I never should have left Florida to begin with—they said. The phone call with my sister was similar. I became the one comforting them instead of the other way around, as intended. I gave them all the information I had on the crash and said how much I loved them. All I could do at that point was wait and see what would happen next with our flight. I just wanted to get the hell out of Nepal … but after a moment, I realized I was being self-centered. Why was I so concerned with *my* flight taking off, when 49 lives had just been snuffed out and their friends and families' worlds had been changed forever?

We spent the next four hours on the runway. At some point, the captain opened the main cabin door, freeing us to walk around on the top level of the jetway stairs. From there I had a clear view of the crash scene. The men were carrying stretchers containing lifeless, charred bodies. It was so fucked up. During our long wait on the tarmac, we were constantly receiving unofficial briefings from the captain and stewardess. This obviously stands in stark contrast to the way litigiously aware American companies handle emergency situations. I couldn't believe that the captain and I were having candid discussions about the crash, based on intel he was receiving from the control tower. He shared with me that the plane flew in for a landing from the wrong direction, and that the plane's wheels caught on the airport fence upon entry. He also divulged that if we had been taxiing on the runway just a little sooner, we could have easily had a head-on collision with the doomed plane! Finally, after sitting on the runway for several hours, our plane was cleared for takeoff with just 20 minutes to spare on the crew's service limit, saving me the hassle of a canceled flight and having to find a bed for another night. Thankfully, I was back in Kuala Lumpur and in Fong's arms by around midnight.

My trip to Nepal was a huge wake-up call for me. In my life, I have had a few major life-and-death incidents (like my logged dive number 89, which I will discuss later). In each instance, my gratitude and appreciation for my life, family, and friends grew stronger. I was reminded that every breath was a blessing. As tragic as that plane crash was, it gave me a new appreciation for my own life, which had to go on. In the short-term, I still had a few more presentations to give and many more places to explore in Kuala Lumpur, its surrounding areas, and beyond. In the long-term, I felt there was so much life ahead of me, so much left to live for. I was grateful for the chance to continue with a life well-lived.

Phil Phact: Kathmandu and many of the airports in that region are well-known for plane crashes. Mountains, winds, and twin-propeller commuter planes often make for bad outcomes. Many of these airlines, like US Bangla Airlines, the airline that crashed, are not allowed to fly in and out of Western airports because of their all-around low safety standards.

With the traumatic experience in Nepal behind me, I was so very happy to be back in Kuala Lumpur. My largest and most memorable presentation in Kuala Lumpur had a turnout of at least 150 people. Two fellow Mangos, Krystal and Victor, showed up to support me. My confidence was at its peak, and I believe it was my best presentation ever! A part of me knew that it would turn out well because I purposely did not plan on recording the presentation on audio or video. Perhaps not having a camera lingering in front of me the whole time helped my swagger. But damn, I wish I had the recording now.

Whenever I am in the flow of a presentation, I enjoy making meaningful eye contact with the audience. Halfway through this one, I spotted my new mentor and dear friend, Dr. Vythi, a fairly short man, sticking his neck out to fix his gaze on me. Our eyes locked, and I spoke directly to him, like it was just him in the room. I could see his broad smile, which could only mean one thing: he was proud. I could feel his reassurance in his stare. We had come to know each other very well in a short time, just like my friendship with Shankar had quickly developed while in India. Come to think of it, my relationships with others were blossoming all around precisely because I took a chance that my laptop could keep me connected wherever I was. He was now an older brother to me, and as the months went on, we stayed connected through social media and WhatsApp.

One of the local restaurant owners attended my presentation. She told me afterwards that even though it was the second time she had heard me speak, she learned several new and notable facts. I was at a point in my presentations where I could give different examples for the same point or emphasize one detail differently than before. It was all within the template that I had developed since I ditched my slides and started speaking from memory. I called this presentation "Total Health – A Vegan Perspective."

After five years of sharing the vegan message through formal presentations, I had come to love the Q & A portion the best. It seemed like there was no related topic in the vegan world, technical or philosophical, that I could not address, sometimes two or three levels deep. I had learned from experience, self-education, and the best minds in the field: Dr. Brian Clement, Dr. Will Tuttle, Dr. T. Colin Campbell, Dr. Michael Greger, Dr. Rabbi Gabriel Cousens, and many others.

One man who, up until now, I have not given enough credit to, is my father, Louis Nicozisis: a charismatic showman, a real force of a man, and a world beater. Many of my stock jokes and comebacks came from my father. Whether it was at the dinner table or in the office of our flagship Carpet Mart store in Lancaster, Pennsylvania, where everyone in our family worked, we all had Dad's "moxie" in our DNA.

Phil Pheelings: "You can't make money in the office," said Louis Nicozisis every working day of his Carpet Mart career. Dad hated meetings for the most part. After spending a fortune every week on company overhead, Dad expected all sales staff to be on the sales floor at all times to make the sale and serve customers. Then, in 1996, when he sold the company and I embarked on a different path in real estate, all we ever had were meetings. We constantly had long, sit-down meetings with architects, engineers, bankers, tenant prospects and landowners. Even though Dad loved being in control at Carpet Mart, he always gave me all the freedom I needed to operate successfully in the real estate business. Following the carpet days, his tutelage helped me turn five commercial properties into 29 properties across five states. I can never thank my parents enough for all that they've taught and given me.

With my vegebrity growing in Kuala Lumpur, my contact list grew even more. I met so many notable people, that there's no way I could list them all. I do, however, want to mention one noteworthy couple, Darkesh and his girlfriend, Rema. He put together the magnificent event on my behalf, which I consider to be the pinnacle of my speaking career. Darkesh was a delightful young man, 32 years old, who spent most of his professional life as a successful civil engineer. He recently decided to go to law school and change his career path, which is where he met Rema. Darkesh was the organizer of the largest vegan group in Kuala Lumpur, which is how I met him, of course. He came from a family of politicians, and I learned more about this during a particularly memorable lunch.

We went to a donation-based buffet located outside in the sweltering heat, choosing it over a fancy indoor buffet, and it turned out to be a wonderful plant-based spread. I had never heard of a restaurant where you paid what you wanted. Darkesh said that he gives about 6 ringgits, or $1.50. After we filled our plates and sat down at our table, Darkesh's face turned pale. Jokingly, I asked him if he had found a cockroach in his curry. Ignoring my question, he leaned forward and whispered that I should look discreetly to my left. I did so and saw a very tall man dressed to the nines. Returning my quizzical gaze to Darkesh, he quietly brought me up to speed. This man had been at the center of a historic corruption scandal a few years back. According to Darkesh, the man had absconded with money intended for a hospital development. He was prosecuted but was never convicted. He went into exile by fleeing to India. Then, a few years later, he received immunity from the Malaysian government. He was now and forever a free man living in Kuala Lumpur.

Just as Darkesh, his girlfriend, and I were about to belly up to the buffet a second time, this imposing man approached our table and began shaking our hands. He was old, stiff, and had a crazy comb-over that looked like a permanent toupee. His skin was very dark, almost black, and his weathered face had distinct Indian features. As if he were working at Walmart, a large nametag was safety-pinned to his lapel. It was like he wanted everyone to know who he was. For my personal safety, let's just say his name was Mr. X.

Mr. X was stumped. He recognized Darkesh but couldn't remember from where. As I would learn moments later, Darkesh's aunt was one of the lead prosecutors in the corruption scandal and Darkesh was present in court for days on end. Darkesh wasn't about to jog his memory! After about ten minutes of small talk and Mr. X trying to figure out the connection, the Dapper Don gave up and walked stiffly and slowly back to his seat on the opposite side of the restaurant. After the brief encounter with Mr. X, Darkesh was visibly shaken. He didn't want Mr. X to make the connection with his aunt. We changed the subject, but the conversation didn't get any lighter. Darkesh, barely touching his food by now, told me that as an Indian Hindu and someone not born in Malaysia, he was basically considered a second-class citizen. Muslims got to buy property at a 7 to 12 percent discounted rate compared to everyone else in the country, while the school system enforced Islamic education as compulsory for every student. Muslims received more lenient treatment in court, while the ethnic minorities in Malaysia, namely the Indians and Chinese, made up the largest populations in Malaysian prisons. From Darkesh's perspective, the Chinese and the Indians were constantly accused and prosecuted for petty crimes, while the real organized crime was found inside the halls of government. As he said this, he pointed in the direction of Mr. X. He continued his passionate talk. The police were complicit and often chose to look the other way when it came to crimes committed by Muslims. Other informed locals had told me that politicians enrich themselves by taking a cut of the city's real estate projects; therefore, hearing all of this from Darkesh confirmed what I had already heard.

Despite the serious subject of conversation at that lunch, Darkesh and I could have been talking about knitting or basket weaving because our camaraderie was automatically brotherly. Again, I was expanding my chosen family with an excellent person.

In my remaining time in Malaysia, I directed my focus towards whatever came across my laptop. Cindy faithfully sent breeze blocks of paperwork through DHL, and I dutifully sent it back. However, I always found time to meditate, take yoga classes, and explore the different neighborhoods with Fong. She was only in her second month of practicing yoga and was already quite advanced. Teachers were amazed that she was merely a beginner. Besides yoga, we went to temples, foot massage studios, street food fairs, waterfalls, malls, and even on a short road trip to the Malaysian island of Penang.

Kuala Lumpur was big on big buildings and big shopping centers. As I mentioned earlier, there was a mall on every street, or so it seemed. The famous Petronas Towers had a huge mall on and below the street level. Our workspace for the month was even located inside a mall, for heaven's sake! One day we took an Uber to Genting Highlands, a hyper-mall, which has to be the largest I have ever stepped foot in. I mean, it contained literally *everything*. You could go there for a pair of jeans, get lost in H&M, hit up the food court for lunch, and even ride a roller coaster. You could go pray in one the several temples, catch the latest James Bond movie in the theater, and then wager some sparkies at the casino to top it all off. You could even stay the night in the hotel, next to another one under construction. The mall was over 15 stories tall, and a great many escalators formed a moving spine through the center of it, transporting thousands of shoppers between floors. As a property owner, I was keen to notice the finishing materials and the fashion-forward designs of marble, glass, wood, carpet, and furniture. And the colors! There was no doubt that the best and brightest architects and interior designers of the world were specifying the latest and greatest décor. The whole experience was stimulation overload. Malaysia was more like MALL-Asia!

One day Fong and I ventured off to the Batu Caves, located about 30 minutes from Kuala Lumpur's center. The caves are a main tourist attraction and a major religious location for Hindus. We held hands as we climbed the 272 steps dotted with monkeys, half-eaten pineapples, and rotting durian fruit. The 100-year-old temple featured numerous idols and statues built in and around the main caves. The caves' interiors were lined with limestone formations said to be around 400 million years old. The most notable feature of the Batu Caves, however, was the world's tallest statue of the Hindu deity, Murugan, standing at 140 feet high.

Before the end the month, I was able to squeeze in one more vegan presentation that involved a day-long road trip to the island of Penang. Again, Dr. Vythi and his connections put me to work. Our driver, Simon, picked us up from Maple Suites, and like many sweet people I have met across the world, he generously showed off his country. The tropical countryside of Malaysia was captivating. Getting out of the Kuala Lumpur megatropolis was a perfect prescription to recharge. We made stops at exotic waterfalls, a tea shop, and a street food market, as Simon whisked us through the lush, mountainous rainforest. The vegan street food was on point, and I gave it five stars on the HappyCow app. He drove us through a small town called Ipoh. I admired all the adorable street art that graced the walls of the tiny town. The colorful building murals gave it so much character and charm.

When we arrived in Penang, we checked into one of the island's waterfront hotels, without much time to spare before my presentation. I spoke in the reception hall of a wonderful vegan restaurant there, which was the only vegan restaurant on the entire touristy island. As I walked into the small hall, I saw that the audience was a decent size but not my largest. It was small enough to walk around and personally introduce myself to people, but large enough to need a microphone. Everything went according to plan. I had really entered a comfort zone with presenting my ideas. After my main talk, I took some engaging questions from the group. Fong and I celebrated with a bottle of wine later that evening, as I decided to fall off the wagon for one night of fermented moderation.

> **Phil Pheelings:** There are people who have been touched by this vegan message and subsequently made lifestyle changes. Knowing that I make a small difference in sharing the message is all I need to sustain my drive to continue. I was definitely going to miss my time in Asia, which was quickly coming to an end.

We flew back to Kuala Lumpur, and I prepared myself to pack up and get ready for another travel day. Packing this time around was harder than I thought, mentally and physically. I was really going to miss Asia, *and* I had so much stuff. Packing and unpacking had become a routine, but now there was more to pack. Fong's and my belongings were spread all over the place. Also, saying goodbye to Fong was tough, but I knew it would not be a final goodbye.

Living and traveling for three months through Asia, gave me way more than I bargained for in terms of cultural elucidation and personal growth. Asia was always a place on the news or in a book—a place I considered "way over there." But now, this far-off place wasn't so far-off to me anymore. Living in Asia affected me in so many positive ways, and it was Asia's culture, habits, and traditions that made the greatest impression. One tradition that will stay with me for the rest of my life is the practice of removing my shoes upon entering the home; that act symbolizes so much of what is right with the Asian culture, in my view. But there are more principles that should be a model for all humanity: the emphasis on cleanliness, the way others are treated respectfully, the way tasks are efficiently and nearly perfectly performed, and so on. What I also treasured about their culture was the strict adherence to punctuality: it's an Asian generalization, but there is a grain of truth in every stereotype. I sincerely appreciated it because I am my father's son: always punctual out of respect for other people and their time. If I had to sum up Asia in one word, it would be just that: *Respect*.

It was nearly time to spend six months in South America, but instead of going with my fellow Mangos straight to Argentina, I made a necessary trip back to Florida. I had some business to take care of, namely a date with fate, otherwise known as the IRS. My business affairs were too complicated to knock out the tax season remotely, and my physical presence was required to sign stacks of tax returns. Oh, what fun. More than once I stopped and reflected: I had half a year of this digital nomad lifestyle under my belt, and a half year to go.

Returning home to my beautiful digs in West Palm Beach was as wonderful as any homecoming should be. I hosted my dear friends and parents at my place, and two cases of Dom Perignon lubricated the lively conversations. One guest in my core group of friends included my music and audio tech, Adam. We had been collaborating in my state-of-the-art music studio for over a decade. Over the years, I had invited Adam to many of my social events, whether it was a Super Bowl party or a chic, Palm Beach air-kissing cocktail party. I always hoped that he might show up, even if it was in his signature hoodie, looking his usual disheveled self. But he always stayed underground and was quite shy on the surface. However, he was one of my best and most trustworthy friends, so having him there for that party really meant a lot to me. It was great to catch up with everyone, but I soon recognized that feeling of wanderlust within me. I had always loved travel, but this new urge was more acute. A voice inside of me whispered, "Okay. I see that my home, my office, my favorite spots, and everyone I care about is still here and okay, but now I'm bored. So, it's time to go. See ya!"

Phil's Phinal Word: Six more months away would be a cinch in my estimation. After the dazzling experiences of the last six months in both Europe and Asia, I had high hopes that the next six would be just as amazing, if not more. There was only one way to find out for sure, so it was time to get back on that steel bird and head southward to new frontiers.

Have laptop, will travel!

Ready for takeoff! Me at my 50th birthday party in West Palm Beach just before I embarked on my year-long odyssey.

*Optimistic beginnings in our first city of Split, Croatia,
here at Diocletian's castle.*

*Surveying the real estate at one of my all-time
favorite islands, Hvar, Croatia.*

*Taking care of business at our coworking space, the WIP
(Work In Progress), in Split, Croatia.*

*The architecture in Prague is simply spellbinding.
Old-world Europe at its finest!*

The iconic television tower in Prague was right across the street from our apartment. It is considered by locals as a relic of the communist era.

Taking care of business in Prague at the K10 coworking space,
formerly the Danish embassy. A very grand structure.

"Our bones wait for your bones," says the sign just above the church entrance. The famous chapel outside of Lisbon, Portugal, built with the bones of Christian monks.

*My lovely neighborhood of Sao Benton, Lisbon, where
I penned some graffiti tags, "Phil Nico."*

*The view from my balcony. For two weeks, they dug up
Rue Fresca (Fresh Street) in Lisbon.*

Me and Alvin shredding the powder on the island of Hakkaido, Japan.

Buddhist shrines are everywhere in Chiang Mai, Thailand,
especially at every shopping center.

*Full of emotion for my Philadelphia Eagles, watching them win their first
Super Bowl at 6:30 a.m. on Monday, in Chiang Mai, Thailand. Coinstein
and Victor, right of center, were rooting for me!*

*Holding a sprout workshop at the Wildflower shelter for young mothers,
Thailand. Looking back, it turned out to be one of the greatest
accomplishments of my life.*

*The Buddha store in Chiang Mai, Thailand, had
all my favorite vegan foods.*

With Fong in Chiang Mai

Top of the world once again at the Sands in Singapore. I had to
make a side trip to break up my Thai travel visa.

The famous Petronas Towers in Kuala Lumpur, Malaysia.
Malaysia was quite hot and humid!

For the month in Kuala Lumpur, Malaysia, I was a "vegebrity" (a vegan celebrity). I headlined five major events there and Nepal.

Perfect weather set the stage for a fantastic day of touring Buenos Aires on our bicycles.

Rocking out with Chris and a session drummer in Buenos Aires.
Felt good to dust off my fingers and rock out!

Bonfire ignited by electrical union protesters in Córdoba, Argentina, 1000 of whom would march to the utility company headquarters nearby. Rampant inflation was getting the best of their paychecks.

Top of the world at the famous Machu Picchu site.

*My beanie hat from the Indian market of Lima, Peru, was
probably my favorite purchase of the year.*

The yurt where Fong and I had a life-changing
Ayahuasca retreat, outside of Cusco, Peru.

Conquering the sand dunes of Peru, broken foot and all.

Taking it all in at Cartagena, Colombia—a great side trip with Coinberg and Coinstein.

Pulling out some sparkies from the ATM. This time it was
Colombian pesos at over 3000 pesos per USD.

The view from our hot air balloon basket, way up in the sky, outside of Mexico City. I nearly fainted from the height!

The famous Teotihuacan pyramids outside of Mexico City.

CHAPTER 7

Buenos Aires, Argentina

"The city and its people are a study in contrasts: European sensibilities and Latin American passion; wide boulevards and cobblestone alleys; steamy tango and romping rock and roll; sidewalk cafés and soccer fanatics."

NATIONAL GEOGRAPHIC ON BUENOS AIRES

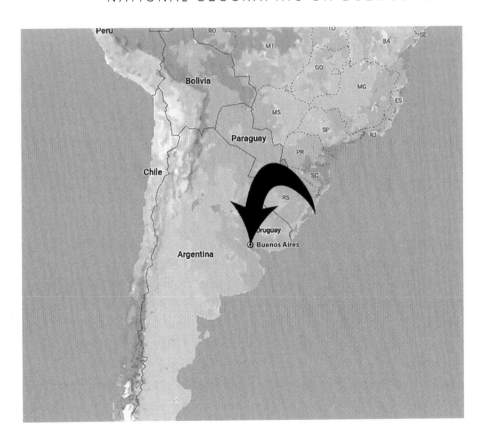

I had hit the six-month mark. No matter what, I had to finish the mission and see it through for the next six. I had to find out if these far-off places really were anything like what I had seen and read about in the news. I also wanted to keep eating my way across the world, vegan style. So, by golly, I would continue using this digital nomad platform and continue journeying with my Remote Year tramily. Oh, and by the way, as you have probably noticed by now, I was having fun!

For better or for worse, we Mangos were to be in Argentina two months: One month in Buenos Aires and one month in the city of Córdoba.

I had romantic notions of sliding back into the familiarity of the Western world, to be sure. Finally, I would be in a time zone similar to home, and I could text and call people without thinking twice. With my olive skin, I look like a South American, too! I hoped to feel less like a fish out of water … but, it didn't take long for my romantic bubble to burst, and for everything to feel out of whack.

I arrived in Buenos Aires on April 9, after my side trip back home to Florida. It was officially autumn in Argentina. The air was crisp, and the bright blue sky didn't have a cloud in sight. It was a welcome change from all the thunderstorms in oppressively hot Malaysia. A decent start. However … if my chapters had names, this one would be called: "(Dog) Shit Runs Down Hill." All of the order and respect I had become accustomed to in Asia was no more, or so it seemed. A tenseness was in the air in my new reality as I walked through the broken-tiled streets of Buenos Aires. Was this really the Paris of South America? The local people were not mean, per se; they were just a bit cranky, tired, and worn down. Unlike the Asians, respect and honor didn't appear to guide their words or actions. No doubt though, it was too soon to make any final conclusions. I came to understand that this common mood was a result of their dysfunctional economic system, where the main symptom of the disease was severe currency inflation. The Argentinians had, for the most part, been living behind the eight ball ever since General Juan Péron founded the modern state. Job creation was nonexistent in this stagnant economy, and their news cycle was a constant reminder. Very often, the front page of the paper featured some kind of drama about the economy, such as a union workers' strike. So, everywhere I looked, I could see that the people were really struggling to make it.

> **No Philter:** General Péron, founder of the modern state, was a strongman who admired Hitler and Mussolini. But mostly, he loved socialist economics. As labor secretary, he ushered in so-called labor reforms that would keep a stranglehold on the country for decades to come. He set up a state-run economy in which socialism was fueled by rabble-rousing calls for social justice. This socialist system turned a once-affluent society into an economic shit show, and as a result, there is a stench around his legacy that modern-day Argentinians are starting to smell.

In just the two months that we lived in Argentina, currency inflation jumped to over 23 percent, as evidenced by the dollar's exchange rate. Imagine if only two months into your job, you received a 23 percent pay cut! Economics comes from the Greek word economia, which literally means "how you take care of your house." As far as I could see, the formerly grand house of Argentina was dilapidated and in danger of falling down at any moment. It needed a new foundation of sound capitalist principals and a total economic refurbishment. If only it were as easy to flip a nation's economy as it is to flip a single-family house.

Actually, there were beautiful aspects about the country, but I was missing my beloved Asia and my girlfriend, which was getting me down now and then. I did my best to take Argentine lemons and turn them into stevia-sweetened *limonada* during the two months I spent there.

Our group of digital nomads was split between two apartment buildings in the Palermo neighborhood, where we each had our own studio apartment. My home was one of the best for that month, complete with a balcony and a full kitchen. It was missing one essential, though: a juicer. So, on my first full day in Buenos Aires, I set out to find the perfect market and stock up on kitchen essentials. I located a promising hypermarket on Google Maps and decided to Uber there, since it was 16 blocks away.

(Uber turned out to be a flop. For some reason, the drivers would always cancel on me, or I wouldn't get connected at all. I soon found out that Uber was illegal in Argentina. I also figured out they would cancel a trip of mine once they realized a gringo was their prospective passenger. They must have been wary of the language barrier. No problem: I changed my name to Felipe Nico on the Uber app. This workaround served me well for the next six months in South America.)

After waiting a while for an Uber that never came, I had to flag down a taxi at the corner of my street. The fare was dirt cheap, maybe two bucks, and the driver knew exactly where to take me thanks to Google Maps. From then on, I used taxis quite often throughout Argentina. The cab drivers, always male, were often gleefully animated, but typically didn't speak a word of English.

I expected the hypermarket to be something similar to a Walmart or a Target, a store that would carry a variety of everything: food, spices, appliances, kitchenware, electronics and more. I was wrong. Well, I say that with exaggeration, because, yes, the store had several departments, but I didn't find the things I needed. Where were the spicy pepper flakes and hot sauces? Where were the food processors and juicers? Where was the tofu!? Where was my beloved Japan? And my biggest question of all: where the hell was Amazon.com?

I left that superstore empty-handed and in a bad mood. I decided to take the long walk home, hoping to find another market. During my errand to nowhere, I encountered many corner markets with colorful outdoor displays of fruits and vegetables, inviting shop owners, land mines of dog poo, and endless broken pavements. It was like an obstacle course. I had to pay close attention to every step, or risking putting my foot in it! Good thing I picked up the habit of removing my shoes when I got home. It was unthinkable to track the Buenos Aires street muck into my apartment. Every once in a while, I would wash the soles of my shoes: that was city living in Argentina.

No Philter: Growing up, I spent a lot of time in the Deep South, specifically Dalton, Georgia, where my dad owned a carpet factory. One summer, I lived and worked there, and the Southern folks had all kinds of sayings. One of them was: "Some days you step in it, and some days you don't." It was their way of saying that we have good and bad days. This saying had relevance during my two months in Argentina in the most literal sense.

I made it home by 6:00 p.m. with a base-model juicer, colorful veggies, some bland red pepper flakes and other spices, and few other essentials for the month. I never knew there were bland red pepper flakes in this world, but I learned that the seeds had been bred to be bland for the Argentinian palate. I now accepted the fact that my vegan diet was headed for a lackluster and somewhat tasteless run. HappyCow, usually my saving grace around the world, was of little help. There were only a few vegan-friendly restaurants listed, and they were all disappointing. However, this forced me to make up for it in my kitchen that month.

For everyday living, a quick trip to the supermarket for a few things could turn into a full-day event. Cash was king, which meant waiting hours at ATMs in lines that were often blocks long. Waits for ATMs were long because the largesse of the public sector was sucking up the physical cash. In addition, people who were on public assistance were hitting up the ATMs at the state-run banks. So, that meant just about everybody wanted sparkies. To top it off, the maximum withdrawal amount was very low, so people had to keep returning to ATMs in order to take part in the largely cash economy. What a mess. I kept thinking about the intellectuals and the elites who romanticize about socialist economics, though they never actually *live* in these places.

But it wasn't all bad. I really got a kick out of the way people greeted each other. Everywhere I went, friends, family, coworkers, strangers, and even dogs in their way, greeted one another with hugs and kisses on the right cheek. Kiss greetings were never given on both cheeks. I saw with my own eyes that Argentina is a kissing society, which I now know reveals the sweetness of the people despite their economic challenges. I'll never forget the everyday examples that I witnessed of such sweetness, reminding me that people can be happy in their lives no matter what.

I was surrounded by the Spanish language and would be for the next six months. In each city where I lived, I tried to pick up a few words and phrases here and there, from Thai to Malay and so on. But this was the first month that I really needed to get with it and learn this language the best I could. Thankfully, Remote Year offered group Spanish classes twice a week. Not only did I enroll in those group classes, I also signed up for some one-on-one tutoring sessions at a Spanish school that I found close to the workspace. I had to laugh because throughout my school and college years, I had required the help of tutors: some things had not changed! Note to self: laugh at yourself once in a while. It's part of loving yourself.

My private teacher was a lovely new mother who brought her infant son into the brownstone house that was home to the language school. Her teaching style was to sit down and start talking in Spanish, and when I got stuck, which was just about every moment, she would jump up from the table and start hashing it out on the blackboard. It was hard on my head. Learning this new language felt like my brain was being bent. And I knew how that literally felt! Allow me to digress ...

My brain was "bent" for real while scuba diving—my logged dive number 89 to be exact. I .was too deep for too long while diving three miles off the coast of Jupiter, Florida, and I got "the bends." The nitrogen bubbles that I had accumulated in my body at 100 feet of depth expanded while I was back on land, causing a circulatory blockage in my inner ear canal (known as the vestibular canal). The blockage created an intense vertigo while I was driving home, which nearly caused me to crash the car. I had just enough wherewithal to pull over, fall out of my car on the side of the road, and wave to the passing cars for help from the ground. I spent four days in the hospital and received several recompression treatments in a hyperbaric oxygen chamber. Fortunately, at the first sign of the debilitating symptoms, I was only ten minutes away from one of the best hyperbaric chamber centers in the world. In the hospital, I couldn't even get out of bed because I was so dizzy, and for long stretches of time I couldn't even pee, which is also a symptom of the bends. The doctor informed me that "inner ear hits" were the hardest to resolve and there was a chance that my vertigo would be a permanent condition. Thank God, my condition resolved itself in about three weeks. That was 600 dives ago, and I can honestly say that I have learned profound lessons, both technical and philosophical, from dive 89.

My brain wasn't starved of oxygen by Spanish classes, but it was in a spin. But, like my dad told us almost every night at the dinner table, "Anything good is worth sweating over." To be sure, I was sweating over this alien language. In class, I took many brief walks outside to clear my head. I was probably taking this language-learning thing too seriously, but I liked my Spanish teacher very much, and we continued with lessons via Skype even after I left Buenos Aires. We spoke about the food and travel that we liked, albeit in my broken Spanish. *No hablo bueno!*

As I have traveled around the world, people would tell me that the English language is easy compared to other languages (including their own). Elle from Croatia and others have shared this with me. After hearing this so often on different continents, I had to believe it. I think that's also the reason why Spanish, like English, is so widely spoken and adopted. I think it's relatively easy, which doesn't mean I'm good at it. I knew I needed to apply myself and learn the vocabulary and grammar. But the rules are pretty simple, and a lot of the words are similar to English. It was just going to take some time and patience to master.

In addition to the kissing everywhere and the language barrier, Argentina was different in other ways compared to my own lifestyle. For example, they perpetually ran on a European holiday schedule. Between all the national holidays, when everything was closed, coupled with the endless European summer holiday schedule, it seemed like they were always on vacation. You could not go to a store and assume it would be open, like you could in the States. Coffee shops didn't open until after 9:00 or 10:00 a.m. Friends sipped wine for lunch at around 2:00 p.m. Dinner wasn't usually served at restaurants until after 10:00 p.m. If you walked in for dinner at 9:00 p.m., which is when they technically opened, no other diners were there, and the waiter looked at you like you had three heads. The "cool people" went out to nightclubs at around 2:00 a.m., which was two hours later than I went out during my Miami clubbing era. GOOD LORD! After six months of travel, even though cultural adaptation had become as familiar to me as the newish wrinkles on my forehead, I would never fully adapt. Many of my fellow Mangos, however, did fall into this alternative-reality, and would begin their days in the mid-afternoon. Techies tended to be night owls anyway.

On the plus side of the region, the women of Argentina possessed a different kind of beauty that I call "pretty and handsome." They were beautiful in a more natural way than were the women back home. (In America I would always joke that I was only one in my Pilates class who didn't have breast implants!) Living in Buenos Aires, I saw more "10s" than I had seen before in my entire life, but I could not seem to get even one of them to glance at me. Was it because I was old? Or was it because I had soul ties to a beautiful young lady on the other side of the world and subconsciously presented myself as "off the market"? Apparently not. I came to understand, as in Japan, the females in Argentina were wary of foreign men who did not speak their language.

No Philter: I also noticed that every other woman in Argentina was pregnant or had an infant attached to her. More fertile? No television in the bedroom? Who knows, but it was a baby explosion everywhere I went!

I managed to create a routine in this new city. I found a hot yoga studio and enjoyed the designated workspace, which was yet again a short walk from my apartment. On display while walking to the hip workspace was an old-school gallery of merchants with their narrow store fronts and aging signage. They offered everything from key duplication to tailoring to home improvement to small appliances. The eateries and small supermarkets I passed were just as charming. One surprise I encountered on the way to the workspace was the "bio store," commonly known in the States as a health food store. These tiny bio *mercados* were sprinkled around the city and sold whole foods like chickpeas and lentils, and other vegan essentials. This bio store even sold kombucha, a fermented tea that was quickly becoming a worldwide fad. This particular brand was low in sugar, but still had all the probiotics, which made for an immune system boost. They were always so happy to see me at the bio store, because I would put a significant dent in their inventory.

No Philter: Around the world, American travelers are known not just for their orthodontic smiles and upscale dress but also for their powerful pocketbooks. From my experience, merchants love us because we are typically generous with our money while traveling. Also, Americans *tip!* Too many travelers from other countries think that "tipping" is just a city in China!

Argentina was now growing on me, but being separated from Fong created a void in my heart. As the second week hit, I made an extra effort to get out and about, hang out with some fellow Mangos, and attend my Remote Year tracks to keep my spirits up. After a few wild nights out, I came to realize that my hard-partying days were *over*. I felt like a legacy band on a farewell tour whose singer couldn't hit those high notes anymore. Getting wasted and partaking in a few recreational drugs left me feeling like death itself the next day. I was relatively healthy thanks to my vegan diet and exercise habits, but it was impossible for me to keep up with the nocturnal club world. Of course, that didn't exactly stop me from trying. I felt safe partying alongside my Mangata brothers. We looked out for each other, especially when we colored outside of the lines.

I attended several Spanish meetups at a local bar, where you would pay a set price, get a name tag, and participate in a sort of (platonic) speed dating activity that involved speaking both Spanish and English. Lola joined me the first time. On our way there, I stopped so suddenly that she ran right into me. I stood on the street staring into the darkened window of what had to be a music studio. I rang the doorbell over and over again until they answered. It was obvious that it was private in nature, and not exactly open to the public. If they had a sign on their door, which they did not, it would have read, "Sorry, We're Open."

At my request, the young guy, who coincidentally was named Felipe, gave me a tour of the studio, and information on renting the space and equipment. I was stoked to be back in a studio setting, like the proverbial kid in a candy store. It had been so long. My inquiry paid off, and I arranged an unforgettable jam session with fellow nomad, Chris, and a female drummer we found along the way. We recorded some of it on my iPhone and posted it on social media. For days after our jam was posted, nomads from the tramily came up to me and said they had no idea I could shred like that. Like riding a bike, I was able to unpack my bag of musical rock guitar tricks, known as "licks," and rock out. I was able to get my musical "Phil."

Phil Pheelings: I wasn't on the level of Eddie Van Halen (an American immigrant success story, along with his drummer brother, Alex), nor could I caress the blues on the level of Stevie Ray Vaughan, but I could play my own brand of awesome! I was on the level of the greats ... in *my* mind, anyway. This thought made me so happy because I knew I would be writing songs for a long time to come.

This weekend was also tracks weekend, and I had signed up for a great one: I was pumped and ready for a full day of bike riding through the famous neighborhoods of Buenos Aires. Our track group met up early Saturday morning and took the 35-minute walking/metro route to Biking BA's headquarters. We signed a waiver, introduced ourselves to our guides for the day, kissed cheeks, and got helmets and bikes that fitted our needs. Then we were off. We rode a total of 34 kilometers that day. Because of the sunny, and breezy weather, it didn't feel like much distance at all. At each stop, the tour guides would let us rest as they explained the history and traditions of each area.

One of those stops was the Bombonera Stadium, where the local team, the Boca Juniors, played their home soccer games. The guides taught us about an important fan tradition. At a game, a fan cuts an empty two-liter plastic Coke bottle in half, and then fills it with a simple yet powerful cocktail: the drink was simply referred to as "Fernet and Coke." More recently, alcohol had been banned from the stadium because fans would get too crazy, and then things would often turn violent. Those Argentinians, along with many South Americans, take soccer (*fútbol*) very seriously.

> **Phil Phact:** The Boca Junior fans sometimes get so worked up during a match, they jump up and down in sync during their fight song. The jumps of so many people collectively will literally cause the stadium to rock and shake. They call this phenomenon "The Bombonera shakes." In fact, in 2012, the shakes hit 6.4 on the Richter scale after they scored a goal.

I came to love Fernet. Fernet definitely goes best with Coke. It is not a low-proof, foo-foo sweet liqueur; but instead it clocks in at 79 proof, just like vodka or other spirits. It's like a cinnamon Jägermeister on steroids. It creeps up on you and hits you like a hammer. Proceed with caution!

After visiting the stadium, we rode over to an area called La Boca, which in English means The Mouth. La Boca is located at the harbor, which was historically the heart of the tango dance. The tango is derived from a form of foreplay between the sailors and prostitutes. Yes, this kissing society could even create romance out of transactional sex! Next, we rode our bikes to a nearby ecological reserve called Bosques de Palermo, an official national park area in Buenos Aires that was built on top of an old dumpsite. It has acres and acres of trails for jogging, hiking, and bike riding. There are several perfect spots for bird-watching and even people-watching. This was my favorite part of the day. The temperature was perfect, and the air was clear in the baby-blue sky. The sun was flitting in and out of the canopy of trees above us, tempting its light to dance on our eyelids. I smoothly glided down the dirt paths in a peloton of Mangos. Riding a bike was, well, just like riding a bike. You never forget, you just jump on and ride.

Phil Pheelings: Buenos Aires means "good air" or "fair winds." I would say that's pretty accurate, and I couldn't help but take that moment to reflect on the six months that had seemed to breeze by. I was forming such strong relationships with many of my fellow nomads. I didn't love each and every person in my Mangata tramily, and I'm sure their feelings towards me were similar. It was not perfect, but it was still incredible.

We all ate lunch in the park, and it probably won't surprise you to learn I brought my own tempeh sandwich, since the options at the food stand were far from vegan-friendly. One of the many things those Argentinians are proud of is their meat. Beef, chorizo, pork, you name it!

No Philter: By the end of my stay in Argentina, I figured out that their meat bragging obsession was largely because their cuisine was actually quite poor. It was famously bland. They purposely stayed away from flavor. The locals would volunteer this information, and even talk down about their food. There was no haute cuisine in Argentina to speak of, and no celebrity chefs to export novel food concepts. So, all they could do was brag about their meat. They weren't above talking down about their country, either. My Spanish teacher was even a naysayer of her nation, as there were many others. Many citizens knew that they were screwed in their economic system, but they would persist. What else could they do?

After lunch, we wrapped up our bike tour with one final stop at the Puerto Madero waterfront area that overlooked one side of the Puente de la Mujer or "Woman's Bridge." We had the perfect view of this narrow pedestrian bridge with its giant architectural needle pointing upward at a 45-degree angle.

We parked our bikes and stood there admiring the Buenos Aires skyline that was staunchly towering over us on each side of La Plata river. One guide pulled out three cups that appeared to be gourd-like vases, accompanied by a thermos of hot water, metal straws with a filter at the bottom of each, and a bag of mixed herbs. For once, with this group of glowtrotters, the herb wasn't pot. The hot drink was Yerba Maté tea, which became my new oral fixation. They called it *mate'* for short, pronounced "mahtay." We sipped from the shared cups as they were passed around. The caffeinated pick-me-up was immediate and powerful. Drinking mate' tea was a social event between the locals. The ritual involved stuffing your cup with loose tea leaves, steeping it with hot water, and then passing it around for sips as the conversation unfolded. Some people went all out with their ornate mate' cups. Then there was the architecture of the straw. Should it be wood or metal, and at what angle should the screen at the bottom be? How big should the screen holes be? In any case, the refreshing dark, rich tea gave us the energy to carry on. Mate' basically tastes like smoky tea, and there are countless flavors and varieties. It has a smooth jolt that seems to go mostly to the head, as opposed to the body. The buzz has a smooth landing with less of the crash that coffee often has. When I was in Japan, I fell head over heels for their matcha. Well, scoot on over matcha; mate' has moved in!

What a day we had riding bikes together along the city's *very* wide avenues! Buenos Aires boasted the widest avenues in South America, maybe 12 lanes wide or more. I was rubbernecking to view the ornate, classic buildings, and tall office towers along these expansive vehicular avenues. Thank you, Remote Year: this track was just wonderful! As the afternoon adjourned, I felt the resolve to take up bike riding back in Palm Beach. The following day, back at the shared workspace, people were walking around kissing each other and then strolling over to the kitchen area to make their mate'. I was no different, but I had to use a cup, straw, and herb that I found in the kitchen. I picked a metal straw, which was recommended by Victor for its screen angle and hole size. Victor always had the best travel hacks and somehow the best local tips.

The next day, Sunday, I joined fellow Mangos Lola, Samantha, and Janet on a trip to the Sunday street market, located in the San Telmo neighborhood. The neighborhood we had sped our bikes through the previous day was now transformed into the largest street fair I had seen so far (the street markets in Prague and Chiang Mai gave me something to compare it to). The Feria de San Telmo seemed endless in comparison. Craft makers, food vendors, and performers lined each side of the street for several blocks, making it nearly impossible to see all of it in one day. As we walked along the cobblestone roads, through the crowds of tourists and merchants, we were drawn toward a large gathering of people surrounding a boombox that was belting out some classic Argentinian melodies. A closer look revealed two performers deep in a dance of tango. The eye contact between the partners was stronger than the tension in a tight rope. When the romantic melody concluded the crowd erupted with applause. For me, this was *real* romance!

After a lunch of margaritas and falafel, our group meandered the streets, taking turns losing one another in the chaos. There were so many trinkets, crafts, and antiques to take in. I found a great deal on a mate' set that included the cup, bombilla (straw), and a bag of organic yerba mate' herbs. I decided not to go too gaudy on the cup, but to stay traditional. I also purchased a gaucho neck scarf with a traditional clip. Best of all, I found an area where they were giving chair massages. I purchased 30 minutes of bliss, complete with sound therapy from a didgeridoo. I hadn't been blessed with such an incredible massage since Thailand. Of course, the price was not nearly as cheap, but it sure was cheaper than the States.

Phil Phact: A didgeridoo is a wind instrument developed by indigenous people in Northern Australia. It makes a very loud, low-pitched monotone sound. The practitioner blows and points the end at an area of a person's body. Often, it is pointed at the throat area where the thyroid resides. The low frequency of the sound waves stimulates blood flow, which is what a lazy thyroid needs in our radiation-soaked world. A study done in 2005 even found that playing the didgeridoo helped reduce snoring and certain forms of sleep apnea by strengthening a person's muscles in the upper airway.

With two weeks under my belt in South America, I joined in on that month's charity efforts led by Remote Year. We had a partnership lined up with a wonderful organization called Sumanda Energias that builds hot water heaters for impoverished families. You mean, not everybody takes a hot shower? I don't think I ever had a cold shower before. Like the others, I always took it for granted. We were to be the *voluntarios del dia,* making solar panels from one- and two-liter plastic soda bottles and aluminum soda cans.

We left early on our last full Saturday in Buenos Aires and headed to the outskirts of the city. The bus dropped us off to continue a four kilometer walk on unpaved and terribly muddy roads, and into a working-class neighborhood. We made it through a labyrinth of single-family homes that were in various states of squalor and privation. We arrived at the house and met the family. Paid staff of the non profit were already hard at work sorting the necessary materials. In the weeks leading up to the build day, we saved all our used plastic bottles and aluminum cans. We brought them with us and got straight to work building the solar-paneled water-heating system.

Here's how you build one. With box cutters, cut the tops and bottoms off each two-liter and one-liter bottle. Next, flatten, sand, staple, and paint the aluminum cans. Those flattened cans are shimmied into the plastic one-liter bottles. Then those bottles are shimmied into the two-liter bottles. Each two-liter bottle and its contents equal one solar cell. Next, assemble those cells onto PVC poles, one by one. Finally, attach the pole systems together and assemble some finishing materials around the conjoined poles to prevent water leakage.

This was no experiment. This was a workhorse design that had been duplicated many times over around the world. For more on the efforts of Sumanda Energia, check out their website: https://www.sumandoenergias.org

We all watched our finished solar-paneled water heater go through a test run. Was this thing really going to work? Raising the large panel of plastic solar cells off the ground and onto the roof was something like an Amish barn raising. Growing up in Lancaster, Pennsylvania, I was fortunate enough to frequently witness a barn raising. We all had a hand in the panel's relocation. Once on the roof, a staffer connected the large rooftop holding tank that fed the panel. We waited and waited as their precious water supply coursed through the contraption … Success! The cells were flush with running water as the water shot out the other side of the panel without leaks. Finally, he connected that open end of the panel to the plumbing system of the house. Mission complete! At that moment, I felt a strong connection to this country and its people. The sun would keep the water just right for a hot shower for many years to come.

> **Phil Pheelings:** While I never plan to spend lots of time in Argentina after Remote Year, and I didn't appreciate their dog-poo-painted sidewalks or hellish economic system, the act of helping a family in need reaffirmed that we are all children of God. We are most assuredly all created equal, regardless of our station in life. The smiles on the faces of that family when they saw their newly installed hot water system are now engraved in my heart. We were able to help a family at a low cost and do so with recycled materials generated from our daily waste: win, win! It feels great to make money, but I've learned that it feels immeasurably better to give one's time, talent, and resources. It might sound corny, but like the sprout workshop I held at the Wildflower shelter in Thailand, the water heater project has to be one of the greatest accomplishments of my life. I must do more.

The last couple of days came faster than I anticipated, though I looked forward to moving on and exploring new frontiers, new surroundings, and new places to learn. I didn't dislike Buenos Aires, but let's just say we didn't get along the whole time.

A few times, we Mangos took salsa dance lessons from our fellow nomad, Erin. This super techno geek was quite the dancer—who'd have thunk it? Over time, her beauty was on the inside and out to me. After one night of salsa lessons, the tramily went out to dinner and to a tango show. I was excited for the next time I would see Fong and impress her with my slick salsa moves. I wondered, *Do they even salsa in Thailand?*

On my last day in Buenos Aires, I went to Chinatown for the third time. I had another 90-minute massage, which was so-so, at least compared to Asia. I also figured out a new travel hack. The supermarkets in Chinatown were by nature very vegan, so I loaded up with food provisions for the next city. My luggage was already overweight, so I had to pay the airlines for my overage. But what's a few more pounds at this point?

It was soon time for the monthly farewell party. I spent nearly an hour in traffic, but the taxi fare was still only about 8 USD. (By now I had a pattern of experiences proving out that everyday costs in Asia and South America were at least half the price compared to daily life in the States.) The adios party was held in an old house in a residential neighborhood, owned and operated by the fiesta caterer. I could not have cared less about where the party was, even though the house had a cool Spanish colonial style. What mattered to me was that I was there with people I now admired and cared about. After seven months together, the bonds between my Remote Year tramily seemed eternal. All the hugs, cheek kisses, smiles, and goofy photographs affirmed what I was feeling. Fernet and Coke lubricated the vibe, although it wasn't necessary for our group's shenanigans. A small speaker played cheesy Latin songs in one corner of the main room, and in the other corner sat a drum set and several percussion instruments. It didn't take long for four of us to start a drum circle, led by Mitch who was a beast on the drums. The Mangos shimmied into the room and started to move their bodies. It was a great party to mark the end of our stay. One more city was in the history books for Mangata, and we had another notch in our belts.

Phil Phact: "Notch in your belt" means a success. In the old days of the Wild West, people used to make a mark on their belt when they killed someone. Not exactly a phrase that honors the values of the vegan message, oh well...

The next morning, on our drive to the airport, I had a moment to reflect on the past month and on what was to come. There was so much more to see, but now that we were over the halfway hump, I could see how quickly our journey would be over. I wondered how many people would remain in our group to the bitter end—several people had already retired from Remote Year Mangata and headed back to their permanent homes. Of the original 49, only about 30 digital nomads would be residing in Córdoba, Argentina, since six nomads had decided to opt out for that one month. Our numbers were dwindling.

I thought about those who had returned and wondered what my life would be like if I were back in West Palm Beach. What would I be doing? Would I be hanging out at the Mar a Lago beach club on a Sunday afternoon? Eating food and drinking wine by the beachfront pool? I most likely would have gone scuba diving in the morning, which I still missed quite a bit. Even though there really is no place like home, I had now come to see the whole world as my home. This voyage of discovery had expanded my horizons more than I ever thought possible.

But with the lack of spices or vegan food options, existential economic tension, and dilapidated sidewalks covered in poop, one month in Argentina felt like it was enough for me. But Remote Year's itinerary was etched in stone, so I mentally prepared myself for one more month here in Argentina: the city of Córdoba. I still missed Fong. I missed the comforts and cultures of Asia. How bad could Córdoba be, though? I kept my expectations low as our plane glided off the runway and headed towards the clouds for the short flight to the northwest.

Have laptop, will travel!

CHAPTER 8

Córdoba, Argentina

"Traveling is a brutality. It forces you to trust strangers and to lose sight of all those familiar comforts of home and friends. You are constantly off balance. Nothing is yours except the essential things—air, sleep, dreams, the sea, the sky—all things tending towards the eternal or what we imagine of it."

CESARE PAVESE

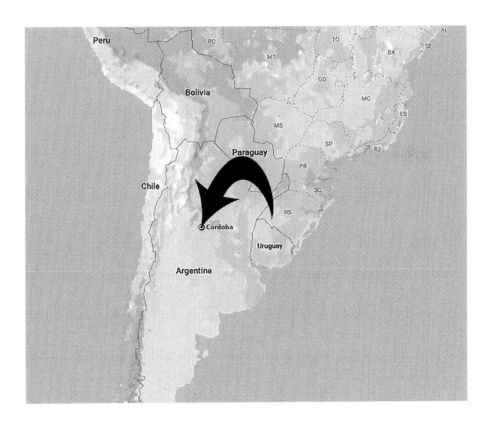

It was a clear and sunny travel day, and the one-hour plane ride to our new home passed quickly. Córdoba would be my first roommate scenario since Prague, and I was assigned Victor and Alvin for the month. By this time, I had come to view the idea of roommates as something like the Uber rating system: I wanted a five-star rating for every gesture, word—or even fart! We settled in to our spacious apartment on a main avenue just above a Starbucks and drugstore. It was an honor that the guys deferred the private toilet and shower to me, while they shared the second full bathroom. Being fifty had its privileges.

Victor is a tech marketing wizard who specializes in building online marketing "funnels." A funnel is a technical term which describes the tracking of an individual's behavior on the internet. A person's online consumer behavior is then used to steer advertising their way and ultimately guide them to the sale of a product or service. Alvin, on the other hand, was getting his MBA online. He was often watching lectures, researching, writing, and submitting papers to a professor he had never met, or videoconferencing for group projects. The digital nomad lifestyle, facilitated by our well-traveled laptops and reliable Wi-Fi, wasn't just the future of work, it was the here and now.

On my first Sunday in Córdoba, Argentina, I had a free morning before the orientation to roam the city. By month eight, and now on my third continent, the streets had become a place where I could gather first impressions. At first glance, the city was run down. Its grandeur seemed nonexistent, and it was not as cosmopolitan as the capital. I was trying to remain positive, but I can tell you, at that moment I was not digging Argentina's second largest city yet.

I took a cab to join the others on an outing to the Artisans Street Market, but because Google Maps wasn't working properly, it directed me to a rundown neighborhood in the wrong part of town. The driver spoke great English, having worked as an engineer in the UK and Germany, so between us we finally figured out the correct location. He was a talkative guy. He said that the Argentinian people are a mix of the worst of the Spanish and Italian cultures, with none of the good. He was quick with a joke: How does an Argentinian kill himself? He climbs to the top of his own ego and jumps off!

Walking around and interacting with folks, I could see that Córdoba had the grunginess of Prague, but without the resplendent architecture. It reminded me of what downtown Miami must have looked like in the early 60s, before the high-rise boom. Block after block of tiny mom-and-pop shops, always shuttered on a Sunday, were slotted into low and mid-rise buildings. Remember when you had to spend the day going from shop to shop to buy what you needed? There were fabric stores, shoe stores, small food markets, and even a place just selling cheap underwear. It definitely gave off a pre-internet vibe. I'm not an unappreciative American. I love the charm of the Old World, but this was a pale echo of the cities in Europe. However, I tried to remember that it was still too soon to make any judgments, so I continued to give Córdoba a chance.

The driver finally found the correct neighborhood. The market was much smaller than the San Telmo Sunday Fair, so it felt more crowded. The booths were smooshed together like dusty books in a library. Paintings, knickknacks, flowers, jewelry, and fried food had all started to mix together in my head with the other markets around the world. The Remote Year city team had warned us about the petty theft problem in Argentina and advised us not to hold our cell phones while walking the streets, and there I was in the perfect thieving location. Thankfully, I was never robbed, but another Mango had her phone stolen from her handbag that was *zipped shut*. She didn't even notice until she looked down and saw that her purse was flopping open. It could have happened to anyone.

No Philter: By now, the Mangos heard me say it more than once: "That would never happen in Japan!" There is a certain larceny in the heart of Latin American culture that doesn't exist in other places, especially not in Japan or in most of Asia. I am not sure why. One friend, who holds a doctorate in education, theorizes that because the colonialists and the natives were always at odds with one another, it created a culture of stealing that has remained to this day. Any other theories out there?

The people in Córdoba, however, were more relaxed than the folks in Buenos Aires. They were calmer and a bit happier. They spoke slower, with almost a more relaxed movement of their mouths. They didn't slur their words or speak lightning-fast like their counterparts in Buenos. I soon noticed many young people walking around with notebooks in hand and book bags strapped to their backs. This, I learned, is because Córdoba is a big college town.

I couldn't have been happier about living with Victor and Alvin. Our apartment was a 3,000 square-foot space, complete with a big kitchen and marble counter tops. My bed was super comfortable. We were headed toward the chilly Argentinian winter with no climate control, and each night I snuggled up with two pillows, a comforter, and the big fluffy blanket I found in my closet. None of our apartments in South America had climate control. This was typical for most dwellings.

The vibe between Victor, Alvin and myself was upbeat, harmonious, and downright fun. We laughed and carried on, even as we did our work. Our apartment had so much brotherly love and optimism, as we brought different things to the table. The guys agreed to keep a vegan home, so I shopped for all the plant-based provisions. They loved eating the vegan meals I prepared in the spacious kitchen. I was obliged to do some heavy lifting, like lugging bottled water back from the Disco. No, not the nightclub. Disco was the name of the big supermarket chain, which happened to be right across the street from our apartment. Because I shopped and took care of the kitchen work, Alvin did all the cleaning, which included my post-cooking messes. And Victor…well, he scored the pot to get us high late at night as we sipped top-shelf Malbec and told stories and howled with laughter.

To make things even more fun, Victor turned us on to coca-powder, which is derived from coca leaves. Cocaine comes from coca leaves, but somehow this powder was legal and widely used, especially in Peru (our next stop). Victor placed a spoonful under my tongue, and soon I couldn't feel my lips. I was super awake, but not quite hyper. It wasn't like a cocaine high; it was just an awakening from the stimulant inside the plant. Night after night, the three of us convened in the kitchen for pot, powder, and wine. We opened the large window to blow the smoke out of and drank Argentina's finest wines. Just like the Billy Joel song says, "We might be laughing a bit too loud!" Fortunately, I never found the powder addictive.

Phil Phact: Coca leaves are a healthy superfood of sorts. Coca leaves can be chewed, or consumed in the form of tea. South Americans use coca leaves to suppress altitude sickness and reduce feelings of hunger, thirst, and pain. The leaves also provide energy and stamina required for everyday activities, such as farming. People usually consume leaves of coca between meals and during their breaks at work. It is said that this plant can prevent development of certain types of cardiovascular disorders, colon cancer, and even dental cavities. It can also be used as a treatment for depression, hypertension, diabetes, obesity, and bronchitis. I used this plant sparingly in the way they have done for centuries.

No Philter: I've never considered myself a habitual pot or drug user, and I still do not. Sometimes when the joint gets passed around, I barely inhale. I take only the tiniest amount into my lungs at the very end of the exhalation. I do that once or twice and then I'm done. I never get stoned; I just get a little bit of a lift and everything is happy and funny. One night, my jovial buzz compelled me to tell the guys an outlandish story from my college days. It almost made it into this book but was deleted after some advice was given to me by a retired secret service agent. Those were different days!

In Córdoba, the streets came alive late at night. Even young families were heading out at 11:00 p.m. Because that's basically my bedtime, I ate most of my evening meals at home. I had brought my juicer from Buenos Aires, so my roommates would join me for spontaneous juicing parties and vegan chef tastings. Day after day, the kitchen looked like the aftermath of a bomb blast. Alvin would shake his head and say that I was so messy, like I was doing it on purpose. But to them (and me), my grub was worth it.

Phil Phood: One night, I introduced my roommates to my new, soon-to-be-famous sunflower seed paté called "Carry Me a Toon-Ah." This is a raw vegan, mock-tuna concoction with a texture and taste pretty close to the real thing. The main ingredient is freshly sprouted sunflower seeds blended with carrots, celery, garlic, and lemon. I coupled it with grilled millet bread and a starter of lentil vegetable soup.

Walking the narrow streets in my neighborhood was treacherous. I had to negotiate the irregular surfaces of the sidewalks, numerous construction zones, and brisk traffic. Much like in Thailand, the drivers came dangerously close to pedestrians, but at least we never got run over. Many of the intersections did not have stop signs or streetlights. It was basically a free-for-all and an every-man-for-himself situation. You could never assume that drivers saw you, and if they did see you, they would cut it really, really close. More than once, I thought, *That would never happen in Japan.*

The first week ended, and I had plans to take a weekend side trip to the famous wine country in Mendoza, which is fairly close to the Chilean border. My immediate business affairs were dealt with that week, and I was feeling as if this weekend getaway was a vacation … from my year-long vacation. Here I was, seeing the best of what the world had to offer on a daily basis, and somehow my weekend side trip was a vacation. Someone pinch me! I had plans to meet up with fellow Mango Lola, who was side-tripping there for a month and staying with her grandma.

More wine is produced in Argentina than in any other country in South America, and almost all of it comes from Mendoza. In fact, Argentina is the sixth largest producer of wine in the world. I was excited to get away from the grey skies of Córdoba and looked forward to sipping tasty wines. As soon as I got off the plane in Mendoza, I could smell the freshness in the air.

I arrived at the hotel, and after a much-needed massage and a productive online lesson with my Spanish tutor, all I had on my mind was *wine*. Lola met me in the hotel lobby of the Park Hyatt Mendoza to kick off the evening. We wasted no time engaging in conversation that was above small talk. You could call it medium talk, or even *big talk!* At this stage in the adventure, a deep melancholy was beginning to infect the tramily and settle into our bones. Too often, both Lola and I felt left out and forgotten by others in the group, and we agreed that only now had we begun to discover who our "people" truly were. The Mangata tramily as a whole seemed in a funk. Some spicy hookups had faded, some people left the RY journey for their normal lives, and the bloom was off the rose for many of us. Traveling seemed to be taking its toll. Yes, I was having mad fun with Victor and Alvin, but that didn't override these feelings.

We arrived at the Fuente y Fonda restaurant at exactly 9:00 p.m. for our reservation. Our punctuality, besides our dress and dental work, was a dead giveaway that we were Americans. Of course, we were still in Argentina, which meant that we were the first people at the restaurant. The staff prepared us a wonderful vegan meal. The main entree was a large pepper stuffed with a medley of lentils and assorted veggies in a thick savory sauce. It was coupled with a side of sweet potato. The entrée was delectable, and so was the wine, of course. I ordered us a bottle of the finest Luigi Bosca Malbec, and as soon as the first drop hit my tongue, I knew the weekend in Mendoza was going to be fabulous.

Phil Phact: The name "Malbec" is derived from two Spanish and French words, "mal" and "bec," translating to mean "bad mouth" or "bad beak." When planted in the hillsides of France, the fruit produced from these particular grape seeds tasted horrible, hence the term "bad mouth." The first European immigrants arrived in the Mendoza region and brought these occidental seeds. When planted in the new region's soil, the higher altitudes and dry climate of the Argentinian Andes Mountains resulted in a superior taste than those produced in France. The rest is history because Malbec still tastes world-class fabulous to this day. It's my favorite type of wine by far!

After dinner, Lola and I strolled back to the Park Hyatt Hotel where I was staying. I was itching to get my hands on the blackjack tables in the adjoining casino. I got my gamble on as I tried to teach Lola the game. I don't think she ever fully grasped it, but it was fun to show off a bit. My spirits and my luck were increasing as the night went on, but by midnight I knew it was time to throw in the towel and get some rest for the eight-hour wine tour. I walked away, up about a thousand bucks, but I was physically holding around 24,000 Argentinian sparkies (Pesos).

Lola arrived at the Hyatt shortly before 9:00 a.m. the next morning. Miguel, our tour guide for the day, met us shortly afterward in his brand-new Mercedes luxury van. After a brief introduction in perfect English (for a change), Miguel drove us toward wine country in Lujan de Cuyo, taking Ruta 40, the longest highway in the country (5,000 km). La Ruta 40 snakes through the rolling hills and lush mountains all the way to Chile.

Phil Phact: Mendoza is one of the only places in the world that still uses the Roman aqueduct system as the city's main source of water supply. You could see the aqueducts all over the place. As the snow from the Andes Mountains melts, the water is collected in a reservoir and released periodically through aqueduct channels throughout the city and its suburbs. The wine industry would not exist if it were not for the aqueduct system, nor would city life be sustainable.

Our first stop was to R.J. Viñedo, a very quaint winery, founded in 1998 by Raúl Jofré and inspired by his four daughters who were known as the "four stars." Our guide, Mica, gave us an impressive tour, as she proudly gushed how their winery is well-known for maintaining a consistently high-quality process in their wine production. The wine masters actually pass through the vineyards, row by row, and manually trim many of the grapes from the vines. This method allows the plant to place more energy and attention to the buds that remain, thus resulting in a Higher Quality fruit. Our tasting of three luscious, savory wines exceeded my expectations. It was 5 o'clock somewhere, so bottoms up!

Mica continued her presentation, informing us that since the grapes grow at high altitudes, they are exposed to lower air temperatures. Yet they receive more sunlight than grapes located at sea level. This combination increases water stress, causing the grapes to demand more water than is available. The result is a grape that contains more tannin and somehow results in higher productivity and superior taste. Who knew?! Mica told us, "One thing never changes: for a great wine, it's all in the grape."

No Philter: As we drove through the countryside along tree-canopied roads, Miguel unapologetically offered his opinion about the people of nearby Chile. First off, he claimed, they speak the worst form of Spanish. Their grammar and pronunciation is low class. I thought, *Wow, tell me how you really feel!* His biggest gripe was how the Chilean men come to Argentina and steal their tall, beautiful women of European descent. Everywhere I went on this digital nomad odyssey, communities seemed to be so ethnocentric, or just plain racist. The Japanese looked down on the Chinese as "sneaky" and "lacking style." The Croatians have their North-South rivalry based on cultural stereotypes. By contrast, the Jews, Muslims, Chinese, Japanese, Chileans, and Argentinians will cooperate quite nicely on the trading floor of a stock market. Private international trade fosters trust and cooperation between otherwise rival groups, and this will continue to be a main driver for eliminating discrimination and prejudices.

Next stop: the Kaiken Winery. As opposed to R.J.Viñedo, this winery grows and maintains their own grape crops on their land. The wine was pretty good, but not nearly as impressive as the tastes earlier in the day. One thing our guide pointed out is that although the climate is near perfect for growing grapes in Mendoza, there is a natural phenomenon that can destroy the grape vines. This threat is hail. When a hailstorm is full-on, sometimes the covered nets aren't enough to protect the plants from destruction. So, the process of using "bombas anti granizo" or anti-hail bombs, comes into play. Airplanes will disperse a chemical explosive to break up the storm clouds that produce the hail. Cool ... except when those chemicals fall onto the crops! In this modern life, sadly, most of us are living in a chemical cesspool.

Phil Phact: Edible algae, like spirulina, chlorella, and E3Live, from the Klamath Lake, chelates (removes) chemical toxins from our muscles and fat cells. We should eat them daily.

Our final destination was Finca Decero, where we tried a selection of five wines accompanied by a six-course meal. The chef came out to greet us and offered the most perfect menu for a hungry vegan. Between the delectable wine, the delicious foods, and the company, my day was magical and romantic. For sure though, Lola and I were not romantically inclined together; no, we were tramily! If I had been there by myself, it would still be terribly romantic.

During dinner, our table was approached by a businessman from a company party on the other side of the dining hall. He was curious about us and wanted to say hello and perhaps practice his English. After finding out that he worked for Banco Patagonia, a national bank in Argentina, I asked him about the rise of inflation in the country. By now, inflation was at around 18 percent since we had first entered the country. He didn't want to talk about it. Despite his fluent English, he completely ignored my question and cut straight to some small talk. I tried following up, but he deflected again. Perhaps the status quo, which was tough for average people, served him and his company quite well.

Lola and I parted ways for the night, and I went on to explore the center of Mendoza on foot. I ate another dinner at a decent Indian buffet restaurant, where the food was served cold, and you paid by weight. My HappyCow app worked like a charm everywhere. Afterwards, I strolled through the pedestrian district on Sarmiento Avenue. It was a cute two blocks. It resembled a miniature version of Lincoln Road in South Beach, Florida, and it was the pride of the city. After visiting three cities in Argentina, I noticed the same street tiles for sidewalks—a cross between the tile flooring in a McDonald's and New York City subway tile. They were always in bad condition and very slippery when wet.

Walking back to the Hyatt, I came across a small crowd surrounding three rappers performing on the sidewalk. Their backdrop included a banner promoting medicinal cannabis. A duo of pedestrian police loomed from behind as they observed the scene. Continuing my walk, I found another crowd of people in between the vendors selling souvenirs and knickknacks at Plaza Independencia. It ended up being a soup line that served meals to the homeless and poor of the city.

Phil Pheelings: I began to feel a new kind of empathy for the underprivileged locals standing in line for a hot meal. The line was no more than 500 feet away from the finest hotel in the city, where I would sleep that night. The contrast between their lives and mine was not lost on me. I had now been outside the Palm Beach bubble for so long that I began to think and feel a little differently. I really *felt* for these people. In my neighborhood back home, I had come to see the homeless as the invaders of my neighborhood and condo building. Their lewd behavior literally challenged my morning commute and my night out on the town, so we were existentially at odds. But now, at this moment, I had deep compassion for the people right in front of me. Yet, there was nothing I could do for them.

On my last full day in Mendoza, I had the idea to drive through the mountains and into Chile. While sipping some coca tea on the hotel patio, I decided not to make the trip. I used the day to rest, de-stress, relax, meditate, and reboot before returning to Córdoba and to my regular routine. One thing for sure, though, I really sucked at geography until I fell in love with wine!

Phil Pheelings: Fear of Missing Out (FOMA) had now become Love of Missing Out (LOMA).

My jaunt to Mendoza was a brief escape from my "new normal" back in Córdoba. I knew that upon my return, I would be battling it out with the eighth-month-funk. Right then and there, I made a deal with myself to stay in Remote Year for the entire 12 months. This had been my intention from the outset, but now my plan was being challenged by the conversations inside my head. If I were to quit now, I would forever consider myself a quitter. There was no way I could let that happen. I'd never quit anything before! I affirmed to myself that I would hunker down the best I could, enjoy my time in Latin America, and enjoy life's journey.

Following my return to Córdoba, Mother Nature gave us 12 consecutive days of rain. I didn't mind it too much at first; it was only a little water, and it seemed nothing in comparison to the summertime downpours of South Florida. The guy on the corner selling umbrellas was definitely making a profit. Gradually, though, the weather got to me. To worsen my mood, I wasn't exercising. I couldn't find a good yoga studio to save my life. I finally found a gym where spin classes were listed, but when I showed up in person, there were just a few broken bikes, no official classes, and no English language to explain why. Everyday life was creating a snowball effect of discouragement. I knew that I had all the tools to pick myself back up and push through this funk. But still, I was off my A-game. I was eating vegan food, of course, but not as healthily as I could. My diet consisted of lots of soy products, processed starch, and not enough whole greens.

No Philter: At least I was still shitting three times a day …

While Lola and I were in funks, we weren't the only ones in Mangata feeling this way. Many of my fellow digital nomads openly shared that they were struggling to find that travel thrill that we had in the previous months and countries. After all, we were humans, not laptops! Maybe it was because for first time we were living in the same country for two months straight. Maybe it was the rain. I even think that the Argentinian inflation, which always weighed so heavily on the nation's citizens, was projected onto us. We were all trying to make sense of our funks.

Midway through the month, some Mangos attended Córdoba Global, a think-tank organization, which also offered college-level classes. Córdoba Global weighed in on the economic problems that exist in their country. We sat together in a circle for 90 minutes while they gave us their take on the economy.

Not surprising to me, the origin of Argentina's inflation problem lay in its addiction to government spending. Starting with the Péron era, the government expanded the money supply through a printing binge that came after many years of overspending and fiscal deficits. We do this in the United States, as well. We call it "monetizing the debt." The difference, however, is that the American greenback is in demand globally, which buoys its price support, thus tamping inflationary pressures. America also maintains a relatively free economic system, which provides a healthy environment for capital formation, wealth creation, and innovation. As new wealth is created, the need for new, physical money grows as well. For Argentina, it is not a coincidence that over the last decade, public spending has bloated from 30 to 44 percent of its country's gross domestic product. Nearly one in five workers are employed by the government. Again, inflation is inevitable because as the money is printed, created out of "fiat," or thin air, the value of the currency cheapens. This is what happened when their government promised too much free stuff to the voters without having the ability to pay for it. In addition, over-regulation, especially in the labor sector, has impeded capital formation, competition, lower prices, and better products for average people. The country, they said, was often on the verge of an economic death spiral.

Phil Phact: By contrast, Argentina's neighbor, Chile, has been enjoying a thriving economy, even boasting a privatized Social Security program. When charted, Chile's economic growth took off like a hockey puck, ever since they initiated their privatization programs by selling off many state-run companies.

As the talk went on, I noticed that many of the Mangos, namely the Obama-loving Trump-haters, sat with their mouths dangling half-open as we learned about Argentina's tumultuous economic history. Some faces were actually looking cross as in disbelief. Who could blame them? Their worldview was just called out and exposed as something that doesn't turn out well, at all! The very policies that they advocated in the States and elsewhere were playing out in another place, where you could plainly see that they didn't work. We lived it every day on the streets while walking to the workspace. On the way to the office, the street sign showed that price of apples had gone up again.

Later that night, I went to dinner with an old college buddy. Doctor Dan moved to Argentina 25 years ago, learned Spanish, and became a dedicated chiropractor in Buenos Aires. He's one of those friends you don't often talk to, but when you do, you pick right back up where you left off. I asked him what it was like living here. He said that he had learned to keep his head low and live simply. He and his wife saved for 12 years to buy a house, because there is no mortgage market to speak of. It made sense. How could a financial institution give a borrower a mortgage with a fixed interest rate if the resulting monthly payment would be a small sum just a few payments later (inflation)? A floating interest rate? That would be unsustainable for the borrower as inflation loomed. Meanwhile, Dr. Dan had been kicking ass financially for years now. He was expanding his business, but not in Argentina. He was opening up offices in Chile, where the business climate and labor rules were more common sense and favorable. He went on to say that there is no national pride in Argentina, and that the collective consensus was always negative. This wasn't hard for me to believe because I could see it all around me. The outlook was bleak, and people didn't seem to plan for a better future. They were just "there." This outlook on life was anathema to everything that was instilled in me as an American, the son of an immigrant war refugee.

One day while walking back to the workspace post-lunch, I was nearly run over, by what must have been over 1,000 electricity-union protesters heading to their company's headquarters close by. I assumed that inflation was getting the best of their paychecks. I was intrigued by the situation and walked a block closer to get a better sense of what was going on. As I stepped off the curb to cross the street, a huge bonfire was lit right in front of me … in the middle of the street! The flames nearly *exploded* as the protesters fueled it with more gasoline. My cheeks felt like they were burning, and I'm surprised my eyebrows didn't get singed from my front row view. This is the kind of thing you only see on the nightly news, and there I was in the middle of it all.

Córdoba, like so many others before, was a truly walkable city. I got in several miles of walking each day. Once again, as in many of the places I had called home, I was waving to the tailor, the coffee guy, the fruit stand guy, and other now-familiar shop owners, on my daily commute to the workspace. My business was doing well, and I even had time for personal projects. My presentations in Europe, India, Nepal, and Asia, which provoked me to speak without slides, had given me a new clarity with which to explain veganism. This inspired a book idea: *The Vegan Manifesto*. With more work than I thought would be required, I registered the idea with the Writer's Guild, copyrighted the logo, and secured a web address. *The Vegan Manifesto* was born.

One day at the workspace, the sun finally decided to make an appearance. I was working at my usual table. My fellow nomad, Andrew, was sitting next to me sifting through some screenplays in search of the next Hollywood hit. At seven stories high, with the sun shining through floor-to-ceiling glass, we could see the magnificent fountain in the quaint square across the street. Behind the fountain and main college building, a Gothic-style Catholic church was standing out from behind. From the looks of it, I could have been in Spain rather than Argentina.

As I sat there, typing away on my manifesto, an angelic song carried itself gently through the cracks of the glass doors. A string orchestra was performing in front of the fountain below, accompanied by the famous Argentinian singer, Patricia Sosa. Her mesmeric voice was so soft yet so triumphant. Andrew and I looked up at the same time and smiled. The moment was so perfect. I swear that I saw folks skipping down the streets below with smiles on their faces, *finally*. It's amazing how both weather and music tend to affect people's moods, mine included. I smiled and turned back to my laptop to crank out some more content. This one moment of magic had altered my opinion of Córdoba; perhaps it was a charming, beautiful city, after all.

I felt a calling to put my vegan views into book form because I made a decision to suspend my public presentations. Since the beginning of all this, my family had become concerned about kidnapping, and when

I got to South America, they begged me to stay out of the spotlight. Respecting their worries and my own, I halted my speaking ambitions for the South American leg of my Remote Year journey, although no one else in Mangata gave kidnapping any thought.

The sun didn't stay out to play for long. I was walking home from the office when something wet hit my forehead. I looked up, and not even three seconds later, I got pelted in the eye with an even larger raindrop. Rain, rain, rain, all the time! I found myself cursing the skies. As I like to say, the most important conversations are the ones you have with yourself. Mine at that moment went something like this: "Goddamn motherfucking rain fucking bullshit, again!" I picked up the pace and entered my apartment building just as it started raining *gatos y perros*. I leaned inside the entryway trying to catch my breath. Suddenly, I felt a sharp pain on the side of my right foot. I'll admit, it wasn't the first time I noticed this pain, but now a certain threshold had been crossed. It was a sharp, debilitating pain. Perhaps it's a bad idea to curse the sky, as I had done just moments before. I knew right away that this required professional attention, so I opened my SOS App and received a referral to a hospital.

The hospital turned out to be just around the corner. Remote Year seemed to have a knack for making everything we could possibly want or need, accessible—in this case, a first-world hospital and physical therapy center. My roommate, Victor, had been receiving physical therapy there for his ruptured calf muscle. At this point, Mangata was like a football team who was well into their playing season: all banged up but still playing on the field. We were hell-bent on making it to the Superbowl triumph of month 12 whatever the physical cost.

I sat in the waiting room twiddling my thumbs and trying not to focus on the throbbing pain in my foot. The waiting room had no cell reception, which to a digital nomad could be considered the worst pain of all! Within 15 minutes, however, a nurse called me into a consultation room where I was introduced to an energetic and healthy-looking man. He shook my hand, ceremoniously kissed my right cheek, and greeted me in English. His name tag read "Dr. Cotter."

Dr. Cotter didn't hesitate to order an MRI, the results of which we had within 90 minutes. In the States, I was always forced to schedule an MRI and wait at least several days for the appointment. Then it was like pulling teeth to get the results, which would have to be discussed in person at yet *another* far-off appointment. The process in Argentina was just slightly more involved than a special order at Starbucks. I was impressed. The doctor even gave me his personal email. And on top of that, all of it cost just 187 USD.

I had a moment of perspective as I exited the MRI room. Another man around my age was coming in for a scan, and he seemed to be in pretty bad shape. I didn't know what his issue was, but he had a catheter coming out of him (ouch), and his urine had topped the bag. He needed help getting out of the chair and getting onto the MRI table. He groaned. There I was, walking away from the MRI room under my own strength. I immediately understood that my problem was trivial.

Phil Phact: All too often for people, myself first among them, *the problem is that there is no problem!*

Within no time, I was back in Dr. Cotter's office, but this time there was no kiss, just bad news. The MRI showed a hairline stress fracture in the fourth metatarsal of my right foot. My heart sank as he told me that I would have to wear a boot cast for probably a month or more. *Blah blah, blah blah* ... I stopped hearing his words as the bad news bounced around in my head. There was that overused South American expression "don't worry" coming at me again. Back home, when someone says, "Don't worry," that's when I start to worry!

The cast was removable, which concerned me because I was afraid of myself (I have a problem following orders). I mean, was I really going to wear this thing? So, there I was, soon after, hobbling around the streets of Córdoba, barely making it to the office and back. The simple act of walking began to negatively impact my right ankle, and it also put a new kind of stress on my knees and hips. It was a classic cascade of problems that can occur when one health complication leads to another. I couldn't help but throw a pity party for myself over and over again in my mind. This mental anguish lasted for several days. On the bright side, at least the land mines of poop, compliments of the house pets, were much less prominent here in this junior city.

Phil Pheelings: I called my mom in the hopes that she could make me feel better. We spoke. I was feeling better already!

I had one more week to go in Argentina, and things were probably more different than at any other time in my adult life. Essentially, I was grounded like a broken fighter jet. I adjusted my routine to include physical therapy each day, which cost me about $30 per session. I also made it a point to sequester myself in bed for 12 hours a day, to allow my foot to heal quicker. For several days my remote office was now my bed, which was very often covered with stacks of my business affairs. Daily physical therapy included double sessions of ultrasound electrical pulses, followed by icing and magnet therapy. My technician, Manuel, knew English pretty well, but since my Spanish was improving, I took the opportunity to practice with him. He was so kind to me, and by the second visit, we began greeting each other with the proverbial kiss on the right cheek. Goodbye kisses, too! By now, the people of Argentina had won me over, especially in Córdoba. At first, I found Argentinians curt and a little rough, but now I saw sincerity at every street corner, restaurant, business, and home. The Argentinian people kissed their way into my heart.

I thought about Fong a lot that month. I knew that if she were with me, I wouldn't have experienced these dark moments so intensely.

Long distance relationships are challenging no doubt. We had our ups and downs during the two months we were apart. Fong was quite the jealous type, and although she had met Lola before, she did not approve of my trip to meet her in Mendoza. I had been single for so long that I had forgotten some commonsense relationship rules. Traveling the world so closely with the tramily also blurred some lines that normally would be clear.

I had a plan to keep our flame alive. So, I offered to enroll her in the Hippocrates Health Institute's Life Transformation Program (LTP) in West Palm Beach. From afar, I arranged her transcontinental trip to South Florida. She was greeted at the airport by the car service I had used for years. They whisked her away to my condo. There, she was greeted by the building manager and given a short tour, which included a trip to the rooftop for the sweeping panoramic view of the Atlantic Ocean, the intracoastal waterway, and beautiful Palm Beach Island.

After a few days of settling in, Fong was deep into the LTP program at Hippocrates, and loving it. I was scheduled to give my signature lecture to the Health Educators during Fong's third week at Hippocrates, so we would be seeing each other soon enough. My parents decided they would come to Florida to see me while I was there, which meant that my Asian girlfriend and I would now be out of the closet. They had heard about Fong, but now shit was going to get real!

It was now time for the Remote Year Mangata to kiss Argentina goodbye … on the right cheek. Months seven and eight were in the history books. Yes, Argentina and I had our ups and downs, but I wouldn't change a thing. Lima, Peru was awaiting us with a Pisco Sour and a bowl of organic veggie ceviche. I threw my clothes and personal effects into a mass that fit into one large suitcase. It was transition weekend, and the tramily knew the drill.

Have laptop, will travel!

CHAPTER 9

Lima, Peru

*"I'm in love with cities I've never been to and
people I've never met."*

JOHN GREEN

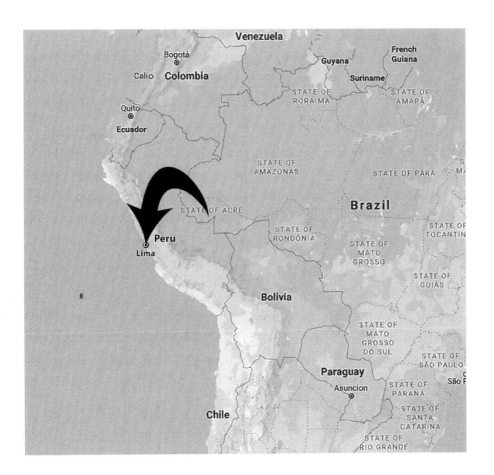

It was 7:00 p.m. when I stepped, broken foot first, out of my apartment to head toward Molly's Irish Pub for the 2018 World Cup Soccer game between Peru and Scotland. This was the first time in 36 years that Peru had made it to the World Cup. There was so much excitement in the misty air.

All around, crowds of people, locals and tourists alike, were waiting in line to get into various places to watch the *fútbol* match. Blaring car radios blended with the street vendors' shouts to encourage last-minute purchases of Peru's team jerseys and other paraphernalia of national pride. The air was filled with scents of beer, fried food, and the afternoon's rain. I was excited for the month ahead of me in Lima, Peru, and felt like being here to cheer on the nation's *fútbol* team was a good omen.

I hobbled into Molly's Pub while the match was in progress, wiggling my way through to meet the Mangos in the back of the bar. At that point, the game was tied and the mood was tense, in an alcohol-fueled way. I joined in with hoots and cheers that erupted every time the soccer ball was spotted near Scotland's net. Ultimately, Peru won. The celebration was nearly as wild as when my Eagles team had won the Super Bowl back in February. The bar erupted with pure joy, and people spilled out onto the streets, where raucous fans were met with like-minded revelers. Traffic came to a standstill in all directions. Hugs, high fives, kisses, and even tears were exchanged between people. Lima was alive!

This month I had roommates again. They were picked randomly by our program leaders: Mitch, the microchip designer from Spain, and Coinstein from Chicago. No, Coinstein wasn't his real name; he was a cryptocurrency trader, so it was my nickname for him and it stuck. He didn't just buy and sell Bitcoin. As I learned, there is a whole world of cryptocurrencies known as "altcoins," hundreds of them. Altcoin is shorthand for "alternative coins." Alvin also dabbled in the blockchain, so I nicknamed him Coinberg. By now, Coinberg and Coinstein had become my homeboys for life, along with their nicknames. Mitch spent most of his time in the workspace designing the next microchip for an upcoming smartphone, so we rarely saw him. He would tiptoe into our apartment late at night and be out the door the next day by 7:00 a.m. Coinstein and I usually mobilized mid-morning for a coffee run. I was grounded from exercise due to my foot fracture, so this chill routine was something new for me.

I had not even lived in Lima for a week when I concluded that I loved the city, the country of Peru, and its people. The feeling amongst the Mangos was unanimous. Lima is a gorgeous colonial city that sits along a coastline of dramatic cliffs. Wherever you are, you can feel and smell the coastline. The Pacific waves and noisy traffic are reminiscent of Southern California, but with a Latin flare. The city's colonial history goes back nearly five centuries. As one of the senior cities in the Americas, Lima offers a multicultural vibe and leaves a person constantly eager to explore more. The vegan scene in Lima is booming, I discovered—not because it was a trend, but rather because of the cost. After all, serving meat, cheese, dairy products, and eggs at almost every meal is a sign of relative affluence. Historically, and around the world, the general population did not always have such affluence.

Little did I know that Peru is known for its haute cuisine. The spices had a phenomenal taste, and there was real flavor in the food. What a step up from the previous two months in Argentina! The city team said that we could assume that the vegetables were organic. Cool! The restaurant culture was a main feature of city life, and Lima is home to some of the world's top restaurants, such as Central, Maido, and Astrid y Gaston. My HappyCow app exploded with restaurant options, which made for a Happy Phil all month long. On the app even popped up an outdoor vegan farmers' market (Sundays only), the likes of which I'd never seen before. I went every weekend except one and got to know some of the vendors. A vegan version of Nutella was my favorite. Everyone seemed to love America. They were eager to tell me about places they had been to there. Very often, they had a relative living somewhere in the States. Most folks at the market could speak English. Obviously, I wasn't in Argentina anymore. It was almost like night and day.

Lima was a nice blend of old and new. Outside the capital city, original tribes that existed for hundreds of years, along with their cultures and their habits, were somewhat preserved with care. Lima and its people, however, seemed to be importing global influences.

The views all over Lima were *breathtaking!* My apartment was just a five-minute walk to the coast, where a wide footpath scaled a rocky cliff overlooking the Pacific Ocean. The clifftop walkway stretched for miles and created a sort of serpentine boardwalk that was perfect for biking, running, walking, and people watching. Along the way were several parks, cafés, and viewpoints.

It was wintertime, however, so the coast was greeted with fog nearly 24/7. There were just grey skies, which I could definitely live with. It rained here and there, but nothing like Córdoba. Even with heavy fog, the infinity view of the Pacific Ocean was more than good enough! In my foot cast, I hobbled along the cliff path making phone calls and checking email. One time, four paragliders swooped in and out of the foggy skies above the rolling Pacific waves; their colorful sails danced with each other. Lima was just plain gorgeous, and the people were fantastic. I could actually see myself living there long-term. For the first time in months, I called up my mom and proclaimed, "I'm moving to Lima!" Over the years, it had become a family joke that while traveling, if I announced my new residency, it was always my way of saying, "I *love* this place!"

I found my rhythm and created a remote office routine along with the usual stuff, albeit without exercise. I kept up my biweekly Spanish lessons thanks to Remote Year. I found the Spanish language terribly romantic, and I was starting to gain linguistic traction. The machine-gun talking speed and slurred words of Buenos were a thing of the past, thank God. The locals articulated their words even more clearly than Córdoba. And even better, one of the pronouns, *vos*, was not used by the Peruvians, giving me one less detail to remember. I found a capable physical therapist and my dream gourmet grocery store, Wong. The Remote Year city team in Lima was incredible and they gushed with city pride. This. Was. My. City.

In my second week, I made plans to meet up with a local friend, Gracia, and her father, Enrique. I knew her from Palm Beach, but she was mostly living in Miami. She is a real beauty, and we were always such good friends. Her father took us to dinner at The Country Club in the Lima Hotel, where a wine tasting event was taking place. While outside on the terrace under the stars, we caught up on our lives, told stories of our travels, and sipped on world class wines. With Gracia, Enrique, his wife, and their friends, I felt less like a stranger in a strange land. With them, I felt like I had family in Peru. Gracia insisted that the local Indian market district was not to be missed, so we made plans to go the next morning.

The Indian Market was not what I expected. The Indian Market had nothing to do with the country of India, but instead referred to Western hemisphere Indians, who are the indigenous people of Peru. The walls and tables were adorned with backpacks, sweaters, shoes, and socks, to name just a few. They were usually made from alpaca or llama wool, and decorated with colorful, bright Inca patterns. Trinkets, crafts, souvenirs and edible goods were scattered around on tables, in baskets, or hanging high above. I wanted it all! I bought a funky hat and a bag of coca leaves. I didn't waste time chewing on some leaves as the effects took hold. I was immediately invigorated. My eyesight was crisper. Even my breathing improved. Chewing the coca leaves and brewing them in hot water had already become part of my morning ritual, and I felt great just knowing I was imbibing antioxidants, vitamins, minerals, fiber, and protein. Adios, coffee, matcha, and maté: here comes the coca train! After about an hour or two spent getting lost in the maze of cheap, local goods, we kissed goodbye and took our own Ubers home.

The next day, I joined 13 other nomads in Mangata for a day trip to a sand desert in the Huacachina region. This excursion turned out to be a bucket-list day on steroids. We had an intense itinerary planned for us that included visiting the Ballestas Islands by boat, checking out a Pisco Sour vineyard, and then finally snowboarding down the famous desert sand dunes. After a restful night, I woke up before the sun, and ordered an

Uber to take me to the workspace. Many Mangos were already snuggled up tightly in the white van. Some of them hadn't even gone to sleep after partying the night before. As in Argentina, the Peruvians partied hard, and many in the tramily would join them. A usual night out involved meeting up at a friend's house around midnight, pregaming with some cheap booze, and then hitting the clubs by 2:00 or 3:00 in the morning. Most people stayed out until the clubs closed at 5:00 or 6:00 a.m. But not me. No can do.

Soon after the tour van left the workspace, I fell asleep to the sounds of the a/c blowing and my fellow nomads snoring. It was a bumpy three-hour coastal ride to our first stop at Ballestas Islands; thankfully, I had snagged the front passenger seat. I always go for the front seat of a van where I can copilot. I made sure that the climate control was perfect and that everyone was happy with the radio tunes. I also kept my eye on the driver to make sure he was happy and driving well. More than once throughout the year, I motioned to the driver to stop texting while driving.

Mountain-to-ocean views were punctuated by poverty-stricken neighborhoods that popped up along the road. It was unbelievable that these shanty towns existed along such a beautiful coastline. Incredible poverty existed outside of Lima's city limits; seeing was believing.

We arrived at the marina to meet the boat. This was Act 1 in the jam-packed day of discovery. We filed out of the van next to a row of restaurants, tourist shops, and tour company kiosks that were just opening for the day's business. It was a misty morning, and the smell of the salty sea and decaying fish filled the air. Seagulls and pelicans screeched at the fisherman carrying buckets of fresh seafood. I stopped to take a photo of a giant pelican flapping its enormous wings at a local who was teasing the bird with a slab of tuna. From there, we boarded a speed boat that awaited us at the dock. We sped atop the foggy Pacific for about twenty minutes. I sat Zen-like, wearing my new rainbow-colored Peruvian hat that protected me from the chilly winds. The pom-poms dangling from each side gave it real style.

Rock formations began popping up from the water as we sped farther away from the mainland. Soon, we were surrounded by the massive and jagged structures. The deep blue of the ocean alongside the blackish-purple rock with hints of red sand, made for a surreal vibe. It was perfectly quiet but for the *Aum* hum of the wind and sea. We were in another world. I was half expecting a sea monster to slither past our boat.

Our vessel slowed to a crawl as we approached a cave-like formation in one of the rocky islands. The guide was pointing towards a ledge at two tiny penguins. I could barely see the penguins, and Alvin joked that they were, in fact, animatronic penguins controlled by the tour company on the mainland. Just as the words passed Alvin's lips, a blob of bird poo splattered across his beard, just below his bottom lip. He didn't know it had happened at first. The entire boat went berserk with laughter. With each finger-pointing laugh, he figured out that he had just been shat on! And since we were out there in the sea nestled in between uninhabited islands, there was no bathroom, soap, or wash rags around for cleaning up. We kept laughing our heads off. Alvin's beard was extraordinary; he had been letting it grow since Croatia, and he was now looking like rock-god Billy Gibbons (a guitar hero of mine), a member of ZZ Top. Someone passed him a water bottle, and he was able to rinse it as best he could. I was just glad it wasn't *me* who was shat on!

As the boat started up again, we headed off to a tiny cove where a family of sea lions was chillin' on a couple of sharp crags. We slowly weaved in and out of these tiny sea mountains. As we got a bit closer, two of the males engaged in an aggressive quarrel over breakfast. They grunted and snorted while taking turns biting each other's necks. You could tell that this scuffle had been going on for some time, as chunks of fur and skin were scattered about. Some tour groups even offered excursions to swim with these wild creatures—since I am comfortable diving with sharks around, sign me up next time, please!

After hitting up a few more rocky islands, the boat took us back to shore. By this time, the sun had started peeking through the clouds, as if trying to set an even better mood for the rest of the day. Next stop was the Pisco vineyards. At the vineyard, we were given a 15-minute private tour on how the grapes were harvested, processed, fermented, and then bottled. As the tour guide spoke, she herded us around through areas stocked with troughs, clay gourds, and distillation units.

> **Phil Phact:** Pisco is a clear, grape spirit. Basically, it is distilled wine with a stronger kick. Cognac and other brandies are also distilled wine varieties, but they normally change color due to how they are aged. They are also made with blander grapes. Pisco on the other hand, is made with aromatic grape plants, such as Muscat, which makes the finished drink attractively fragrant. Both Peru and Chile claim to be the original land of Pisco, which adds to the existing rivalry between the neighboring countries. In reality, this elixir was probably being made in both countries before their borders were even set. Pisco used to be exported through the Peruvian port of Pisco (hence the name), so maybe Peru has a slight upper hand in this argument.

After the tour around the property, it was time to sample the goods. Siting in a circle, we were taught the traditions of drinking Pisco and Pisco Sours, sampling at least ten different varieties. Some were flavored with fruits, such as passion fruit and berries. Others were more concentrated, and thus had a higher alcohol content. A traditional Pisco Sour cocktail is made with an egg white, which is what makes it a "sour." So, for this vegan wine aficionado, it was hand over the Pisco but hold the sour, por favor! After we all got a little buzz going from the tasting, we piled into the van and headed to the Ica desert region of Huacachina. Staring out the window, I watched the landscape around us transform into giant sand dunes and massive cacti. Were we on Mars or some other planet? It was unbelievable that only a few hours before we were gliding along the Pacific Ocean spotting pelicans, sea lions, and penguins. This was another pinch-me moment.

We arrived at the hostel and headed inside to anticipate our snowboarding-turned-sandboarding adventure in the desert. We were given the choice of riding the sandboard down the dunes on our stomachs like a sled or strapping in and riding it like a snowboard. I am a skier, not a snowboarder, so for me it was a belly-only endeavor. Others, like Alvin and Victor, decided to speed down the sand dunes standing up as proper snowboarders. Damn, I loved them and their spirit! Instead of ski lifts, there were dune buggies outfitted with monster truck tires ready to give us a thrill ride to the top. They were a cross between an ATV and the Mars Exploration Rover. We took our seats as the driver strapped us in like we were in a rocket ship. Prepare for takeoff! I think it's fair to say that none of us were prepared for what was about to happen. The strong rumble of the engine tickled our butts and made our heads wobble a bit. Without forewarning, we went from 0 to 60 mph faster than I could say "supercalifragilisticexpialidocious!" The spinning tires made a long turkey tail in the sand behind us as we sped off. For about 25 minutes, we raced up and down huge mountains of sand. Each time we climbed up a new dune, our driver floored the accelerator causing us fly off the top and catch some air. More than once, my stomach dropped to the floor. We made donuts in the sand much like I had done in my neighbors' front yards during my short career as a juvenile delinquent.

After being jerked from side to side on this trackless roller coaster ride, our driver ascended to the highest sand dunes in the desert. We unloaded the boards, while rubbing grains of sand out of our eyes, ears, and hair. We took custody of our sandboards and took our lives into our own hands. From the sun-soaked apex, it looked so expansive it could have been the Sahara Desert. From there, we were given instructions on how to ride and control our speed while sliding down the dune. My turn snuck up fast. I still had my broken foot to deal with, and I was nervous about making my injury worse. But, as is my way, I wasn't going to seek a doctor's approval. I was just going to go for it.

> **Phil Phact:** As I often say, "Don't ask for permission, ask for forgiveness."

In order to brake and steer, the technique is to dig your feet into the sand. After seeing the others go before me, I realized just how dangerous this was. They went fast! Wiping out could mean a serious injury. I lay on my stomach on the board, held tight to the rope rings, but before I was ready, I was pushed off the steep hill. Those 15 seconds felt like forever—boy, did the speed feel fast! I felt the grains of sand hitting my cheeks and pelting my sunglasses as gusts of wind whizzed past my ears. I'm pretty sure I held my breath the entire way down; I just wanted to make it down that hill in one piece. Whew! I made down intact. I rolled off the board, wiped the sand from my body, and walked toward an applauding group of Mangos. Hours later, I came to realize that I had lots of sand in my foot cast as well, but my belly ride down the dune thankfully went off without a hitch ... at least compared to the crazy dune buggy ride on the way up! One thing was for sure, sand is not snow. I flashed back to the fresh POW in Japan. I still missed Japan for so many reasons.

Like children going up and down a playground slide, we repeatedly shot down the dunes over and over. There was a scare for a moment when Lola wiped out on the way down. Both sides of her hearing aid went flying off her sweet little head along with her sunglasses. It looked like a horrible wipeout because her head smacked down hard on the sand. I rushed to her side worried that it was serious. When she sheepishly looked up at me, embarrassed, I realized she was going to be okay. I dusted off her personal effects and helped to put her back together again.

By now the sun was setting. The Mangos were bundled up in our sweaters and jackets, admiring the pink cotton-candy clouds and pastel hues that painted the sky's canvas. I've never seen anything so surreal. We were spent from an outlandish bucket-list day, but this moment was not lost on us. The sun sliding behind the sand dunes; it looked like a raw egg yolk. We took tons of pictures trying to capture the moment forever.

Phil Phact: The desert oasis of the Huacachina, pronounced "Waka-CHEE-na," was the featured scene in the iPhone X launch video. To see it in person is stupefying. Its desert beauty can't fully be appreciated on a computer monitor or tablet.

The next day I packed my bags and headed back to the States. It was Fong's last week at Hippocrates in Florida, and I promised to be there for her graduation. I was also scheduled to present the latest version of my signature vegan lecture. I saw some familiar faces, ate some of HHI's delicious, renowned, raw vegan meals, and spent the day with the Health Educators. Three times a year, HHI offers a nine-week course for those who want to deep dive into the vegan nutrition field. I was mainly there for Fong, though. I felt so proud watching her graduate from HHI after three profound weeks there. Her HHI credentials means she was now fully vegan. Seeing her on stage at her graduation filled me with great joy.

Fong met my parents for the first time during this trip. That's always a big step for a couple, and it definitely was for us. Unfortunately, Fong's first meeting with my parents started some doubts in me. As timing would have it, upon my return from Peru, I walked into my condo at about the same time that my parents and Fong descended on me. My baby hadn't seen me in three months, and my parents hadn't seen me since Christmas. My parents were in my kitchen when Fong walked through the front door. As she crossed the threshold into my home, she jumped up and down with excitement and leaped into my arms. They were startled by her outburst as they viewed the scene from the kitchen doorway. I turned and noticed their expressions, and it felt like they already did not approve. When they were officially introduced, Fong folded her arms in prayer, which is how the Thai people greet one another. That simple gesture seemed to throw my parents off. I'm pretty sure they had never met a Thai person before, so how would they even know what it meant? I'll never quite figure out the spell that seemed to be cast at the first meeting, but all at once I had a sense of the big picture. I wasn't in Asia anymore. I wasn't Asian. And for the first time, I asked myself, "Does this young woman fit into my life?" Nevertheless, I couldn't wait to take her back to Peru to spend the rest of the month there together.

> **Phil Pheelings:** I've never been a mama's boy and, truth be told, I've always gone against the grain of what my parents "expected" of me. But as I've gotten older, we have come to agree on so much. In business and personal life, along with my sister, we have all become a team. My brother was also a part of the picture, though he has chosen his own path, going on to become a very successful and internationally recognized orthodontist.

We left Florida and headed back to Peru to join the others. With only two days in Lima, Fong and I were off again to explore the Cusco region of Peru and experience an Ayahuasca ceremony together. The night before our flight, we held a small dinner party with my roommates and a handful of my favorite Mangos. Fong made a delectable vegan spread for dinner, Thai style.

As I waited in the kitchen for my guests to arrive, in my new, relaxed-fit Armani sweater-blazer, I felt very dapper. I opened a bottle of wine and thought about where I was, how I'd gotten there, and what was to come. As I've said, the most important conversations are the ones you have with yourself. At this moment, it went something like this: "Wow, you really are on top of the world, Phil. You have a young lady who is getting ready in the bedroom and loves you to death. You have friends coming over who admire you as much as you admire them. You are a healthy 50-year-old man traveling the world and experiencing life to the fullest." All of this was true. Yet, I kept finding voids in this "perfect" world of mine; voids that still revealed a certain unhappiness. Why was this? Throughout my life, I had never been able to fully resolve a certain unhappiness or dissatisfaction. This had been both a blessing and a curse. This desire for more, more, and even more, had brought me to where I was today. But here I was, nine months into a once-in-a-lifetime mega-odyssey, and somehow things were still "missing." I tried to keep my worries and uncertainties in check as we had planned to attend an authentic Peruvian Ayahuasca ceremony that weekend.

But what is Ayahuasca, you might ask? Deep in the jungles of South America, an obscure root called Ayahuasca (pronounced "eye-ah-WAHH-ska") was found to have hallucinogenic properties. However, the effects only lasted a few minutes. While the indigenous people were under the influence, however, the Mother Spirit of all creation enlightened them about a plant located 1,000 miles away that when mixed with the Ayahuasca root would create a trance lasting several hours. The substance taken at an Ayahuasca ceremony, therefore, is a concoction made from the *Banisteriopsis caapi* vine and the *Psychotria viridis* leaf. Far from a recreational, mind-altering substance, it is a transcendent healer, and without a doubt, it is a powerful tool for mental and physical ailments. A few recent studies have shown that Ayahuasca therapy can be effective in the treatment of depression, addiction, and PTSD. I hope that someday it will be accepted into the mainstream. Whereas the government of Peru recognizes the role of the Mother Plant for her healing properties, both mental and physical, it is illegal in the United States. Do you think this stops a truth seeker like me? Pahleeze! Most people seek out these transformational retreats in Peru or Colombia, where a more authentic experience can be found. The ceremony itself is considered sacred, and my Peruvian Ayahuasca ceremony took place in Peru's Sacred Valley, right outside of Cusco on June 14–17. Most importantly, Fong agreed to join me.

> **Phil Pheelings:** As a Buddhist, Fong had never been a drinker and had never even tried drugs. When I invited her to the Ayahuasca retreat in Peru, she said that she would go because she trusted me. As she often says, "I follow you." This meant a lot to me.

Fong and I flew into the valley of Cusco early in the morning. I spotted the sign with my last name on it among the crowd of short, dark-skinned Peruvians dressed in colorful ponchos and their hair in neat Amazonian braids. The air was chilly and dry: we were 3,400 meters above sea level, *and* it was winter in the Southern Hemisphere. At least here the sun was always shining.

We drove for about two hours up and down winding roads that took us around limestone mountains and lush, green hills. We passed run-down dirt houses, roaming chickens, and local women walking with baskets of household goods upon their heads. These villages are like places that time forgot. We were heading to Pisac, a tiny town in the heart of the Sacred Valley of the Incas.

When we arrived at the retreat center, we checked in and dropped off our bags. The boys and girls were separated, so I shared a room with two young men from Germany and Australia. After that, Fong and I were called into the examination rooms. All participants of the Ayahuasca ceremony are required to undergo a full physical. The medicine is so strong that a participant must pass a basic health test, which concerned me because I had suffered from chronic respiratory infections here and there during the past few years and had suffered one recently. I was winded during the physical exam and was worried that I would not pass. Right out of the airplane, I could feel my lungs working extra hard for each breath because the air was so damn thin! Fortunately, though, Fong and I both passed, and we were given the green light to participate. In addition to the physical, a psychotherapist interviewed us both extensively. He wanted to understand our purpose for attending this sacred ceremony. My purpose was to be physically healed in the hopes of improved breathing, to be detoxed, and to also get some clarity and hopefully some direction on my relationship with Fong.

All participants had to follow a strict vegan diet for at least four days prior to the ceremony. That was a given for us. After our physical, and one day before the actual ceremony, we drank a special mineral water that tasted foul, like sea water, that made us … *ahem* … shit our brains out. The port-a-potty toilets were lined up like soldiers across the grass. Within 20 minutes, we were both on toilets. It was a professional operation, but it was no Ritz Carlton. It got to the point where we were literally squirting clear water out of our butts. It was a new form of togetherness for a couple. We joked that couples who have been married for years don't get to that level of closeness! The group then abstained from food for the next day and a half. The Great Purge, combined with the vegan diet, properly prepared everyone for a hopefully positive Ayahuasca experience. If these rules were not followed, it would mean trouble for the participant during the ceremony. I saw it before and during the West Palm Beach ceremony last year. You *will* have a bad trip if you don't follow the protocol!

Phil Phact: It is well understood that animal foods contain toxins that are harmful to our physical bodies. But it's not a stretch to say that they also contain *metaphysical* toxins. The metaphysical toxins of fear, anger, pain, death, and an entire worldview of might-makes-right supremacy are ingested with every bite of flesh. This is not lost on the shamans, who recognize the physical, spiritual, and emotional components of the ceremonial medicine. This is why they insist on dietary preparation of the vegan kind. When we eat animal foods, we are accumulating these toxins, both physical and metaphysical.

The first ceremony took place on the second night in the main circular hut known as a yurt, about 40 feet in diameter. Each participant (there were ten of us) was given a sleeping bag and lots of heavy blankets and pillows. Two shaman priests, dressed in traditional Native Indian garb, officiated the sacred ceremony. Their outfits were of a colorful Aztec design adorned with a few bird feathers here and there. They didn't just look the part, they were the real deal! Their leathery faces were straight out of an old Western movie. One of the shamans drone-chanted in his native language of Quechua (pronounced "Ketch-wah"), while the other swept flowers over us to expel negative spirits. Also on hand was a medical doctor, a nurse, and a designated helper. The Etnikas Retreat Center was top-notch.

We started out with a brief introduction ceremony that included more chanting and getting comfortable in our bedding. We drank our first two ounces of Ayahuasca medicine. It tasted like bitter prune juice, with the consistency of the coffee grinds found at the bottom of Turkish coffee, just not as thick. The lights went out, resulting in almost total darkness, and we sat in the pitch-black waiting for the medicine to take hold. Within half an hour of ingesting the dose, I began my journey through time, space, mind, body, and soul.

This may seem completely nuts, but a big part of the healing ceremony involves the process of "purging." In simple words, this means that you might puke your guts out. Everyone gets a bucket that stays by their side like a security blanket. I probably puked three or four times during this ceremony. I learned that water is the gasoline to this physical and mental healing. The more water you drink, the more you purge. If you're lucky you double purge from each end of the body. The compassionate helper lady springs into action when a bathroom trip is required.

Each purge represents some kind of healing via the medicine. On this occasion, I experienced more of a physical healing. I asked The Mother to heal me of asthmatic symptoms, induced by respiratory infections, that often dogged me. After receiving the initial dose of Ayahuasca, I began vomiting and wheezing up a storm. It was my own concert of bodily noises and fluid elimination. No one seemed to mind or to even notice, though, because they were all going through their own personal expedition, even Fong. Although she was right next to me, and everyone in the room felt a connection to each other, the experience involves deep inner work and no one else matters at that moment.

I began to travel through what seemed like large distances between planets. I was being thoroughly entertained in a spiraling tunnel of trippy imagery, and then, suddenly, a microchip-like motherboard appeared in front of me. It was a very intricate panel that stretched from one end of my view to the other. The image was the size of a drive-in movie screen, and I felt like I was standing right in front of it. I immediately recognized that the medicine was showing me that She (The Mother) was scanning through my genetic disease paths and pinpointing what needed help. At that moment, one of the shamans came to my feet and began chanting. Somehow, he knew there was deep healing taking place. His spiritual chanting filled the room for everyone to experience, but I could feel him praying directly on my behalf. Perhaps he was relaying messages from The Mother.

The schematic quickly vanished, and a large basket of French fries popped onto the big screen. I wasn't sure what it meant, and before I had a chance to ponder its meaning, a giant wine bottle appeared, replacing the French fries. The meaning then became clear to me. The Mother Spirit conveyed to me that if I wanted to be *truly* healthy, I had to be alcohol free and eat whole foods, not simply vegan foods. As I pondered the message, I could literally feel the medicine trying to heal the damage that had been done by the pesticides and other toxins within my body. It was true, I had consumed my share of non organic plants and alcohol.

> **Phil Phact:** It was recently reported that 100 percent of California wines were found to contain glyphosate, commercially known as Roundup. Glyphosate has been linked to cancers, leaky gut, hormonal disruption, and it has been determined by the World Health Organization to be "probably carcinogenic to humans."

The messages that came next turned down a darker path. For sure, I wasn't even in the room anymore. I was far, far away. But there, right next to me, was my dead body. I couldn't look away. It was as if my ability to move my eyeballs was disabled. I could hear familiar, distant spirit voices asking me if I wanted to be buried in a coffin or cremated. I couldn't tell them. I was already dead. The "real" me was trying to scream my answer, but no sound escaped my mouth. I felt paralyzed. I was able to "change the channel" by focusing on the shaman's chanting, a technique that they had recommended whenever things got scary. It worked. Although the nightmare stopped, the message was sent and received. Besides carrying life insurance, I've never made any post-death plans because of my unspoken fear of dying, coupled with a sense of forever-ness. At points in my life, especially when things were going well, I thought death would never happen to me; somehow, I would figure a way around it. But now, during the ceremony, The Mother was forcing me to accept my own demise someday, showing me that we are all mortal beings whose fate is always to transition out of this physical body. The time had come to accept this reality and the concept of dying. I had no choice but to dispel this immaturity that I was holding on to. At the same time, I was shown the beauty of the transition from the physical shell, the body, to this new other world I had seen.

I was shown the first-fruits of heaven.

These visions that I am telling you about are known as the "visionary trance." They put us face-to-face with the Mother Spirit. The trance is personal to each one of us, based on our physical condition and what we need at the time of ceremony. Trances can be good, bad, or scary, but they almost always end up being euphoric. In the ceremony, we very often have the opportunity to emotionally metabolize past or current relationships or any fears or questions we may have about the future. It's both a reflection and an outlook. It's the truth and never delusional. We laugh or cry depending on what we bring to the table that night. I laughed *and* cried. Ayahuasca can heal physical ailments when one is fortunate and open enough to receive. We learn that our ego is the root cause of most problems.

If I were to describe these Ayahuasca ceremonies in one word it would be "healing." If I could have one more word to describe it: "sacred." We are given the grace to forgive ourselves and others, while getting rid of negative thoughts, feelings, and events.

Please reread the last sentence. This is a big deal!

Following the conclusion of the ceremony, many people are inspired to make changes in health, lifestyle, and goals. I was profoundly grateful, but not surprised, that a physical ailment of mine was resolved during the ceremony. By the next morning I had the lungs of a baby, although the altitude was still a little tough on me.

After the weekend, I could not stop thinking about all kinds of people who could be healed from various physical and mental ailments such as PTSD, depression, and maybe even cancer. For me, breathing more clearly again was a gift I shall never take for granted. I was forced to accept my mortality and see that the ego is the biggest problem for most people, especially me.

Let's talk about the fun aspects. The images and colors that appear are unimaginable and unlike anything you may ever see in real life. Billions of kaleidoscopes with an infinite number of vivid colors form shapes from patterns to graphics, from animals to people. These images morph into and out of symbolism that is both relevant and irrelevant. For me, it was like watching one giant Las Vegas strip at night, continuously melding one theme with another. I saw a lot of colorful dragons for whatever reason. I call it "The Grateful Dead Picture Show." This all takes place while the shaman priest chants rhythmic tunes that synchronize perfectly with the medicine's dancing visions. It reminded me of the chanting in my own faith tradition, the Greek Orthodox Church, but the chants in this ceremony were more tribal and primitive.

The ceremonial trance allowed me to feel the power of love so, so deeply. I felt love for family and friends very intensely. It wasn't within the context of an artificial high, either. Instead, I was revealed the big picture of life, the only thing that mattered: God is LOVE. The Mother of Creation, in the form of a multi-jeweled glass dragon, firmly expressed to me that the power of creation is all about love, and nothing else. I dwelled on this love for hours as the cartoon-like, kaleidoscopic laser light show continued to bring me joy and make me laugh and cry. My laughs were parroted by Fong, who had her own journey going on in the darkness, just a few meters away. I would never forget the simple yet profound message of love that I had received. As the shaman chanted on, and while people were streaming vomit, I resolved to reach out to the many people who hold special places in my heart by any means necessary: emails, phone calls, texts, smoke signals … whatever the method, I would be letting them know how much I loved them. If you didn't get a call, email, or text from me, I'm so sorry. There's always next ceremony!

There is no hangover, depression, withdrawal, or addiction after coming out of the Ayahuasca trance. It was like a well-engineered anesthetic. With a snap of the fingers, after the journey, the effects of the Ayahuasca are gone. There is no desire to keep taking it. What could an Ayahuasca experience mean for you, the reader, if you were to participate in a ceremony? First off, understand that we are dealing with Godliness, Herself. The plant doesn't play games and it never lies. The medicine does not waste time tricking you into falsehoods. That is not its purpose. The purpose is to bring out truths, healing, and clarity for your own unique life. The Mother Spirit will both punish you and reward you. If there are unresolved issues and you haven't been honest with yourself, you might have a rough ride. If you truly love yourself, you will love yourself and others even more. You visit and discover dimensions that exist beyond our senses and our 3-D world. I still think Ayahuasca is a window to heaven. I'm guessing that when we leave this body, we will travel, much like I have traveled in ceremony. I have wondered if it's just the mind playing tricks, induced by the plant medicine, but I'm pretty sure it's real.

The sacred Ayahuasca ceremony usually lasts about five hours, and it often results in a strong bond between fellow participants, be they good friends or strangers. Fong and I did two ceremonies over the weekend, and I now have three ceremonies under my belt. My experience in attending this ceremony with a loved one (Fong) opened new doors and shined light on some important lessons.

Fong and I felt very bonded as a result of the first ceremony, but during the second ceremony, we hit a bump. She felt the wall that I had put up, and she cried the whole time during the second ceremony. She could sense that I wasn't 100 percent committed to her and that I had doubts. In our debriefing following the second ceremony, she shared that her sobbing was also over an ex-boyfriend who broke her heart. He had gone back to his wife following a separation. Everything that needs to come out in ceremony, comes out. I knew that Fong had been allowed to peer into my heart. I felt it. Again, the medicine doesn't lie, nor does the heart. I realized I had put up a wall during the ceremony because I wanted to see Fong stand as her own person. She had always been my "follower." But I knew me: I could not be in a long-term relationship with someone who was merely an extension of me. I needed to see her strength. Without planning it, it turns out that I was I giving her a test. She had confided in me about her past, and I knew she was hurting. Her hurt was necessary for the pain to be resolved. This was how the medicine worked.

In addition to the relationship stuff, somehow almost everyone I had ever met flashed across my mind while in the second ceremony. This is not unusual. Some people can remember people and events as far back as the womb! At one point, I was introducing people from my past to other people in my life in the form of a receiving line. It was like they were winning Academy Awards. Words don't really capture the scene. It was so loving. Everyone loved everyone, just like heaven I presume.

In between the two Ayahuasca ceremonies, on a sunny Saturday, our group of ten visited Mother Teresa of Calcutta's orphanage in Cusco. I was not prepared for the experience. After an hour of traipsing through the mountains back to Cusco from Pisac, we pulled up to a plain building with large, bare concrete walls around its perimeter. The clouds had drifted in front of the sun, making the day seem dimmer and the air chillier. A shiver went down my spine. My first thought was, "Are we at a prison or an orphanage?"

We entered the main gates to an outdoor courtyard, where all at once a crazy cacophony of screams, outbursts, and yells spilled out from the darkened rooms that were connected together like a dormitory ... or prison cells. The children who weren't bound to wheelchairs swarmed all around us. Dozens of children, who each had some sort of disability, physical and/or mental, attached themselves to any free arms or legs they could find. One boy tried to pull me away from the others. I sensed that, like my special friend at the Wildflower Home, he really needed a father figure in his life. The others were confined to souped-up wheelchairs with their hands tied down to arm rests and their heads strapped against headrests. They were freely making outbursts, spitting up, laughing, or crying uncontrollably. It was a fucking horror show.

We were there as volunteers, so the lady in charge took a few of us to a room that was piled high with clothes that reeked of mildew and cheap detergent. Fong and I began the chore of folding the children's clothes, which lasted about two hours. The clothing was pretty beaten up. It was heartbreaking.

After that, we went to the dining hall where it was time to feed the children a snack. Sadly, the snack was a purple congealed goop, full of sugar and flour. Nevertheless, we all picked a kid and began playing the airplane game with our spoons. As we stuck slurp after slurp of the slop into their mouths, I remembered back to the Wildflower Home in Thailand where I had given the sprouting workshop. It was such a beautiful property, situated on a lake with lots of foliage and positive vibes. And now I was here in this hell hole of despair. It was quite a contrast.

Phil Pheelings: I was happy to leave, but I had witnessed firsthand how humanity continued to suffer in the unseen cracks of society. Here I was again seeing and doing at the ground level, as opposed to stroking a check at a Palm Beach charity ball. The people in charge of the orphanage had committed their lives to this type of work, caring for those kids, and not just for one long afternoon, as I had. What dedication! Once again, it was not lost on me that I continued with my charmed life while the challenged youngsters I had just left were stuck in a disability loop. On the ride home, our group discussed the controversial idea of euthanasia. It was actually me who put it out there on the table. At that moment it seemed like the best option to me. Someone countered that we couldn't possibly know what was going on inside their heads. Could they actually be happy? It's certainly possible. One thing I did know for sure was that the children at that orphanage would know little more in life than the horror we had just witnessed. They would be stuck forever. I remain heartbroken about this.

Phil Phact: I learned that these Mother Teresa orphanages had chapters all over the world, not just in Cusco. These places for unwanted children represent some of the untold, uncelebrated work of the Catholic Church.

After the second Ayahuasca ceremony, I vowed to become sober. No more wine or spirits for me. I didn't want to take a chance in reversing the miracle of my healing. My body felt so purified that the thought of alcohol actually disgusted me. I felt reborn. I was ready to experience the rest of my Remote Year in good health and high spirits. Fong and I left the retreat with the highest level of gratitude and much excitement for the next leg our trip: the ancient site of Machu Picchu.

Before departing for the Sacred Valley, HappyCow led us down a narrow pedestrian street to a local restaurant called The Garden of Vegan, which had only been open for four months. We met the owner, a nice young American girl with a seven-year-old son. Her life partner was busy in the kitchen. The menu consisted of vegan versions of Western favorites like mac & cheese and loaded nachos. Not exactly the healthiest menu, but I'm sure the restaurant was accustomed to tourists who love comfort food like that. Me too! I had a beautiful burrito bowl made from whole foods: beans, Peru's giant tooth-sized corn, guacamole, sweet peppers, lettuce, and quinoa. It was just what a hungry tourist needs. I still needed to lose some weight, but this day wasn't the time to start my diet!

It was bucket-list time once again. We had train tickets to take us to the touristy town of Aguas Calientes, which is closest to Machu Picchu, and the next morning we set off. That train ride was, by far, the best train experience I had in all my travels. Oops, I forgot about the bullet train; so, okay, it comes in at a close second. We were served complimentary beverages and snacks, including unlimited coca tea. The staff was extremely attentive and friendly. Some were even modeling ponchos and hats available for purchase. The windows extended across the ceiling of the train, giving us a spectacular all-round view of the mountain landscapes, farms, and rivers for the 90-minute ride. The sun shone brightly through every inch of the train as we climbed to higher and higher elevations. The mountains began to show their snow-capped peaks. This was no Disney World ride. This was the real thing! Our hotel was an over-the-top, five-star lodge complete with its own dedicated train stop. We went to sleep early so that we'd be refreshed for the 6 a.m. train to the famous Machu Picchu.

We arrived at the Aguas Calientes train station and met up with our private tour guide. Aguas Calientes had a gaudy village feel that obviously relied on tourism. Restaurants, shops, spas, and hostels were shoved neatly next to one another in what looked like a Swiss Alps village. We waited with our private guide to get on a bus that would take us up to the mountain site. Bus after bus drove past us as staffers came down the line to check everyone's tickets and passports. We hopped on bus 16 and followed the bus in front of us over the bridge and up the mountain that eventually led us to the entrance of Machu Picchu. It was still dark and foggy, and we couldn't see much of anything. I could tell, however, that the steep, winding, uphill road was scaling a mega-mountain. It was a long way down for sure. Given my fear of heights, it was terrifying and exciting all at the same time. As we reached the gates, the sun was beginning to rise, but it was still hiding behind the mountains and thick layers of fog.

Our guide led us through the gates as soon as they opened, at 7:00 a.m. Panting and out of breath at 8,000 feet, we learned about the history of the Incas and how Machu Picchu came to be. As we reached the top, the fog began to fade into the ozone, as if it were cued to do so. There it was, the view of a lifetime! Better than the Acropolis, better than Hagia Sophia, better than the Eiffel Tower, better than *anything!* Steep and jagged mountain peaks of green coupled with the ancient ruins of Machu Picchu created the perfect scene. Behind them was a flawless blue sky with puffs of clouds adorning the dream. In all the excitement and anticipation, I had left my boot cast in a taxi cab before we departed on this trip. Typical me. The doctor's orders had me for one more week in the cast. So, even though my foot was pretty much healed, I found myself live without a net, scaling the irregular surfaces of the mountain with my cast-less and tender foot. Thankfully, I would make it out of there just fine.

There we stood, above the ruins of about 150 ancient structures that included grain warehouses, temples, sanctuaries, and residences left behind by a long-forgotten civilization. The scene was spellbinding. It was no wonder they made this a holy place where they prayed for a productive harvest. Photos could never do it justice. I was breathless, both from the sight and from the altitude. Fong and I took hundreds of photos from different vistas, as our guide took us all over the site. In fact, the cover of this book was taken at the incredible spot. Okay, I admit it: I was not actually working on my laptop at Machu Picchu ... Did you really believe I would be working at a time like this?!

Phil Phact: According to our guide, Machu Picchu was considered by the elders of the time to be such a resplendent and holy place that they did not engage in animal agriculture, nor did they sacrifice animals there. This obviously resonated with me.

Our visit to Machu Picchu had to be the finest tourist experience of my lifetime. The weather was perfect, and it was so well organized. It wasn't that crowded either. You know how some tourist hotspots can be overrun with people and can just become chaotic and dysfunctional? That was not the case at Machu Picchu. The Acropolis in Athens is mobbed during the summer. Saint Sophia in Istanbul is crowded, super smelly, and pretty boring. Venice, Italy and its narrow pedestrian streets and water canals are always overrun with tourists from all five continents (especially Asia). Machu Picchu is in a class all its own.

Phil Phact: Machu Picchu was built around AD 1450 as a symbol of the Inca Empire. It was initiated as a UNESCO World Heritage Site in 1983 and was named one of the New Seven Wonders of the World in 2007. In the Inca language of Quechua, Machu Picchu means "Old Peak" or "Old Mountain." Machu Picchu was built in a hidden location, invisible from below and nearly impossible to find, making it one of the most well-preserved Inca cities to have ever existed. Unfortunately, most of the cities and villages built by the Inca civilization were abandoned following the Spanish conquest. It is believed that hundreds of men pushed the heavy rocks up the steep mountain side for the construction of the city.

Fong and I took the majestic 45-mile-long train ride back to Cusco. I reflected on how incredible the last few days had been between the Ayahuasca ceremonies and our visit to Machu Picchu. The Ayahuasca ceremonies were also powerful for Fong. She felt as if she had new eyes, mind, body and soul. We spent the last week of my month in Peru together, and then Fong flew back to Thailand. When we said "goodbye," it meant "until our next embrace." No one had ever loved me the way Fong had.

During my remaining days in Lima, I dove right in to all the work I had missed during my side trip and caught up on my Spanish lessons. The city was still celebrating Peru's advancement in the World Cup. Everybody wore white and red on game days ... and on non-game days. Businesses would stop their commerce, and employees and customers alike would huddle around TVs and radios to cheer on the game. Everything basically shut down during a match so that no kick would be missed. Back in the States, everybody has their favorite team, but imagine an entire nation rooting for *the same one* team. The euphoria was so widespread that even in the countryside there were flags and banners in support of the Peruvian soccer team. Peru didn't make it far in the month long tournament, but there was pride throughout the nation nonetheless. As a Philadelphia Eagles fan who was still basking in the glory of our first Superbowl win, I loved the Peruvians' team pride. They were true-blue fans, just like us Eagles fans. It was in their DNA. Hell, yeah!

Peru had such an optimistic vibe. I could see that they always wanted to improve themselves and their country. I admired that. I respected their humble and gentle nature. They held fast to their morals, heritage, and customs, which had been passed down from indigenous tribes. All of this somehow seemed to harmoniously meld with the culture and customs of their European counterparts, who were also steeped in centuries of their culture. It was a melting pot and a tossed salad at the same time. Collectively, they were still open to the outside world, and because of this they were in a perpetual state of acculturation.

As I'm sure you have figured out by now, I really loved my stay in Peru. It lifted me up and placed me on a brighter path. I felt physically and mentally stronger. My foot was almost 100 percent healed. The Ayahuasca ceremonies were profound beyond words, and my respiratory system was better than it had been. My mind felt clearer. I was ready to take on Colombia.

Have laptop, will travel!

CHAPTER 10

Medellín, Colombia

"Travel is fatal to prejudice, bigotry, and narrow-mindedness."

MARK TWAIN

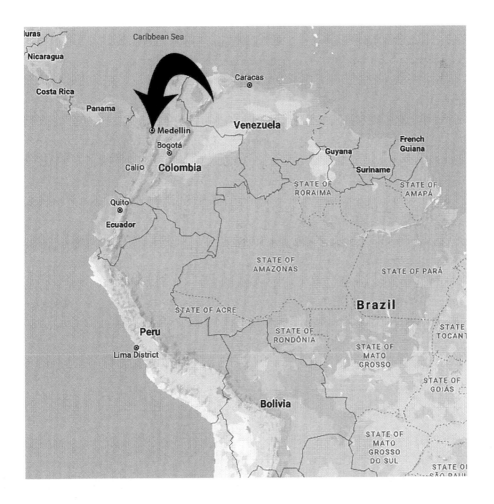

With a hop, skip, and a connecting flight, our band of digital nomads arrived in the land of drug dealers, prostitutes, and government corruption. At least, those were the stereotypes reinforced by Netflix dramas like *Narcos*, a series based on the dark history of the violent drug trade in Colombia. Medellín, home of the notorious narco-terrorist Pablo Escobar, turned out to be nothing like the stereotypes we were fed in the States. I think we all had preconceived notions that Colombia would be unsafe and unstable. Damn, stereotypes can be so wrong, especially where this city was concerned.

Our luggage made it safely into our custody at the airport. Okay, so at least they weren't riffling through our luggage and stealing our traveled laptops. Good sign. It didn't take long to realize that Medellín is far from what it used to be just 20 or 30 years ago. It is now considered one of the most innovative and thriving cities in the world. It gets high ratings for quality of life, which includes the very low cost of living. This is why many expatriates and digital nomads choose Medellín.

As in Argentina, we were going to live in two Colombian cities for the next two months: Medellín, then Bogotá. I was excited to discover the mysteries of Colombia, although I had my guard up about being targeted ... for ... kidnapping! Yep! My parents and sister were still very concerned about this. My dad confided to me that he even had nightmares that this would happen. They, along with many others, had heard or lived through horror stories about this place. My parents never wasted an opportunity to repeat a certain Greek phrase to me: *ta matia sou dekatessera*, which means "your 14 eyes." It's a warning that you should somehow have 14 eyes all around your head to keep from falling into harm's way. Oh, we Greeks and our drama!

> **Phil Phact:** Drama is, in fact, the name of a town in the northeastern corner of Greece near the Bulgarian border, population 44,823. Yeah, that's how you know that we Greeks invented drama, too!

It was an honor that Victor and Alvin requested to live with me this month. From our high-rise apartment, we had a stunning view of Medellín's hillside metropolis, nestled in a gently sloping valley and surrounded by lush, green mountains. Prague had spellbinding architectural ornateness, but Medellín took first prize in both great weather and nature's beauty. The surrounding mountains formed a giant bowl, and filling it were countless buildings of all sizes, styles, ages, and uses. Due to the elevation of the city, the clouds danced close to us. Blue skies watched over the city and later were transformed by the fiery palette of sublime sunsets.

Over the last 20 years, the Colombian government has been upgrading the public spaces, transit infrastructure, and neighborhoods in order to steer the country into a safer, more prosperous future. Some of the poorest spots, such as Plaza de Cisneros—one of the seediest drug dens—even underwent a renewal. It is now a thriving hamlet, and a representation of hope for Medellín's new and better quality of life. The city added a cable car system, trams, buses, and a metro that connects the once separated impoverished hillside communities to the prospering city below.

Medellín is known as "The City of Eternal Spring" thanks to its pleasant, year-round climate courtesy of its elevation of 5,000 feet above sea level. It took about a week for me to get acclimated to the higher altitude, although I knew it would be much higher still in Bogotá. The day was always a sun kissed one, with just enough chilly breezes to cool me down after traversing the city's steep hills. Of course, we had the occasional thunderstorm, but without those, Colombia wouldn't be blessed with an abundance of lush vegetation that was all around.

My apartment was located only five minutes from the Selina Hostel and coworking space. These walking hills of Medellín were a few notches steeper than the pedestrian hills of Lisbon. I didn't think that was even possible, but there I was scaling the hills of the city on foot, huffing and puffing. Going to and from my apartment was a vigorous cardio experience. I was worn out by the time I arrived at the workspace. I'll admit, I took an (illegal) Uber ride the first few times I made the trip. I had an initial shock the first time the Uber app displayed the trip's bill because it was 6,254 Colombian pesos! Thankfully, that's only about 2.25 USD.

The Selina coworking space was one of my favorite office spaces so far. (I think I said that about every city.) It was in a great location, and it had all the amenities a digital nomad could desire. It was located inside of a hotel/hostel complete with a hip café, trendy restaurant, and nightclub. The open-air club carried on with a party almost every night. Selina also abutted a natural creek that gave off a pleasing sound of running water. This was no Bose sound machine: this was the real deal, and it made for a peaceful environment for working or participating in the free yoga classes held outside on the deck. There was also a kitchen area, a meditation room, plenty of desks to work at, fast internet, and modern decor that incorporated motivational quotes and awesome graffiti. I loved it there … *but*, I still had the chip on my shoulder about living in Colombia.

My guard was up for any shady shenanigans that I might encounter. Plus, my relationship with Fong was beginning to get a bit rocky, and I was unsure of where it would lead. More on that later. Thankfully, I was pleasantly distracted by all the beautiful Colombian women that walked past me on the streets, stores, and restaurants. And I mean every single one of them was gorgeous. I went to the supermarket and saw beautiful women. I went to get my haircut, and a breathtaking woman was sitting right next to me. I went out for lunch and encountered some real stunners. Do not even get me started on yoga class. It was almost like a gorgeous-female, circus sideshow in the yoga room. Beautiful women were so common that Colombian men didn't even turn to look at them. But I nearly gave myself whiplash.

I was living with the guys in the neighborhood of Poblado, which happened to be in the heart of the entertainment district, full of bars, clubs, parks, shops, and restaurants. To sum it up, Pobaldo was safe, affordable, and wonderfully walkable. Once I found my routine of yoga, work, and massages, I could tackle the uphill walks with more ease. Removing alcohol from my lifestyle also helped me a lot. I could clearly see an improvement in my health and my breathing. I was sleeping better. When

I went out with the boys, it was club soda with a splash of cranberry all the way.

The World Cup tournament seemed like it would never end. I cheered on Peru while I was living in Lima, but now my allegiances were with Colombia, and they were still in the tournament. They were scheduled to play a semi-final match against England during our second week there. It was a big deal because the winner would move on to the final championship match.

Just like in Lima, everyone stopped what they were doing to watch or tune in to the soccer match, which happened to be on Sunday this time around. Bars and restaurants opened early to accommodate the influx of customers and fans. Street vendors were posted on every corner selling jerseys, t-shirts, scarves, and other paraphernalia donning the bright yellow, blue, and red Colombia team colors. The streets were packed. Reservations were a must if you wanted a table at the restaurant to watch the game. People were just as happy to stand without a table to sit at. The amount of national pride and support for this Colombian *fútbol* team was over the top.

No Philter: For the first time on this digital nomad journey, I experienced the highest level of intense, nearly fervent national pride. I had never seen this level of enthusiasm in the States. The Japanese and Thai people were too reserved to express their nationalism, if they had any. The Malaysians had a young country with simmering socio-religious tensions, so national pride wasn't exactly noticeable to me. The Europeans were way too cool for school and a bit cynical, so they didn't exhibit any patriotism that I saw. The Argentinians were simply too negative to express pride for their country (for good reason). The Peruvians were proud, but it was as if they had less to be proud of. But the Colombians were loud, proud, and all-in for their country!

Colombia and England were tied 2 to 2 at the end of 90 minutes, so they went into 15-minutes of overtime, but still no goals were scored. Because no one scored, it was now a game of sudden death. Five players from each team were chosen to take the penalty kicks. Everyone in the bar was on the edge of their seats and biting their nails. In the end, Colombia lost in sudden death when England scored the winning penalty kick, so England moved on to the final round. The Colombian locals were great sports about losing. Even after a loss, the Colombians knew how to party. They were vibrant and optimistic people, and always looked for the silver lining. I was surrounded by overzealous fans who hugged it out in defeat. I figured since they had been through so much historical turmoil, especially in the 1980s and 90s, that perhaps they were keen to celebrate the real victories in life; the things that really matter.

Later that week, wanting to learn more about Colombia's famously violent history, I signed up for a Pablo Escobar city tour. Like I've said before, "An ounce of experience is worth more than a ton of theories." I looked forward to comparing the facts and sites of this tour to what was projected through the lens of Hollywood.

Several Mangos departed from Betty's Bowls, the vegan-friendly breakfast bar next to Selina, following a scrumptious cup of Colombia's finest coffee. About ten of us stepped away from our laptops and got off the grid for a day of discovery. Our tour guide, Federico, was quick to emphasize that he was good friends with Escobar's son. He was the real deal and knew where to take us. As the saying goes, he knew where the bodies were buried. At age ten, Federico became friends with Juan Pablo Escobar through his mother who sold real estate to Pablo Escobar. They played on the same soccer team while the bodyguards stayed very close (and even traveled with the team). Nobody ever went near or challenged Juan Pablo during a game, so his team always won. Later in life, Federico was kidnapped and held for ransom. Kidnapping for money was a cottage industry in the '80s and '90s, and since his family had some money, he was successfully targeted. His family paid the ransom after he had spent several days in a closet on a damp concrete floor. The kidnappers pistol-whipped him, broke his nose, and gave him gave him barely enough water and bread to survive until his release. When the nightmare was over, he fled to Europe where he lived for a few years. He wanted nothing to do with Colombia. Eventually, his mother convinced him that conditions had changed post-Escobar and it was safe for him to return home. Voice shaking, he spoke with great emotion that his country "had now become the country he knew it could be." I got chills from his words and his feelings. His restaurant, tour, and coffee businesses were all thriving. These successful enterprises exemplified the country's vibrancy and economic upswing. I became sold on Colombia in that moment.

Through the winding hills of the Medellín, we drove to the safe house where Pablo Escobar was eventually found and killed in December of 1993. A Colombian electronic surveillance team, led by Brigadier Hugo Martínez, used radio trilateration technology to track Pablo's phone transmissions. One day, Escobar's conversation with his young son went on just a little too long, and that allowed them to pinpoint his whereabouts. The military police rushed the house, leading to a shoot-out on a rooftop where they killed him. After all the binge-watching of *Narcos* and drug cartel documentaries, I couldn't believe that I was *there* in that nondescript, middleclass bario. From a higher-level street, I had a clear view of the roof where the final shoot-out took place—it was just a plain-old tiled roof that blended in with all the others.

Phil Phact: Pablo Escobar suffered gunshots to the leg and torso, but the fatal gunshot went through the ear. No one will ever know whether the kill shot was fired by police or by Escobar himself.

After the safe house, Federico drove us to the now-famous Comuna 13 neighborhood. Medellín is a city divided into 16 neighborhood sections, called *comunas* in Spanish. Although the Mangos lived in the neighborhood of El Poblado, that was not the name of the comuna. All 250 neighborhoods in Medellín are identified by one of the 16 comunas in the city. El Poblado is actually located in Comuna 10, which is pretty far away from Comuna 13. The common misconception, even with the locals, is that the *comunas* are the "slums," but, in fact, every area of Medellín is classified into a specific *comuna*. Some are safer than others, some are richer than others. They each have their own vibe.

In the 1990s, Comuna 13 was considered one of the most dangerous places in the world. Amazingly, it was now a top choice for tourists on TripAdvisor. The violence began with two waves of migration from other areas of Colombia: one in the late 1800s, and another in the early 1900s. Many of the migrants left smaller cities due to conflict and strife. They also sought better economic opportunities. Unfortunately, their skill set was primarily limited to agriculture. Comuna 13 was not ready for them, with its poor infrastructure and contaminated farmland. This privation left the area susceptible to gang crime and the drug smuggling scene. Everyday life was hard and unsafe; even to simply walk around the small hamlet was risky. Comuna 13 was built on the side of a mountain, which meant lots of stairs and vertiginous sidewalks. On the flip side, for us anyway, that meant some of the best views in Medellín. The vast city view and mountainous backdrop were simply stunning.

Throughout the late '80s and early '90s, this strategically located area was used as a distribution hub for cocaine and weapons. Rival gangs and drug lords were constantly in dispute, and violence was a given. Comuna 13 was literally a battlefield in the Escobar era and beyond. It was not until 2002, when Alvaro Uribe was elected as president of Colombia, that things finally changed for Comuna 13. Uribe led ten military campaigns, which eventually pushed out the drug gangs. Many people, both good and bad, were killed during this time. It was a harsh way to establish law and order, but positive outcomes were achieved.

Phil Phact: In 2006, the government lifted a law that forbade passengers from riding on the back of a motorcycle. All too often during the Escobar era, the rear passengers were the hitmen, spraying their victims with bullets as the bike sped past. The Spanish word for assassin is *sicario*, and at the height of the Escobar era, Pablo had 5,000 *sicarios* on payroll. Thankfully, times have changed!

As I walked through Comuna 13's steep and winding pedestrian streets with my fellow nomads, I gawked at the giant graffiti art that decorated the exteriors of many structures. A kaleidoscope of color formed famous figures, symbols, animals, and other designs that represented the dark decades of drug smuggling and gang warfare. In my mind, I kept going back to what I had seen on *Narcos*. I felt that, hands down, *Narcos* nailed the vibe and scenery quite well, although many Colombians felt that shows like that reinforced negative stereotypes. Colombian music, modern salsa, and merengue drifted out of kitchen windows as we walked past. At every home, café, park, and bar we passed, we heard the music of the people. It blended together as one celebration of life, culture, and community. Rock and roll in the 4/4-time signature was *nowhere* to be found on the playlists! It was apparent that a positive transformation was very much in progress. The past was gone, and the flourishing of art, culture, expats, and tourism seemed like it was all here to stay. Take a graffiti tour through Comuna 13, mix with the locals, drink a freshly squeezed juice, and buy a souvenir ... But go in a group, and please don't go at night! While there is significantly less violence now in Comuna 13 and in other areas of Medellín, gangs, trafficking, and street crime still exist. The streets are often occupied with soldiers and policemen strapped up with machine guns. I felt safe but also wondered if these officials were in cahoots with drug traffickers.

Our last stop on the Pablo Escobar tour was to his main family home, Edificio Monaco. Located right in Poblado, it looked like an army fortress with a penthouse apartment on top of the stark, white building. In 1988, the rival Cali Cartel set off a powerful, roadside car bomb that ripped through the second-story window of his daughter's room. She lost her hearing in one ear as a result of the assassination attempt. This savage act against Escobar's family continued to fuel a deadly rivalry for the years to follow. On the other side of the house were stairs leading down to a basement where tortures and killings took place. It was all in a day's work for Escobar, who presumably would emerge from the basement after a day of bloody carnage just in time for dinner and to help the kids with homework. Monster!

Earlier this year, the mayor's office decided that the Escobar home would be torn down and turned into a memorial park commemorating the lives lost from the drug wars. More than 220,000 people died as a result of Colombia's drug war since it began around 1960.

> **No Philter:** Legalize it, all of it! Portugal decriminalized all drugs in 2001, and it's working! The numbers don't lie. Drug abuse and addiction is down due to Portugal's decriminalization policies.

At some point, it popped into my head to look for an over-the-top luxury apartment for the upcoming month in the capital city of Bogotá. I loved having roommates the last couple of months, but I was ready for some solo living. More than that, I felt that the Mangos needed some spice in month 11. I wanted to make new memories that harkened back to the glory days of my Chiang Mai rooftop parties. If only I could find the right apartment. On the very first search on my Airbnb app, I found it! There were a few top choices, but one place stood out. It was in the right neighborhood and close to the workspace. The landlord was very responsive and agreed to meet me the very next day. I grabbed a direct flight to Bogotá, which cost me less than some cab rides back in the States.

I arrived in Bogotá without a hitch and took an Uber straight to the condo where I met Manny, the landlord. He greeted me in the lobby like a long-lost friend. He struck me as a born salesman, but he would turn out to be so much more. He was a well-dressed, avuncular, balding man in his early 60s who probably hadn't had a bad day in a long time. He was so charming, friendly, and eager to know me. His English was perfect. Manny explained that he was a realtor and landlord, and that his family had acquired rental office buildings and apartments over the years, starting with his father in the 1950s. The condo was rented at that time, so the tour included a meet and greet with the existing tenant at no extra charge. Manny's tenant was an expat from Washington D.C. who had hit the jackpot selling off some business technology. In the apartment that could be mine, the three of us were hitting it off in a round-robin of storytelling and laughs. Our personalities clicked, and I felt a sense of belonging and fortuitous timing. Once again, synchronicity abounded.

Manny's apartment was even more beautiful than the online pictures. Blond, dark, and caramel wood warmed the home, contrasting with the cool white walls and marble countertops. It was just across the street from a quaint little park and walking distance from numerous cafés and restaurants. The apartment was on the top floor, which featured a private rooftop deck with views, views, views. The coolest thing was the retractable roof. Like a kid in a candy store, Manny began an enthusiastic demonstration. First, he grabbed a remote control, pressed a button, and the roof quickly disappeared. He pressed another button and down came a giant movie screen. And with the press of another button, modern salsa rang out and the sub-bass throbbed. And then the *pièce de résistance* on the roof deck: comfortable, inviting seats that surrounded a modern fire pit that overlooked the park! He pressed his favorite button, and the flames of the fire pit came to life.

Manny thought of everything when he fitted out this spectacular condo. This place was decorated to the nines; it was totally upscale and totally *me*. Manny proudly declared that the maid would come three times per week to clean, do laundry, and even to make breakfast and lunch for me and my guests. I could get used to that! But now, there was only one problem. The place was so amazing, I lost all my negotiating skills. As the saying goes: real estate and emotions *don't mix*. Even though I brought along a stack of Benjamins sufficient for his asking price, I had planned to bring it down. I tried to "Greek-him-down" several times, but he was cheerfully firm. By now, I was irreversibly in love with the place, so I paid his price and secured the condo for month 11 in Colombia's capital city. Truth be told, the rent was still a lot less than it would have been in Los Angeles, Miami, or New York.

My time in Medellín would come to end soon, and I was ready (and excited) to take on Bogotá. I had a great feeling about the city. As the capital, it boasted taller buildings and wider avenues than the twisty-turny streets of Medellín. As I would soon discover, it was replete with a variety of restaurants, grocery stores, malls, boutiques, and a more sophisticated nightlife. Bogotá was more cosmopolitan and more my vibe, for sure. It was a bit cooler in temperature, though, and at a higher elevation of 8,000 feet above sea level, this would prove to be a respiratory challenge for me. I left that evening not only with a new home for our second-to-last month, but with two new friends, as well. Win, win.

Phil Pheelings: Although I was excited for Bogotá, I came back to that feeling I got whenever I side-tripped: a comfortable satisfaction of "coming back home." So, even though I was away for just a short a weekend trip, I missed Medellín. I guess there's some validity to the saying, "Home is where the heart is." But, with a Phil Twist, I'd rather say, "Home is where your personal belongings, clothing, and backup cash are."

Before departing Medellín, I participated in an exotic-fruit-tasting track, where we learned about and ate more than 15 different fruits, some of which were native to Colombia. From coconut to star fruit to pineapple, we sampled them all. There were so many fruits I had never heard of. For example, I tried a lulo (that looks like a cross between a tomato and an orange) and a tomate de arbol (or tamarillo)—two tangy, bitter fruits. A few of the fruits had jagged points on them and looked like giant yellow hand grenades. It was a short and sweet track that really opened my eyes to the incredible biodiversity of Colombia.

> **Phil Phact:** There are about 55,000 species of plants and wildlife in Colombia. About 3,000 of these species are plants native to Colombia, along with almost 18 percent of the world's bird species. Oh, and there are nearly 400 different species of bee. Talk about biodiversity!

It didn't take much convincing to fold up our laptops and get off the grid, yet again, to attend an interesting track. This time we would head deep into the mountains surrounding Medellín. We were meeting a farmer who made CBD oil from cannabis, the kind that contains no psychoactive THC. After 90 minutes of riding in a van up to even higher altitudes, our driver turned down a dirt and gravel path into the secluded farm. We piled out of the van and were warmly greeted by the "jefe," which means "boss" in Spanish. He was a thin, weathered-looking Colombian man about my age, who had obtained his master's degree in botanical chemistry from the University of Miami. He obviously knew his stuff. His slide presentation convinced me even more deeply about the therapeutic and healing benefits of the marijuana plant. I never did get his actual name. Let's just call him the "Pot-boro Man," because, unlike the Marlboro Man, he was not selling cancer; he was selling something that could relieve your symptoms and, quite possibly, heal you too.

His supply of the cannabis plant actually came from the southern end of the country, from an indigenous Indian tribe. Because the tribe had sovereignty over their ancestral land, their laws allowed them to grow pot legally. On a regular basis, Pot-boro man would drive south to purchase their harvest and transport it back to his property. He performed the oil-extraction process at his facility. We performed an extraction of CBD oil, and it was a surprisingly simple process. All we needed was a common kitchen appliance (a slow cooker), some edible cooking oil, and the plant itself.

Soon after our extraction demo, things got interesting for us Mangos. The Pot-boro Man led us to a makeshift gift shop of sorts where his offerings were spread across one large table. There was CBD oil in one-ounce tincture bottles. In addition to those, he offered "other" oils in a speakeasy fashion. He implied that a certain batch of bottles on one side of the table contained psychoactive THC in addition to the CBD. We learned that the Colombian government had not fully banned psychoactive pot in oil form. It was still a legal grey area. Pot-boro was very confi dent about this when he explained the intricacies of the law. We could buy as many bottles as we wanted for $22 each, while back in the States the same amount would cost us $200. Don't ask me how I know this—I just know.

The tramily loaded up! I bought four of the fun bottles. I gave two away to some locals later in the week and kept two. I had a fi rm rule to *never* travel with contraband, and with travel day coming up for Bogotá, this weighed on me. My solution involved my fellow digital nomad, Chris, who was still making a nice living head-hunting for engineers and software programmers. He gladly accepted the role of my mule for the plane ride from Medellín to Bogotá. I offered to give him one of the two bottles for his transport fee. He was happy with the offer and went on to perform the task successfully. Problem solved. I used a few drops here and there to help me sleep. It works.

As the buying frenzy ensued, the Pot-boro Man informed us that certain amounts of various drugs were allowed to be on your person at one time. A person could have up to eight joints, a few grams of coke, and a few tabs of acid. What!? During one recent night out on the town, many of us in the tramily were searched for drugs by police who were holding back uber-aggressive dogs on leashes. The crazy part is that the candy and cigarettes street vendor offered us drugs under his breath with those same damn police within sight. It was a racket, and they were obviously in cahoots.

> **No Philter:** If someone were naïve enough to fall prey to the racket and get caught, the police would escort them to the nearest ATM to extort funds. I guess that was considered paying your debt to society as well as *time served*. It's hard to imagine a time when people would get locked up just for having a joint in their pocket, especially as we are now studying the countless benefits of the various marijuana extractions. I wonder how many people are still rotting in a jail for the petty "crime" of carrying around some herb?

In the final week of July, with the Remote Year finish line in sight, I gave two vegan talks in Medellín. I was no longer afraid for my personal safety; things were checking out just fine. One of the talks was a success, and the other was not. I shared the vegan message first at the Yolo Hostel, which was the home of my beloved Betty's Bowls café. I really hit it off with the two couples who owned Betty's, and after getting to know me, they offered to promote and host a lecture there. We had become good friends after so many weeks of going there almost daily.

They held the event in the large lobby area and took care of all the advertising and technical equipment. Forty truth seekers came out to hear my vegan message of health for self, and compassion for animals. To top it off, I asked my fellow Hippocrates Health Educator colleague, Barbara, to translate the presentation in Spanish as I spoke. I met her just weeks before when I gave my presentation at HHI in Florida. Barbara and her husband, Seth, were part-time locals in Medellín, and owned a gorgeous luxury condo in the same neighborhood. Their uber-luxe apartment boasted sweeping views of the mountain bowl and the sloping cityscape below. Spending time with them got me thinking that someday I would also be a part-time local in the City of Eternal Spring. It was serendipitous that Barbara, Seth, and I had connected just weeks earlier. Now they were pumped about being involved in the presentation.

It was Barbara's first time translating, and it sounded like she did a great job. We were communicating harmoniously, like we were singing a duet but speaking our parts back and forth instead. Speaking with a translator is something I always enjoy. It challenges me to think differently and choose my phrases carefully. It requires me to use more easily digestible bite-sized phrases, while also affording me a break to evaluate my next thoughts as the translator is still speaking. I get a kick out of hearing my words being communicated through foreign sounds and hopefully into someone's heart.

My presentation was followed by a lively Q and A, and there were some great questions that night. I fielded the usual ones like, "Where do you get vitamins B and D?" I also answered some of the common mythical questions like, "If we stop eating the animals, then won't they take over the earth and overpopulate?" And then there was the question that never goes away: "Weren't the animals put here for us to eat?"

The most rewarding moment came at the end of the presentation, as I was approached by Sonny, a co-owner of Betty's Bowls. He said that he was ready to go vegan and that his wife was also on board. He had watched the videos I had recommended earlier in the month, such as: *What the Health* and *Cowspiracy*. Since he was a dedicated athlete, his concern about physical performance on a vegan diet was eliminated when he watched some YouTube videos by Rich Roll, a top vegan athlete who ran five Ironman triathlons in a row, across the five main Hawaiian islands. I gave Sonny all the support, advice, and tips I had swimming in my head. I saw the look in his eyes and could tell he was going to embark on a successful vegan adventure. Fast forward two months later when I received an email in English from Sonny:

Dear Felipe,

Hola Amigo! I wanted to thank you for introducing me into the plant-based universe. Three months since I became vegan, I feel much more energized and happy. I regret not doing it before. I had always used the common excuse, "Where will I get the protein from?" I like to exercise daily, and I used this excuse all of the time, as I was afraid of becoming skinny and sick looking.

Also, I certainly feel more at peace and whole with the Mother Earth knowing that I am not contributing to her destruction. I am also not causing to the animals. More specifically regarding my transformation, I can happily say that I've obtained more muscle, and my recovery time between workouts is shorter. We miss you! Come back and see us!

Sonny

Sonny's email gave me that same feeling I had when I received the follow-up note and picture from The Wildflower Shelter in Chiang Mai. Helping people help themselves is the main reason I give my lectures. That's what it's all about. On the flip side, I gave my second presentation in Medellín the Friday evening before we left for our month in Bogotá. I hosted it myself at the Selina coworking space and only four people showed up. But, hey, I was happy to be available to *any* number of people looking to improve their lives and our world through the vegan diet. As I stood in front that audience of four, I imagined I was onstage at Madison Square Garden in front of thousands. As it turned out, two of the gals who showed up were totally into it. They were in the beginning stages of setting up a vegan advocacy group in Medellín. We exchanged contact information, and they promised to invite me back for an event they would promote. We vegan advocates are constantly planting seeds (no pun intended!).

Our Remote Year transition day was now upon us. Several Mangos had decided to leave the program for various reasons. I always took their departure personally, even though I knew their departures had nothing to do with me. While our group was decreasing in size, from 49 to the low 30-something, I was determined to cross the finish line. I was tired of traveling, but I was looking forward to further exploring incredible Colombia.

Medellín was a real eye-opener, serving as a true-life lesson about believing what I read or see in the media. In reality, Medellín was nothing short of a paradise. The stereotypes about Colombia faded each time I stepped out of my Poblado apartment. When I walked the streets alone to find a bite to eat, go to the workspace, take yoga, or whatever, I always returned unscathed. I could even say that I felt safer walking the streets of my Poblado neighborhood than I did walking around some places back in the States. With the economy's rapid and positive growth, the natural beauty, incomparable weather, low cost of living, and overall high quality of life, Medellín had now become one of Latin America's exemplary success stories. Even city planners in Mendoza, Argentina, for example, were now studying Medellín's best practices for improving the economy, transportation, and safety. You could call it "The Medellín Miracle."

Medellín was now at the top of my list of favorite places in the world. I had another month of Colombia ahead of me and I was grateful about that. My bags were packed again. Each time I left for the next city, I paid less and less attention to packing. I just squished it all in to the suitcase and zipped it up.

I was excited for this magic carpet ride to keep flying. Month ten was officially over, and in just two months, this year-long odyssey would end. I mulled this over on the way to the airport, and immediately reminded myself that there never is, in fact, a final destination. The Mother Ayahuasca confirmed to me that the journey continues long after our short time on this earth.

Adios Medellín! Que tal Bogotá (what up Bogotá)?

Tener laptop, viajará!

CHAPTER 11

Bogotá, Colombia

"To travel is to learn that everyone is
wrong about other countries."

ALDOUS HUXLEY

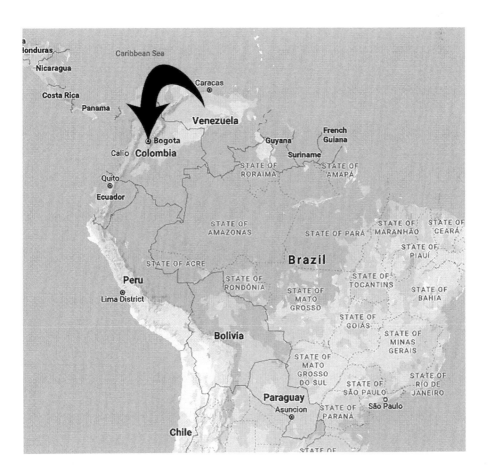

The Mangos arrived in the capital of Colombia on Saturday evening, all of us unscathed and not kidnapped. My brief visit to Bogotá during the previous month didn't give me a complete feel for the city, so I was excited to explore more. I quickly discovered that the city had a sophisticated charm all its own. It was a real gem.

In Bogotá, modern culture, high-rise buildings, and colonial landmarks all intertwined within the vast city grid, and like the other places I had seen in South America, there was a blend of old and new. The city is home to just over eight million people who all teemed within the business districts, lush parks, vibrant nightlife and cultural scene, and amazing views of the Colombian Andes mountains. Best of all, though, was the spectacular apartment I rented from Manny overlooking Parque Virrey. From my eighth-floor rooftop, I could gaze at the multi-colored, billowing trees that swayed collectively in the gentle breeze. Joggers, dog walkers, commuters, and families flowed in and out of the park down below.

Phil Pheelings: I had been assigned an apartment that month with fellow digital nomad Sal. I set foot in that apartment only once, simply out of curiosity, since it was on the way home from a bar one night. The tiny apartment was dimly lit, old, and reeked of Sal's cigarette smoke. Despite the dilapidated digs, part of me was disappointed I did not get to room with Sal, who was on RY taking a yearlong break from his computer programming career. He was, in his own way, a sweet man with a heart of gold, but he struggled with his weight and addiction to cigarettes and booze. I tried to inspire him to embrace some better habits, including exercise. He was so kind and sweet that for the first couple of months I assumed his sweetness was phony. By the third month, it was obvious that his kindness was genuine. I always felt compelled to help and encourage him. At the same time, I've learned in life that the only person we can change is ourselves.

Thanks to my new bachelor pad, I was blessed with many blissful mornings on the private rooftop. With the press of a few buttons, I retracted the roof, cranked up the fire pit, launched a playlist, and sipped my coca tea in the lap of luxury. I sure was living it up this month in Bogotá. The main floor boasted floor-to-ceiling windows that slid open to further reveal nature's beauty. Travel books on Iceland, Japan, India and other bucket-list hot spots were stacked nicely on each cocktail table, as they were always big hits with my guests. My housekeeper, Cielo, was a sweetheart. Between her, Spanish classes, and the Rappi app, my Spanish was improving by the day. My brain was no longer getting bent from this language.

Phil Phact: Rappi is a mobile app that provides home delivery for groceries, restaurant food, liquor, and drugstore medications. All the main chain stores are on the app, and every SKU that they carry is just one simple click away from being at the house in a few minutes. It even has the option to receive cash, as if to provide a chauffeured ATM service! In the States, we have Uber Eats and Instacart, but Rappi surpassed them both, big time! Rappi added spice to each city we lived in, but I used it most often in Bogotá. A stream of orange-shirted bike couriers with their payloads strapped to their backs weaved through the city streets. Happy customers waited for their orders to arrive at the front door by the friendliest people you've ever met. Oh my Rappi!

Our workspace for the month was at a WeWork location, one of a large chain of modern, beautiful, shared coworking spaces found in many cities, including New York, Hong Kong, Miami, and Buenos Aires. They, much like Remote Year, are true examples of the future of work and the digital nomad lifestyle. They were committed to providing an alternative platform to the life-sucking nine-to-five.

One day, an email from a national tenant popped into my inbox, suggesting that I build a prototype store on one of my Pennsylvania properties that had been sitting vacant for two years. I was so distracted by my travels that it had not even occurred to me to build there. I will always have fond memories sorting out the details of the new project from the WeWork tenth-story rooftop. I would be getting record rents, but not without a world of hurt from the state and local government in the process of obtaining building approval. Why should anything be easy?

> **Phil Phact:** There are 3 secrets to success:
> 1. There is no substitute for persistence.
> 2. 80 percent of life is showing up.
> 3. I'd rather be lucky than talented. An old real estate guy told me that a long time ago, and I really took it to heart. But then I tweaked it a little bit, and now I follow this mantra: be lucky *and* talented!

I woke up one morning during that first week in Bogotá with the sunlight peeking through the blinds over my bedroom window. I threw on my yoga clothes and walked into the kitchen to prepare some coca tea. Then I grabbed my phone off my nightstand and headed up to the roof for my morning ritual. I took my phone off airplane mode (always switch on airplane mode when you sleep to reduce the exposure of radiation emitted from the cell service towers and satellites) and stared up into the cloudless blue sky as the phone caught up with the backlog. A stream of WhatsApp messages blew up my phone. I had 15 notifications from Fong. Still not fully awake, I couldn't believe what I was reading: she was finished with me. Done. Broken up with me via text! I was shocked. I could not read the text messages fast enough. She was 12 hours ahead of me and was probably asleep. I tried calling, but she wouldn't answer. I could almost hear the fibers in my heart muscle ripping apart like heavy-duty Velcro.

She explained that she couldn't handle the long distance and wanted me to quit Remote Year. She had given me an ultimatum: No more travel. If I didn't take the ultimatum, she was going to follow through with an invitation from a professor to live with him in Spain. Just like that. Whiskey Tango Foxtrot?! This was an awful manipulation. She had set a jealousy trap, and it almost worked. This was hurting me bad!

I sat there on the roof letting the memories of our relationship flash through my mind like a slideshow. I desperately wanted to connect all the pieces to figure out what went wrong and why this relationship was failing. Even though I felt like a failure, I had insight enough to know that it really wasn't about me; it was about her. I was so smitten with the idea of love and the possibility of marriage that I had been blind to some of the red flags.

Truth be told, after Fong's visit to Florida, I realized that she didn't exactly fit into my world. She was like a square peg in a round hole, and power tools would be needed in order to make her fit. Her parents would not let their daughter come to the States for an extended period without being engaged … *plus* they wanted a chunk of money in exchange for their daughter—essentially a reverse dowry. On top of that, we were expected to send money to them on a regular basis. This is standard in Thai culture, in lieu of social security checks. I couldn't get my head around it at the time, but under the spell of infatuation, I was willing to acquiesce to all of it, including when it got weird and they abused "the ask." I was expected to pay for her parents' upcoming vacation. I was expected to buy a car that would sit idle in Thailand, along with a condominium that would sit vacant. Huh?! We were not married, nor were we even engaged! All of those things were possible, but for me it had to happen organically and on a timeline that made better sense.

There was also the constant jealousy Fong spit-fired at me nearly every day via text. It was exhausting, and I tried my best to calm her down and reassure her. I believe that her possessiveness was exacerbated by our long-distance separations; the inflammatory texts would not have happened had she been by my side every night. However, in the end, our relationship was just not meant to be. I wasn't Asian, and I wasn't in Asia anymore. But I will always love you, Fong.

I was single again, and although there was a hole in my heart, I knew I had to move on. Sitting under the bright blue sky and looking at the mountains standing tall and proud in the background, it was as if the whole world was embracing me: it wanted me to know that it had bigger things in store. I was in pain. Yes, I was going to grieve. It wouldn't be easy, but I was going to rise above this situation, stronger than ever, and finish RY on a high note. There was no way in hell I was going to throw away this once-in-a-lifetime experience for anyone, let alone a woman I had only been dating for five months. I imagine that's why I'm still single. Sigh...

I pressed the phone's home button with my thumbprint, opened the messaging screen for Fong, and texted:

> I love you, and I am shocked and hurt that our relationship has come to this. I will not leave Remote Year! I will give you the space you need. No one ever loved me like you.
>
> Yours always, Phil.

My text shot up into the sky, in and out of satellites, then back down to the other side of the planet to Fong.

Phil Pheelings: A part of me will always keep the door open for Fong. If it is meant to be, it will be.

I refused to let the sadness sink in, so I filled my days with as much activity as possible. I went to yoga every day. I meditated for an hour a day because by now I firmly understood, more than ever, that inner work was just as important as diet and exercise. I immersed myself in my work, setting up phone calls and conference meetings throughout the day. I pressed on with my shopping center project in Pennsylvania. Digital nomadism worked well for this new real estate development, and I was able to sign contracts with, and send voluminous amounts of information to, engineers, architects, brokers, tenants, and bankers—all from my smart phone and laptop. I had video conferences to review site plans and architectural drawings. I wired money from my mobile app to keep the development train moving. I had no partners, and I already owned the land. Cha-ching!

No Philter: What do real estate and a kiss have in common? LOCATION, LOCATION, LOCATION!

I was so busy distracting myself from the heartache, that I almost forgot about my side trip with Coinstein and Alvin (Coinberg) to Colombia's coastal town of Cartagena. The timing could not have been more perfect for a guy's long weekend getaway.

Before we knew it, the boys and I were touching down into the tropical paradise of Cartagena. My friends knew about the recent breakup, but they didn't press me when I sat in silence for most of the plane ride. As we drifted upward through the sky, I stared out the window in a trance, mesmerized by the colorful shack houses forming a shantytown. There were stuck together, too many to count. These were the impoverished *barrios* of Colombia. The houses have been built outside of the Colombian legal system and are referred to as "invasion properties" or, more euphemistically, an "informal settlement." The settlements rivaled the privation I had seen in India. Some homes are abandoned, while some units might be home to a family of ten. In such slums, the plumbing systems are often missing septic tanks and sewage will drain, untreated, right onto the ground. The streets were often unpaved and filthy, and I couldn't bear to think of the smell.

Phil Phact: *The Mystery of Capital,* by Dr. Hernando De Soto, calculates that the squatters of the world are sitting on over $14 trillion in untapped real estate value. But because these houses are "extra legal," meaning that they were built outside the legal system, they are not able to obtain mortgages, which is the main vehicle for tapping into the $14 trillion. Because of the extra-legal status, people are less likely to make upgrades and improvements, which keeps values down and trades to a minimum. The book was written in 2000, so of course the value of the land that squatters live on now is much higher. One solution to eradicating poverty around the world, in addition to allowing free trade, is to unleash the value of the squatter's real estate. I admit, though, that for a host of reasons, this is easier said than done.

Coinstein, Alvin, and I spent four glorious days in Cartagena. We relaxed, partied, and relaxed some more. Our top-notch AirBnb was quite the pad. Two nice women came every morning and stayed all day making us breakfast and lunch. I was bummed that my RY brothers had the housekeepers make them eggs each morning, but nothing is perfect in life! I kept my views on the hazards of eggs to myself. We hosted a pool party with some fellow digital nomads who were in town. There were two pools actually: a small one on the roof and a large one built in as a feature of the open-air living room. I want a house like this! We made fast friends with Jorge, the CBD oil shop owner across the street. His store was quaint, but he carried himself as if he were Steve Jobs in his garage during the beginning stages of Apple. In his estimation, he was pioneering the future of medicine in his new country of residence, Colombia. Jorge was an expat from Venezuela. During the five months I lived in South America, I met many Venezuelans who had fled their country for a better life. From my own firsthand experience, I concluded that Venezuela has suffered a major brain-drain. The best and brightest seem to have left the homeland.

Jorge took us on a private boat and island tour. Our perfect day was filled with ocean swims, snorkeling in crystal clear waters, white sand soccer scrimmages, and plain-old chilling out under an umbrella. Reggaeton music—rap mixed with Latin and Caribbean influences—which I now loved, played from start to finish. We got back to the mainland just in time to catch the sunset at the famous Cafe Del Mar. Situated on the waterfront in old town, this open-air club featured chillaxing live lounge music. Their playlists are sold commercially around the world, and they are the gold standard for down-beat house music. I've been listening to their music for years. Visiting Cafe Del Mar was one more bucket-list experience for me ... Check!

Fong's name didn't come up once during the entire long weekend. This was a good thing. I needed that weekend to escape my hurt feelings. I had a month and a half left of Remote Year, and I just wanted to come in for a smooth landing. I wanted to coast.

Even though I was tired from this year-long voyage of discovery, I accepted the role of host for my best friend, Gabe, and my niece, Elena. Gabe was the first person I met when my moving truck pulled up to my Clematis Street office in West Palm Beach, 15 years ago. Back then, he had just received his real estate license and was transitioning out of professional poker. A brilliant Georgetown University graduate, Gabe was "my people." So, I was stoked that he finally made it out to see me in one of my RY cities. Gabe's visit was quick because, as a home builder, he had to return to West Palm Beach to babysit his projects. While my livelihood is conducive to the digital nomad lifestyle, building new homes and rehabbing old ones, like Gabe does, is not.

Gabe's visit was brief, but I was able to knock his socks off with the grand tour of my digital nomad lifestyle, including a Remote Year track to the salt mine. One hundred feet below the earth's surface, this mine produced salt for centuries to the people of the region. The role of salt has been almost as important as water throughout history. Many wars have been fought over salt because it was necessary to preserve animal products before the invention of refrigeration. Salt also brings out the taste in food. Now defunct, this salt mine has been transformed into a tourist attraction. Artists had carved beautiful designs into the shimmering salt, which were set off by a rainbow of soft lights. There was even a Catholic church, the size of a cathedral, down in the depths. You could touch and taste the walls. I always loved salt air for its healing properties. It even helps with sleep. I wanted to bring my pillow and sleeping bag, and sleep there for a solid day or two!

After Gabe left, I only had a day to regroup before my niece, Elena, came to visit for a week. How honored I was that at 22-years old and fresh out of college, she wanted to hang with her almost 51-year-old uncle.

Phil Pheelings: Proud Uncle Spoiler Alert! My niece, Elena, is a child prodigy who received a full scholarship to Ohio State University. She graduated summa cum laude (as opposed to magna cum laude) and had already landed a big New York City job at Ernst and Young in the mergers and acquisitions department. On top of her many, many accomplishments, she is respectful, beautiful, and can parlay confidently with all kinds of people of all ages. Elena is way ahead of her time and her age ... take note, young ladies and gents!

Hosting Elena in Bogotá was a joy. Sometimes hosting family members can be draining and burdensome, but not with my niece. She is used to traveling the world, and she is independent. Of course, we spent plenty of time together, but because she had her own sightseeing agenda, she often came and went as she pleased.

One fine afternoon, Elena and I hosted my landlord, Manny, and his wife, Nicky, for a rooftop lunch. Fellow Mango Lola joined us as well, since she had now reached sister status with me. She took a long lunch break from a logo design project to hang with us. I began to refer to Manny as "The Prince of Bogotá" because of his vivacious personality and impressive real estate empire. Manny and his brothers were born into a successful family business but slowly grew the portfolio of rental properties. I think we admired and respected each other on a certain level as real estate owners. Nicky was also a business maven by birth. She enthusiastically showed me pictures of her large extended family on her iPhone. As she explained, the pictures were taken at their annual family meeting, where parents, siblings, aunts, uncles, and cousins all came together to "discuss" the family business (involving the production of chemicals and steel). Only the patriarch and a son ran the businesses day to day, so the main reason for the big meeting was to allocate the "allowance" that everyone would receive just for being a family member.

No Philter: In South American countries, and elsewhere, it usually goes that if you are born into a rich family, you are "set." You will have a pretty easy life, free from the toil experienced by "average" people. You will be raised by nannies and looked after by housekeepers for the rest of your life. You are born into an economic station, and that's where you'll most likely stay, rich or poor. What sets the United States apart from nearly every other place on earth is income mobility. Each person in the States has the opportunity to climb the economic ladder based on luck, ability, and determination. In fact, research from Cornell University revealed that 50 percent of Americans will find themselves among the top 10 percent of income-earners for at least one year during their lives. After traveling and seeing the world for nearly a year, I was beyond certain that my beloved United States was the most egalitarian and non-elitist country this side of heaven. We don't look down on waiters or Uber drivers; we look them in the eye, thank them, and call them "Sir" or "Ma'am." We Americans fundamentally recognize them as our equals because we are almost completely free of traditional hierarchies upon which most cultures are built.

Elena, Manny, Nicky, Lola and I savored a three-hour lunch extravaganza, courtesy of Cielo, the Rappi app, and UberEats. Veggie burgers, pesto zucchini pasta, steamed veggie dumplings, Indian dal, tofu and broccoli stir fry, and a sprout salad were passed around over and over. We drank this colored liquid known as wine. Yes, I was back to drinking wine on occasion … I remind you that I am a vegan, not a saint! There were lively discussions about business, travel, and life. Manny and Nicky shared a passion for exploring the world. They especially loved India, which challenged my restraint in the conversation. After all, I had seen *the real* India with Dr. Tuttle and Shankar. We had so many stories to tell and photos to show, that the lunch could have easily carried over into dinner. The weather was impeccable, too, with just the perfect amount of cool breeze blowing across the retracted rooftop. The rooftop soirée was nothing like the Great Gatsby parties I had thrown in Chiang Mai, but by now, my vibe was more kicked-back. Besides, following Chiang Mai, our group had dropped from 49 digital nomads down to 30, and many of my favorite Mangos had left me. Boo hoo!

Before Elena had to leave, we decided to be tourists together and catch the famous cable car to the top of Mount Monserrate. This imposing mountain overlooked the city and simply could not be ignored no matter where you might be. In no time, we were on the mountaintop at nearly 12,000 feet. It was so damn high, I could barely breathe. From that vista, we took in the sheer scale of the capital city. The buildings just went on and on. We lit candles in the Catholic church built in the 1600s. I said a prayer for my family and tramily. Then, I couldn't get down quickly enough!

After Elena had gone, I was so honored when Manny and Nicky reciprocated my rooftop lunch by inviting me to Nicky's apartment across town. They had been so impressed with the vegan cuisine at "my place," that they researched and rolled out some of their own vegan creations for a fabulous daytime feast. Even their maid got in on the vegan wagon, and proudly presented some dishes that we devoured. We smoked cigars and drank rosé by the fireplace. I loved it when Manny told a story: he would yell in his burly voice and move his arms all over the place. He carried on with so much expression I thought he might pop a blood vessel! The Prince of Bogotá and Nicky had become like family.

> **Phil Phact:** Bogotá has no change of seasons throughout the year. Because it's located at 8,000 ft above sea level, the four seasons are experienced daily, throughout a 24-hour cycle. Morning is fall, noon is spring, afternoon is summer, and night is winter. I had never experienced anything like that. I mean, who would have believed that four seasons in one day was possible? Little did I know that the next city to come, my last on Remote Year, Mexico City (CDMX), would have the same weather pattern.

As the month drew to a close, I reflected on my four wonderful weeks here. Bogotá was definitely one of the more cosmopolitan places we had lived on this Remote Year journey. It was more upscale, lively, and first world compared to some others. Bogotá was also the ideal backdrop for me to heal from lost love and stay busy with all the interesting opportunities and activities that were right in front of me. There was a never-ending list of places to eat and explore throughout the city. Despite the altitude, I truly felt at home in Bogotá, thanks in large part to Manny and Nicky. It's definitely on my short list of cities to return to, especially since it's so close to South Florida. Make no mistake about it, Colombia has everything: perfect weather, beaches, mountains, world-class cities, a vibrant culture and, truth be told, some of the world's most beautiful people.

But once again, it was time to move on. It was the same scenario playing out yet again: just when I learned my way around town, my time was up. Moving on to the next place was still like a drug. I was eager for my next apartment, neighborhood, gastronomic explorations, and newfound friends. Even though I was worn down and tired in all ways, on all levels, I was addicted to the change of nomadic travel. I was ready for the next high, the next adventure in a new city … our last one on Remote Year.

Adiós, Colombia! You were good to me, but Mexico City is now my home for the next month.

Have laptop, will travel!

CHAPTER 12

Mexico City, Mexico

"Travel is about the experience, not just the appearance. Luxury travel may be glamorous, but it's not always meaningful. Local culture may not always be glamorous, but it's always meaningful."

NYSSA P. CHOPRA

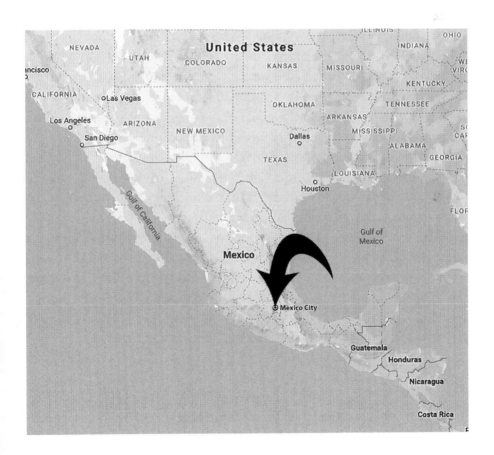

We were now in the wonderful metropolis of Mexico City, otherwise known as CDMX (Cuidad de Mexico). The land of the Aztecs and home of the taco welcomed us digital nomads with open arms.

Remote Year was almost at the end, and I couldn't believe I had made it to month 12. A few guy friends back in West Palm Beach had made a bet before I left for Croatia, almost one year ago, that I wouldn't make it past month three. They lovingly insisted I was too high-maintenance to travel around the world as a digital nomad—especially at age 50—for one whole year. Of course, they were correct, but they "misunderestimated" me (thank you, George W. Bush). As my odyssey unfolded, the over-under bet kept changing. Well, I couldn't wait to return home to collect my winnings in the form of expensive wine and dinners. Those knuckleheads!

Mexico City was quite different from Bogotá. The Colonial Spanish architecture rolled on for countless miles of city blocks. The neighborhoods, including my own, known as Condesa, featured tree-lined streets, stately homes, apartment buildings from different eras, and lots of public parks. Like pieces in a jigsaw puzzle, traditional cantinas, intriguing museums, and ancient canals nestled comfortably next to residential buildings, funky new restaurants, and bike stations. Street vendors mostly sold fruit, and they were everywhere. Much like the other cities, it was nearly impossible to see and experience everything in just one month, but considering it was the final city, I wanted to see all I could.

There were only a few skyscrapers, which had been assigned to one small area of town. Why not more? The city was built on a lake system in the valley of a plateau region, leveling at about 7,380 feet above sea level. As the city population grew, this lake was filled in, and building on clay does not make for strong, structural foundations. Besides that, the city was one giant subduction zone (an area where one slab of the earth's crust is slowly sliding under another). In Mexico City, the Cocos Plate is gradually sinking beneath the North American Continental Plate. As time passes, friction between the slabs causes stress build-up, and when the tension reaches capacity, all the pent-up energy is released in the form of an earthquake or tremor.

Mexico City experiences about 20 tremors (minor earthquakes) a day. I was pretty sure I experienced one while singing in the shower, which was one helluva way to start the day. In our welcome orientation, the city team gave us safety instructions in the case of an earthquake. Commercial buildings prominently donned earthquake safety signs. I had never lived under the specter of earthquakes, so this was a new, existential reality for me. As time went on, I realized that cars on our street could cause our apartment building to vibrate. Because the city surfaces were built on wet clay where there formerly had been a lake, the roads and sidewalks were very broken up, which allowed vibrations to travel. The streets were so bumpy in CDMX that I was not able to read my emails while in an Uber. More than once, the road threw me around so much that I hit my head on the passenger window. Yes, even with my seatbelt fastened!

> **Phil Phact**: As I mentioned above, the ancient settlement of Tenochtitlán (the original name of Mexico City given by the Aztecs), was built on a lake. This was definitely not an ideal foundation upon which to build a sprawling megatropolis. However, it was done, and now the city is sinking at a rate of four inches (10 cm) each year. When I visited the Metropolitan Cathedral, the sloping floors and sagging rooflines confirmed the narrative. Inside the church hung a swinging pendulum that revealed the building's increasing tilt. I could see more proof of CDMX's unstable foundation in the way that the sidewalks were so broken up and unleveled. There were blocks and blocks of buildings leaning this way and that.

The altitude in CMDX was high enough to bother me a lot. While not quite as high as Bogotá, the city's poor air quality made things pretty bad for my breathing. It was the worst air quality of any city to date.

I may sound like a broken record, but maintaining my regular yoga practice combined with lots of walking, were key factors in enabling me to acclimate to the higher elevations. Nevertheless, during my entire month in CDMX, I was never fully comfortable with the simple act of inhaling, which confirmed my feelings that it was time to go home ... to my real home.

By now, all those Spanish lessons had finally started to pay off. I was able to have some basic conversations with Uber drivers, with people in restaurants ... and on online via dating apps.

> **No Philter:** Reading Tinder profiles is the best way to learn a foreign language. I was able to understand just about everything in any given Tinder profile. They all love walks on the beach, romantic dinners, and traveling!

I loved my little Parque Virrey across the street from my apartment in Bogotá, but I was in for a much bigger surprise in CDMX. Mexico City is a city of parks. Our city orientation included a walking tour of Chapultepec Park. Chapultepec means "grasshopper hill" in the ancient Aztec language. This park was a massive ecological green space that dwarfed Manhattan's Central Park. At 1,695 acres, it earned its place as one of the largest city parks in the Western Hemisphere.

The park was a whole world unto itself. It was separated into three sections, with a giant rock in the middle. It was home to museums, amusement parks, winding paths, commemorative sculptures, lakes, fountains, and lush foliage. Most importantly, though, it functioned as a giant green space for the Greater Mexico City area. It acted as the "lungs" of the city, where all the oxygenating trees and plant life teamed up to filter the overabundance of carbon dioxide. Nevertheless, the air quality still sucked! Thanks for trying, though, trees!

The sounds of buzzing insects, scurrying reptiles, and loquacious birds filled the air as we stopped at a secluded nook of the park. This was a perfect spot for bird-watching, reading, or snuggling with your better half. We moved on, and the shady walkways suddenly became a main pedestrian boulevard. The sun was now beating down on us, and my peaceful headspace was obliterated by the hundreds of vendors lining the pavement on either side of the boulevard. The merchants shouted incessantly from their festooned carts, offering souvenirs and food. Behind the vendors stood a massive lake dotted with paddle boarders.

On the walk home, I got the sense that Mexico City was definitely Mexican, but with an American influence. This was not necessarily a bad thing. Massive state-of-the-art shopping centers were filled with American tenants, like Forever 21, Armani Exchange, and Sunglass Hut. If nothing else, it was familiar to me, which gave me comfort. I will forever be an American.

CDMX was special, in large part, because I was warmly embraced by members of my family who live there. No, not the tramily; this time it was real family! My brother-in-law's sister, Angela, had been living in the city for decades, along with several first cousins. Kenny and Angela have 51 first cousins living all over the place, as their father—originally from Syria—was one of 11 children. Within my first week in Mexico, I had coffee, lunches, and a Sunday brunch with some incredible distant relatives who rolled out the red carpet for me. I had peace of mind knowing that they were there for me if I needed anything. It was especially comforting for my parents who always worried about my safety. I was now living the closest I had been to my beloved United States in almost a year: I could almost taste it!

Kenny's sister, Angela, was married to a kind man, Sam, who owned a large chemical factory that produced makeup. On the second Sunday, they insisted on picking me up and taking me to their estate home across town. For their approach to hospitality, Uber was simply out of the question. Their affluent neighborhood was heavily wooded with wide, hilly, (still-bumpy) streets, and lined, block after block, with stately mansions. I've seen lots of mansions in my day, but one thing stuck out: the tall fortress-like walls that lined the perimeter of each home. When we entered their compound, the security wall was quite tall like the others, but I also noticed barbed wire on top. A sign was prominently displayed warning that the wires were electrified. I was aware that members of the family had been kidnapped in years past, so they were doing a top-notch job of protecting themselves now. Damn.

Phil Phact: Kidnapping in South America and Mexico still is a bit of a cottage industry and an existential threat to wealthy residents. In the U.S. and Europe, there are people struggling for money, but there is really no need for kidnapping because income mobility, purchasing power, social programs, and good law enforcement all serve to discourage this awful crime. Not to say that it doesn't happen, of course, but it's certainly not that common. There is an extremely low probability of being kidnapped in America, although I actually know someone who tried kidnapping a member of a wealthy Palm Beach family. He was caught, and later killed himself in prison. Crime doesn't pay.

Angela's family received me like a prince. When I walked into the mansion, I was bowled over by the explosion of kisses, hellos, and hugs welcoming me to Mexico. It certainly wasn't a normal day for a digital nomad to be so warmly hosted. The little children wasted no time running circles around me in the expansive yard within the fortress walls.

It never ceases to amaze me how non-vegans always want to learn all about the vegan lifestyle. I don't typically preach—well, I try to not to—but folks sure do ask questions! Knowing about my plant-based diet, Angela made traditional Arabic dishes from scratch. Laid out on the backyard platform for us to indulge were the Arabic classics: chickpea hummus, eggplant baba ghanoush, tabouli pasta … and those were just the appetizers! Even the pita bread was made from scratch. For the second round of food, we feasted on an indulgent cornucopia of plant-based haute cuisine. Kenny's sister had mad skills in the kitchen! Stuffed peppers and squash, colorful salads, veggie burgers, and Mahmara walnut paté graced the center of the large, round outdoor table. On this table, under a calm blue sky, we sat and broke pita bread together.

Sam, the patriarch, came to Mexico 40 years ago to start his business and now ran the company with his children. He kept holding me and hugging me like I was his long-lost son. They were not fake people; they were genuine and pure class. They were Mexicans from Syria, exemplifying the signature Mexican *and* Arabic characteristic to host and to please. Having collected me from my apartment across town, they also insisted on driving me back.

I spent the rest of my month in Mexico feeling like I had some kind of family force-field around me, protecting me. In the abstract, I guess I always had a loving, Mexican family through my sister's husband. But now I was connected to them in a meaningful way.

My yoga classes in CDMX had turned *hot*, namely Bikram Yoga hot. Classes were held early in the morning, allowing me to have a full day of work or exploring afterward.

Happily, Uber was legal in Mexico. The drivers drove around the city proudly and always seemed to go out of their way to impress passengers. All through Latin America, I ended each and every Uber ride by asking for "cinco estrellas por favor (five stars please)." It was quite the joke with the Mangos. To some in the tramily, the idea of asking for something was a bit too assertive. But if you don't ask, you don't get! My Uber rating was now 4.95 which is pretty unheard of for a score.

I'd been in Mexico for a week, and I had already fallen in love with it. Starting with the baggage handlers at the airport, I noticed right away, then over and over again, that the signature feature of the Mexican culture was *the desire to please*. It wasn't the fake kindness you get with luxury tourist travel, either. Whether I was Ubering across town, at the tailor, or buying fresh papaya from a street vendor, the Mexican people were out to please, and they always went the extra mile. In almost all encounters, they were deeply sweet.

On top of all that amiability, they were second only to the Japanese about doing things *correctly*. Coming from me, by now, I think you understand that's saying a lot! Mexico is a country that works—be it farming, trash collecting, or servicing people. From what I saw, they took their jobs seriously at all levels, and they were always working *hard*.

Nothing is perfect, though, and at the end of my first week, I was hit with Montezuma's Revenge, which affected many of the Mangos. The bacteria in the water resulted in a mean bout of diarrhea. Even if you don't drink the water from the tap, some restaurants, especially the street vendors, wash their food with the tap water. I won't subject you to too much information, but my situation was pretty extreme, and I could barely get out of bed. I had it bad, but only for about fourteen hours. That's because our property manager, Diana, came to my bedside, diagnosed me, and ran to the drug store to pick up some antibiotics. She brought me the medicine but would not take my money; she just wanted to help me. In this instance, she was exemplifying Mexican culture. It's worth repeating: *the signature feature of the Mexican culture is the desire to please.* Fortunately, the pills began to work immediately, and it was all over quickly compared to some of the other nomads.

Our "Publico" workspace was situated in Roma, about an 18-minute walk from our Condesa apartment. It was, once again, an incredible space, set up to provide the best of the best for digital nomads. And, what became my favorite vegan restaurant of *all time* in the entire world (!!), Los Loosers, was located right across the street. It had an odd name for sure, but I probably went there 15 times or more. They used no processed junk in their dishes, only whole foods. So, for example, their cheese sauce was made from whipped cashews instead of plant fats synthesized in a laboratory. One page on the menu offered crazy-good varieties of ramen soup, one page featured Asian dumplings, and on another page (my fave of them all) was the taco omakase platter. Small, colorful, open-faced tacos, called taquitos, formed a circle around the large plate, and omakase, as I will explain later in this chapter, would characterize my birthday celebration later in the month. Los Loosers offered me many "food-porn" photo ops.

The Publico coworking space featured fun furniture: green-painted industrial benches and seats were stacked on top of each other like bunk beds. They were elevated to a level where you need a ladder to climb up to a seat. It was funky, modern, and fun.

The workspace rooftop area became my happy place, where I spent several afternoons with other Mangos, playing guitar, holding conference calls, and enjoying the remaining time we had left together. On the rooftop, we had a clear view of the skyscrapers as if you could reach out and touch them. I kept wondering about earthquakes, but apparently there is some mad engineering which, in theory at least, would allow the office towers to sway, not fall. However, I for one wouldn't want to see these engineering theories put to the test.

The famous Parisian designer, Hermes, was one of the few permanent tenants in Publico. Hermes is a well-known luxury brand for clothing and accessories, especially for scarves, and it also produces the outrageously expensive Kelly and Birkin bags. One afternoon, I decided to stop by their small office to see if they had any samples for sale at a special price. I was looking for their "scratch and dent" department. They had no such department, which was a bummer for a bargain hunter like me. They only distributed perfume to boutiques and other retailers. An associate offered to sell me perfume, but I declined. Without any inhibitions, I explained how perfume is filled with harmful, synthetic chemicals that mimic estrogen once inside the body. Since our skin is the largest organ, things that go in and out of this organ are consequential. It is well understood that outside sources of estrogen, including those from animal products, are cancer-causing in humans. The store worker was polite upon hearing this Phil Phact. I mean, what else could he do? Mexicans, like the Asians, tend to avoid confrontations.

Phil Phact: My parent's generation typically worked for one company, in one spot, for 20 or more years. But today's millennials can expect to change jobs every two to four years. Also, one in two people are projected to be working as freelancers by 2027. This means, very soon, people will pretty much be able to work from anywhere as location-independent professionals.

As always, I enjoyed the walk from the apartment to the workspace. I could pick up fresh fruit on the way home from the now-familiar street vendors. To enhance the taste, they cheerfully offered chipotle powder and lime juice onto the freshest, tastiest papaya this side of heaven. Mexico's streets catered to pedestrians. Yes, the sidewalks were broken up, but mutual respect and patience were facilitated by orderly crosswalk systems.

I have to admit there was still some paranoia left in me regarding my personal safety. A friend of my parents—an executive at a company who frequently traveled to Mexico City—warned me about street thugs who randomly pushed people into traffic for no apparent reason. So, there I was, at each cross walk, vigilantly looking over my shoulder, as locals zipped passed me in their normal behavior. That same friend also said he would never wait outside the hotel for his driver. Instead, his driver came into the hotel lobby to pick him up for meetings. They would walk out to the car together in a literal embrace so that no one could snatch him. Thank God that none of my fears ever turned into reality, but I continued to be alert.

Phil Phact: It isn't paranoia when they *really are* out to get you.

Alvin and Tommy were my roommates for the final month. Alvin and I were well acquainted as roommates, but it didn't take long for Tommy to fit right in. I got the master suite again ... of course! Our vibe made for the perfect situation in the final month of Remote Year. Our apartment featured a good-sized modern kitchen, a huge outdoor patio, and a very chic interior design. Our pad was on the first floor, which meant no steps or elevators. Our comings and goings always included a warm greeting from the 24-hour security guards, who became our friends. Each bedroom had a marble bath and shower. There was beautifully finished dark wood everywhere. We agreed that this Remote Year apartment was the finest accommodation yet.

We spent a lot of time together that month. We bonded, fought, and made up. The fights were petty. One of the "issues" that came up is that I am an early riser and tend to make noise in the kitchen in the wee hours. Tommy might just be getting to sleep around then, if he even came home at all. He loved to crash on OPC ... other people's couches! Tommy was quick with his emotions but was even quicker to seek forgiveness and make peace. He was such an easy forgiver, it was a powerful reminder for *me* to seek forgiveness and make peace. I wouldn't have changed a thing about how things played out between us. We had lively discussions about race, history, and economics. We hosted (late) lunches and dinners, vegan-style, for many in the tramily. There was this feeling that we had to savor every moment of these gatherings because they would be some of our last moments together. Things were going to change soon and never be the same again.

It was now time for a Mexico City track: Lucha Libre wrestling matches. It was like RY had been saving the best for last! "Lucha libre" means "freestyle wrestling." In the States, the matches would be known as professional wrestling. Tommy, Alvin, and I took the bumpy Uber ride to the Lucha Libre arena, where we met up with the rest of our track group. We were led not through the main entrance, but through a side door that read "NO ENTRAR" on a tiny white plaque. This would have been Elvis's entrance into the venue. We shuffled down a hallway lit with flickering fluorescent lights, and then through another door that opened into to a small practice ring. We were officially behind the scenes of Lucha Libre!

The Mexicans are proud of their unique version of professional wrestling that focuses on entertainment, dazzling athleticism, and dramatic plot lines. The sport boasts a heritage that goes back for generations. It has developed into a distinctive form of the wrestling genre, characterized by flashy costumes, rapid sequences of holds and maneuvers, and never-ending storylines of good vs. evil. The good guys are known as *Los Tecnicos;* the bad guys as *Los Rudos.* Female fighters started competing in the 1980s, and at some point in the history of the sport, midgets got tossed into the ring. Anything goes at the Lucha Libre.

Four masked fighters or *luchadores,* stood in the ring and greeted us from afar. We had the opportunity to ask some questions, and through a translator, someone asked a wrestler about the glittered character masks, which are a powerful symbol of the sport. We discovered that the designs can be somewhat of a family crest. In certain key matches, the losers remove their masks, thus revealing their identity. This is the ultimate humiliation, and it basically spells the end of their wrestling career. To be accepted as a *luchador,* the aspiring wrestler must first create an original character and present it to the Wrestling Council. If they lose a key match, they have to wait things out for a while, reinvent a character, and come back with a new persona. Many of the famous *luchadores* characters run in the family, and masks can be passed down to the next generation.

Most of the *luchadores* come from impoverished neighborhoods and rural villages. One of the luchadores there went by the name Atlantis. He was a champion who had no problem bragging that he had never had to remove his mask, so his identity remained a mystery to us and the community at large. As he walked from one end of the ring to another, he appeared very stiff and walked with a slight limp. This reflected the hazards of the job I'm sure. I asked Atlantis if he recommended this life to his family. He nodded, and the other wrestlers also nodded in affirmation. Indeed, many of their family members had joined the sport.

A half dozen people had died from injuries suffered in the ring over the years. And then it clicked for me. I saw the sport as a symbol of the working man's challenges: he would fight, even if being in the ring resulted in permanent injury or death. Lucha Libre, for the wrestlers and their fans, meant that the struggle was real. Suddenly, it was time to stop talking and start doing! The wrestlers invited us into the ring to try a few moves. Alvin was the man of the moment, and the *luchadores* joked that he should apply to be a fighter. If I hadn't been so exhausted, I would have easily jumped into the ring and kicked Alvin's ass with some flips and body slams! (I jest.)

After our amateur taster, we were pumped up and ready to experience the professional show on the main stage. We left the training room and entered the large arena where thousands of people were pouring into the seats holding their beer and popcorn. The Mangos were seated just three rows behind the wrestling ring, front and center. The house lights went down, and high-energy music blared across the arena. Off to our right, seven dancers in tight-fitting, sexy costumes, emerged from smoke clouds, swaying their arms and hips to the beat. Four *luchadores* came trotting out, donning their gaudy masks and costumes as the announcers introduced their wrestling names. Names like, "El Samurai," "El Santo," and "Blue Demon" echoed through the large hall. The good guys got the ear-splitting cheers of adoration, while the competing villain teams were greeted with exaggerated "boos" and shouts leveled against them. Of course, the night would not have been complete without some drunken fans hooting it up for the bad guys. Thanks to them, I picked up a few new Spanish swear words that night!

We were treated to five matches, each one leading to the main event. Tag teams of male wrestlers, midgets, female wrestlers, and champion wrestlers took turns shoving, kicking, flipping, choking, pulling hair, and flying through the air until winners were declared. Each victor exuberantly jumped up onto a corner post of the ring and screamed in victory. The audience howled back and threw loose change into the ring in celebration. It was so real and yet so fake. Sometimes the falls and fights would spill over into the area outside of the ring. More than a few throw downs took place right in front of me, since I was in the aisle seat. What a way to make a living!

> **Phil Phact:** Is this wrestling real or fake? I can tell you that many of the hits, tumbles, and falls I witnessed were shockingly real. But there is always a predetermined winner in each Lucha Libre match in order to move along the planned, soap opera plotlines. The wrestlers are usually acting out orchestrated moves during the matches, and they don't actually hate one another. Don't ever bet on one of these matches unless you have insider information!

My 51st birthday was approaching fast, and I wanted to make a celebration plan. But I had to face reality: I was exhausted. I had gained a few pounds, was suffering from the crappy, big-city air quality, and had my share of aches and pains. Yoga could only do so much. I missed my organic, tree-rubber foam mattress back in West Palm Beach. Nevertheless, I hatched a plan for a dinner with my favorite bros in the tramily.

On the eve of my birthday, I was signed up for a hot air balloon ride at the Teotihuacan Aztec Pyramids. My alarm went off at 4:45 a.m. None of my aches and pains could quell my excitement as I left our apartment at 5:30 a.m. and briskly walked the 20 minutes to the workspace where the vans were waiting. I tried to but couldn't wake Tommy, who had also signed up. He eventually came out of his slumber but ended up taking an Uber to the wrong address and missed the trip. That was typical Tommy: a beautiful, disorganized, hyperactive genius.

Fifteen digital nomads piled into the van. We all craved caffeine and breakfast. Many of the Mangos were showing the toll taken by months of traveling and remote working, as well as Montezuma's Revenge. Some had also partied the night before. Some were still recovering from recent injuries. Most of us were just plain worn out. I was tired, too, but my almost-birthday excitement gave me that extra "somethin-somethin." Unfortunately, someone snagged my usual spot in the front passenger seat of the van, so I reluctantly found a spot in the very back. There was no attention to the radio station, which was very crackly, the air was off, and who knows what the driver was up to. I braved the one-and-a-half-hour drive over bumpy, potholed roads to the headquarters of Sky Balloons Mexico. The sun had not yet risen, so the air was crisp and nippy.

I had never seen a hot air balloon up close and personal before, and then there they were, lying on the ground like a discarded silk sheet. We watched intently as our balloon filled with nothing but hot air and rose to life, turning from a sad rag into a mighty bulb of color.

We climbed into what seemed like an oversized picnic basket. The captain positioned himself in the middle alongside the propane tanks. I was the last to climb in. I have always been afraid of heights, big time, but I tried not think about it. However, expecting an overthinker not to think was like expecting a parent not to worry about their children. I was climbing into a wicker basket that would carry us thousands of feet into the sky, held aloft by a nylon sack and propelled by wind and fire. Wicker, nylon, human flesh: all the things that should not be in close proximity to naked flames. And how the hell do you steer the thing? Ummm, you don't! Besides all that, there was nothing to worry about. Once inside the smallish laundry hamper, a few hombres untied our balloon from the pegs on the ground. We gently lifted off and went up, up and away, as the sweet smell of propane wafted through the calm air.

Before I knew it, we were just *too damn high*. The scenery below was a speck of this or that. I fell apart, involuntarily, as my fear of heights overtook me like never before. I crouched in one corner of the basket, my eyes shut tightly, while tiny whimpers escaped my mouth. Yes, I was whimpering like a child and could not control it. I needed to be bitch-slapped but no one was "up" for it (excuse the pun). I was stuck in the circular thought that we were just too damn high. Suddenly, one of my favorite records of all time, "Too High to Die" by the Meat Puppets, popped into my head. The opening track, "Violet Eyes," took over my brain like music always does for me. "Mother Master, some things must be …" In my mind, the song played louder than a stadium concert. I began murmuring the words and tapping my hand to the beat. I was trying to work out the guitar parts in my head that I once knew so well. Through music, the spell was finally broken. I mustered the courage to stand, and I held on to one of the padded cables for dear life as I cracked one eye open and peeked over the edge of the basket. A ball of warm orange was rising in the east and staring back at me. I took in a deep, cool breath. I looked around and noticed everyone else in the basket taking selfies and having a gay-ol' time, as if this was something to be enjoyed. Oh, me!

The Aztec pyramids slowly came into view as the nighttime sky gave way to the dawn. I must admit, it was pretty awesome! When I kept my cool, I was able to take it all in and really enjoy the bird's-eye view of the pueblos (towns) below. Cemeteries, neighborhoods, and farming fields were laid out beautifully below our floating magical mystery tour. After a 45-minute eternity, our balloon began to drift slowly downward. Our captain clicked on his radio and contacted his ground crew. Hot damn! I actually understood his chatter, as he gave them orders for our pickup. It looked like we were heading toward someone's backyard. Before I knew it, we were hovering just a few feet over a corn field, and then … we landed on the train tracks! The crew was laughing as if landing on train tracks was a hilarious joke. I had to assume that they knew the train schedule! I spilled out of the basket more than grateful to be back on land.

Phil Phact: Soon after our ride, a friend told me that the typical hot air balloon accident occurs when the flames set the nylon alight. The poor victims must then choose between jumping 2000 feet to their death or burning alive. I'm glad I found this out afterwards, or I probably would not have taken the ride.

And now it was time to head to the famous Aztec pyramids. I was still hungry after a brunch stop that had very few vegan options, so once in the van, I cracked open a bag of cheesy kale chips from my stash. From out of nowhere, Hannah, who was notorious for her moods and sassy disposition, spun around in her seat and harangued me about the stench of the kale chips. Who can even smell kale chips? In an act of high drama, she pulled her hoodie up over her face to protect herself from the fatal kale fumes. Although she was on my last nerve, I played it down and jokingly told her to quit being so sassy. By now, I had learned that these little altercations were unavoidable on this bizarre social experiment called Remote Year. Brothers and sisters of the tramily were merely getting into a tussle. Our brief spat blew over, but it reminded me just how conditioned we all are, especially about food. Somehow, my kale chips were considered gross, but decomposing flesh, tendons, and chicken periods (i.e., eggs!) on a plate were somehow not gross? The irony was lost on everyone else, I was sure. But I kept it to myself.

Ten minutes passed before we arrived at the Teotihuacan Aztec Pyramid Heritage site. Our guide regaled us with some facts about ancient Aztec culture and religious practices. We walked in the dry heat to the Pyramids of the Moon and Sun. I was emotionally drained from the trauma of the balloon ride. I couldn't summon the energy to climb the stairs to the top of either pyramid with the others, so I stayed at ground level and took some photos. The preserved architecture was another great sight to see, but it was no Prague. Forgive me—I know that's not a fair comparison—but I was kind of irked knowing that these massive structures were used primarily for animal and human sacrifice. The guide conveniently left out that main purpose of the pyramids. Of course, I'm the guy who raised his hand and brought it up. As you know by now, yep, I'm *that* guy! She acknowledged my Phil Phact and quickly moved on to a different historical narrative.

Phil Phact: Archaeologists have excavated the bones of human and animal corpses that prove sacrifices really did take place at Teotihuacan. Scholars believe that the native people offered human sacrifices, usually enemy warriors, as part of a dedication to ensure the city's prosperity and successful harvest. Some men were decapitated, some had their still-beating hearts removed, and others were killed by flogging or other savage methods. It was believed animals such as cougars, wolves, eagles, falcons, owls, and even venomous snakes were sacred and possessed mythical powers, so they were also sacrificed atop the pyramid altars.

After the ballooning and pyramid excursion, it was time for my birthday celebration, which had morphed into guy's night out. I wanted to go all-out, so there was only one place that would fit the bill: Nobu. This Japanese restaurant, with locations in New York, Los Angeles, Miami, Las Vegas, the Bahamas, and Mexico City never disappointed. Dining at Nobu is more like an *event*. Wear your stylish threads, bring your appetite, and make sure there's enough money in the bank for your debit card to cover the bill. Several of my *brochachos* had organized their own "trip" to the pyramids the day before my birthday, though. They had planned to take LSD and commune with the pyramids, so was I worried that they wouldn't make it back in time. The WhatsApp text thread was very quiet, so I figured they were somewhere on that wild ride. I was invited to trip along with them, but acid was never my cup of tea. The Mother Ayahuasca and I had our connection and our understanding, and I felt no need to push the envelope. I was good.

No Philter: We have to ask why alcohol is legal throughout most of the world, yet psychedelics are illegal. The conscious and safe use of psychedelics or "visionary medicines" has been shown to assist in mind expansion and to initiate spiritual experiences during which people commune with the Divine. The use of psychedelics has helped people heal numerous physical and spiritual ailments, increase intelligence, repattern the brain in a positive way, align people with their soul's purpose, and inspire them to create great works of art and other innovations. It seems to me that these substances would only be banned and discouraged if there truly were an agenda seeking to oppress the human potential and to keep us "in the dark" regarding who we are as spiritual beings. Perhaps those in power want to stop us from discovering our innate potential, and from achieving our own empowerment. Whatever we do, we should always hold onto our personal sovereignty. No one but you is looking out for you.

September 10 had finally arrived. On this day 51 years ago, all 6 pounds and 12 ounces of me entered the world. Thank you, Mom (and Dad). I had made it past a half century of life on this earth. Everyone but Victor had recovered from their weekend "trip." I couldn't stop smiling when I saw Chris, Alvin, Gillionaire, Sal, Coinstein, Tommy, and Andrew come filing through the grand entrance. The outside of the building looked a lot like the Playboy Mansion but was even more ornate. Following the receiving line of man-hugs, we sat down at the long table and anticipated our bacchanal feast. I planned ahead and requested a vegan chef's tasting, called *omakase* in Japanese. There was no menu to browse; instead, the servers brought wave after wave of shareable, delectable bites. Every course was a surprise.

> **Phil Phact**: *Omakase* is Japanese for "from the heart." It is available in better Japanese restaurants that feature the chef's finest curated offerings on that day. It's my favorite style of eating!

As we filled our stomachs with fresh, haute vegan cuisine, spontaneous storytelling broke out. The guys took turns sharing their favorite "Phil Story." I was very moved by their words. Many of my fellow nomads said I was always so optimistic and that my sunny outlook had actually rubbed off on them. I never really saw myself that way, but hey, I'll take it! Others said they gathered wisdom from my now notorious "Phil Phacts." I'm never comfortable hearing people talk about me when I am present, especially when what they have to say is flattering.

As the Argentinian Malbec flowed, coupled with a few sips of cold sake in between, the stories and roaring laughter rolled on. After the Phil stories, came the anecdotes about everyone else—story after story. We were reminiscing and feeling emotional about the year that was about to end. For me, it was truly one of the best nights in all of Remote Year. Brotherly love was all I could have asked for on my special day. Thank you, my Mango brothers.

The celebrations kept coming even after my own had ended. Five days later, it was Mexico's Independence Day, known as *El Grito*. It's okay, don't feel stupid: it's not on *Cinco de Mayo*, May 5, but on September 15. And to be even more exact, September 15 only commemorates the cry of Miguel Hidalgo as he shouted through the town of Dolores in northern Mexico with a declaration to revolt against the Spaniards. The *actual* day that Mexico obtained independence from Spain was September 28, 1821. (Just like the rest of Latin America, here in Mexico, any reason was a good one to throw a party, shoot fireworks, eat a ton of food, dance, and sip on spirits. I'm no party pooper, but there are so many national holidays in Latin America that stores, banks, and post offices are closed *a lot*. This created challenges if the holidays fell on transition days into or out of a city.)

The main celebration for Mexico's Independence Day occurs at night on September 15, in the Zocalo, Mexico City's main square. The president typically comes out onto the balcony of the grand Palacio Nacional and rings the Independence Bell. He belts out the words of el Padre Hidalgo: "Viva Mexico!"

I joined other Mangata nomads and headed in an Uber to Zocalo. Traffic was a mess, so we hopped out a few blocks away and walked to the square. The giant square, built centuries ago by the Spanish, was packed full like a scene from Times Square on New Year's Eve. People were moving about trying to get their snacks and drinks before the president emerged. At exactly 11:00 p.m., President Enrique Peña Nieto popped out onto the balcony with his wife and greeted his Mexican citizens with arms held high. It resembled an appearance of the Pope in Vatican City, except that this couple looked like movie stars. I could see them clearly on giant video screens. He rang the bell, and everyone in the plaza screamed in response to his words, over and over, *"Viva México!"* The crowd's response was so powerful, I could feel the collective, exhaled air moving through me. What an amazing moment!

Phil Pheelings: Emotions were high at this point in our final month. The end was drawing closer and closer, and I was still processing exactly how I felt at this time. I wasn't sad, per se. I was definitely tired of the digital nomad lifestyle and ready to return home. Yet, my life had been enriched and positively changed forever. I was still in one piece, and I was grateful.

At long last, our much-talked-about farewell weekend arrived. Our program leaders, Jenna and Lidia, had organized a spectacular weekend retreat for us to relax, bond, and create some final memories together as a group. We were going glamping at a large ecological complex.

> **Phil Phact:** Glamping is a growing trend in ecotourism, where camping in nature meets modern luxury. It's a way to enjoy remote places without having to give up day-to-day comforts. It was a great way for a luxe traveler like me to digitally detox and plug in to the amazing lush landscape that surrounded the metropolis.

We left as a group early in the morning and headed to Las Estacas in Morelos. Las Estacas is a national reserve and spa resort that provides a unique ecosystem where wildlife can thrive while tourists revitalize and relax. As the Mangata stepped out of the van, without our laptops, iPads, or any other work-related electronics, we descended upon the glamping area reserved for us ready for our digital detox. Without our smartphones or computers, we could relax and focus on social interaction in the physical world. I think all of us could use a digital detox more often.

We all shared three-person tents. As Lidia gave us our rooming details, I wondered how the hell she and Jenna had put up with us for an entire *year*. I was unsure about glamping, but after seeing three plush beds in my assigned tent, it was starting to seem plausible. I shared the oversized tent with Mitch and Chris, who both loved the outdoors. Mitch was into rock climbing, hiking, and biking when he wasn't designing computer chips for the next smartphone. Chris was an outdoorsman through and through when he wasn't head hunting via Skype. Three natural swimming holes and a river encircled the entire complex, and floaties, innertubes, and even snorkeling gear were at our disposal. It was beautiful there, and we were free to explore as we wished.

Las Estacas boasted natural springs so clear that I could see the fish swimming in between my legs as I doggy-paddled from one waterfall to the next. Swing sets that were built into the natural pools rocked back and forth with smiling, happy people. The swings were hung low enough to climb onto, but high enough so that my toes could gently graze the surface of the water. The girls of Mangata took turns taking photos on the swing sets. Others, who weren't splashing around, were either napping in hammocks, playing chess on picnic blankets, or off on a hike. Alvin and Tommy decided to climb a tree that was so high I could no longer see them. My fear of heights extends to fearing for others' safety.

We gathered together for lunch around 11:00 a.m. on our second day of glamping. We shared one of our final meals together and held our final farewell presentation. By now, we were in full-on hippie mode. I half expected to turn around and find Coinstein and Alvin (Coinberg) sitting in lotus position on yoga mats with flowers decorating their beards. I laughed to myself at that vision. We shared tender reflections of friendship and tramilial love. I was now in the mode of trying to make sense of the last year. I was trying to understand the huge impact that this travel odyssey would have on me. It was by far the most out-of-the-box thing I had ever done in my life; so much so that it will probably take the rest of my life to fully process it.

Paper bags with our names on them were lined up like soldiers across the grass on a colorful kaleidoscopic quilt. From the night before, we were asked to place handwritten notes to each other and place them in the individual bags, and following lunch, we were allowed to take possession of our goody bags. Since the notes were not compulsory, the pessimist in me was certain I would have only a few notes, if any, from my fellow Mangos. But when I picked up the bag, there was definitely some extra weight; the bag was full.

I set off to a shady spot underneath a large tree to read my notes, one by one. Some notes were anonymous, and some were authored. My fellow Mangos expressed how much they had learned from me, and how much they enjoyed my point of view on certain aspects of life. Some wrote how much they admired my commitment to the vegan lifestyle. I read one note that said that I was "unique, distinguished, and incredibly young-looking for my age." Millennials can be tough, yet here they were, saying such positive things in their own handwriting.

When I pulled out and read Victor's note, tears streamed down my face. He poured his heart out to me in his way. He was a very big guy, but his heart was way bigger. A flood of memories flashed through my mind: shredding the fresh powder on the slopes of Japan, and the rogue toe warmer; his life-threatening last night in Thailand; the wine-inspired nights at our Córdoba apartment, where we told stories and howled with laughter; his valuable teachings on e-commerce, travel hacks, and technology tips ... I had come to deeply love and admire this *brochacho*. He wrote:

> Phildo Baggins, you sandbagging son of a bitch! *[Phildo Baggins was my nickname to some in Mangata, a play on Bilbo Baggins from The Hobbit.]* I love that you don't mind that the boys give you a hard time, but you, Phil, are honestly one of the most genuine, nicest souls I have ever encountered. And you know ... I had to put you in check every once in a while, bro. This year was a real pleasure to be with you, and you were also an amazing roommate. You are one of the most caring people, and I can't wait to hang out with you back in the States. I love you, man. You are an incredible person, and I am forever grateful that we got to meet, and to call you my friend.

I wiped away more tears. It wasn't that I needed my ego stroked; it was what lay *behind* the words that gave me such powerful emotions of joy. We had shared so many touchstones through the year's journey, and because of that, this was a moment of crowning glory. Victor and I, and several others, would be friends for life. I resolved to extend many key friendships beyond Remote Year. I kept saying over and over during the weekend, "We did all of this together, now what are we going to do about it?" What I meant was, what can we do in the future to leverage the experiences and knowledge that we gained? I think I will always be checking in with myself and asking this question. If I were to stay as mindful as I felt right then, I should be so lucky. I was filled with gratitude that I *went for it* on this crazy one-year odyssey. I now owned it 100 percent, and no one could take it away from me.

There were other notes that also typified the farewell weekend's vibe in the bag, but at the bottom, like the prize from a Cracker Jack box, there was one more note. To my surprise it was the postcard I had written to myself one year ago in Split, Croatia. Oh jeez, I had forgotten all about it. I stared at the postcard for several moments as the words just danced around the card. More than a prize at the bottom of the box, it was more like a transcontinental message in a bottle. I didn't remember a single thing I had written to myself. I was a different person when I had written it 360 days ago. Or was I?

I read my own words quietly to myself:

> Dear Phil,
>
> How are you? What did you accomplish? Which place do you want to return to? What was your favorite place? How was the vegan food? Who is your new family? What did you accomplish and what does it all mean? So, now what? LOL!
>
> Love, Me.
> P.S. Habla Espanol?

The words that stuck out the most when I read the postcard were "Love, Me." I can be hard on myself, and not really feel satisfied with my so-called achievements. But after this year, I can honestly say that I love myself and that I also actually *like* who I am. My self-love was affirmed during the deep soul dive I took during the Ayahuasca ceremonies. I have learned that too many people just don't like themselves. Let's never forget it is our birthright to be happy and love ourselves.

Twelve months later, and with all that transpired, I was still the CEO of my life. From my perspective, the opportunity of adventure would continue as new opportunities beckoned. It felt weird, like *really weird*, that I wasn't moving on to the next digital nomad spot and working from my laptop in a new and exciting city, workspace, and culture. As much as I wanted to return home, I was afraid that normal life would now be too boring. I guess I would find out soon enough.

We returned to CDMX after a fantastic send off. One by one, the Mangos disbanded to the far-off lands they called "home," with their own itineraries this time. By the last night, Friday, September 29, I found myself solo in the apartment. I was the last one to leave and was packing for the last time. This final pack was playing out in slow-mo. I made the choice to show up in Croatia, and I made the choice to show up every single day until our final days in Mexico. So, thank you, Phil. Thank you, me, for showing up, and owning the unknown, along with 48 other digital nomads who were just as clueless about what they were getting themselves into.

EPILOGUE

The Journey Continues

"Dearest Philip. We'll be thinking of you daily and praying for your experience to be a safe and enriching one! Keep this icon card with you as a special blessing from us for Panaghia [Greek for Virgin Mary] to watch over you. Keep in touch … call at least once a week. Filakia [Greek for kisses] and hugs, Mom and Dad."

Mom's note to me was written in a greeting card with an image of the Madonna and Child on the front. I kept it with me throughout my travels. My perfect keepsake.

I was buckled up tightly on my flight from CDMX to sunny South Florida. A nice, older man, who split his time between Miami Beach and Tel Aviv, happened to be sitting next to me in business class. He was the kind of guy that easily sparks up a conversation with his neighbor on a flight. The topic of this book and my travels came up, of course, because everything was at the forefront of my consciousness and swimming around in my head. I had just parted ways with some of the most inspiring people I'd ever met, who had started out as total strangers, no less. I had just been on a fantastic voyage of self-discovery.

After hearing me out, he then asked me, "So, Phil, what is the *purpose* of this book?" I was somewhat stumped. I couldn't quite articulate the actual meaning other than to say that it was a travelogue. But then I was able to think on my feet while sitting in my seat. I told him the book was a travel memoir that aims to introduce the joys of being a digital nomad while inspiring others to see the world through new eyes, sample different cultures, and make new and lasting human connections. He nodded and pursed his lips. Enthusiastically, he began to pepper me with more questions about the trip.

During the year, I touched down in 16 countries in all. I wasn't joyriding or doing it for kicks and giggles; I wanted to see the world with my own critical eye. Now that this travel odyssey has adjourned, I have had the opportunity to reflect on how I had changed. I didn't know it at first, but it would take me some time to unpack the experiences of the last year ... More than that, it would probably take me an entire lifetime to process it all.

I estimate that I walked about 1500 miles across all kinds of streets and sidewalks. There were broken-up sidewalks, major city avenues full of buzzing traffic, pedestrian markets with people practically crawling over each other, and cobble-stoned alleyways leading to secret bars and cafés, just to name a few. I can't help but think this raises the bar for what it means to have "street cred." If you spend enough time on the streets, you become "street"—a quality I certainly didn't have before. I am proud to say that the city street, almost anywhere, is now a comfort zone for me. I learned to use the eyes in the back of my head, while avoiding the cleverest of pickpockets and sketchy vendors. I eventually learned my way around every neighborhood that I lived in. I knew which areas were "bad news" and which would welcome me with smiles and open arms. I was far from being a tourist in these cities: I believe I was a resident.

I gained first-name status with the local shopkeepers who I befriended and gave regular business to. They were all too happy and grateful to take my sparkies ... I now even love some of them like family, like my dearest friends at Betty's Bowls in Medellín. And then, just as I got to know a place and its people, it was time to *move on,* which was often very sad. That's the beauty of it, though. Traveling taught me to "let go." For years, yoga had become my portal for dealing with attachment issues, but this travel year really set a new standard on that. Holding on to the past— or to material items or even certain people—can become heavy and burdensome. The airlines punish us with fines for overweight luggage, but life will also penalize us for holding on to things and people that do not serve us in a positive manner. Minimizing attachments, and minimizing just about everything, is not only the key to successful travel but also to a successful life.

As I learned, traveling the world wasn't always sunshine and rainbows. It was exhausting. There was rain, illness, and injury. There was love and heartbreak. It was difficult to live away from home for an extended period of time and not gain weight, even for a strict vegan like myself. When I got on the scales back at home, I had gained nearly ten pounds. Every city had its specialty food and drink that I couldn't say no to trying. With each new city and its food, I was like a kid on Christmas morning. But, in the long run, tasting the flavors of the world expanded my gastronomic horizons, and not just my waistline.

In addition to HappyCow, there were other tools that helped me survive and thrive. There was no way I could have successfully completed the trip around the world if it weren't for a regular yoga practice, my NUCALM app, and my Transcendental Meditation (TM) practice. When it comes to TM, I marvel over it. Who would have thought that three little words, mentally chanted over and over again for an hour each day, would bring such joy and peace? Mantras are tried-and-true: they work!

Around the world, I had the privilege of experiencing many styles of physical (hatha) yoga, but I thrived most with Bikram Hot Yoga. I am proud to say that I kept up a regular yoga practice in 9 of the 12 cities. Physical yoga has the ability to give us what we are lacking. If we are stiff, we will loosen up. If we are flexible but not strong, we will gain strength. It tightens the "screw loose brain," which was crucial rehab for me. Attending yoga classes resolved back pain from poor mattresses, helped me cope with high altitudes, zapped general aches and pains, and helped me maintain a certain level of happiness. I solved many problems in the yoga room, both business and personal. Furthering my yoga practice helped me understand just how important "inner work" is for a life well-lived.

One of the biggest questions I asked myself throughout the year was, "Is America special compared to all of the other countries?" The shortest answer is: "Kind of." Who decides which country is best? People do. I have seen with my own eyes that a human being has a good life in a hut or a mansion. At the end of the day, the same sun is still shining on both roofs. Sometimes a rich man can have everything materially, yet he has nothing spiritually. Walking the sunken, muddy roads in the outskirts of Buenos Aires, I saw people who had nothing but seemed to have everything: Family, community, and a stress-free, uncomplicated life. In Palm Beach, I know some very miserable people, even suicidal ones, who happen to be fantastically wealthy.

However, so long as more people want to come to the United States than leave it, this makes a strong case for American Exceptionalism. A recent poll conducted by the Gallup organization found that about 750 million people want to leave their country for good. They further found that 158 million of them want to come to the U.S. My hunch is that the number is probably much higher. The thing is, almost no one wants to leave America, and many, many people aspire for a better life there. I could have filled many airplanes with people I met who expressed a desire to immigrate to the US. In my year abroad, I grew to love the United States of America even more, with all of her struggles, flaws, opportunities, freedoms, and drama. However, in the grander scheme of things, Planet Earth is now my home, and I am part of wonderful and wide interconnected world. So, in a very real sense, who the hell cares if America is exceptional or not? Go out there and be great whoever and wherever you are!

In addition to all that, I now have personal connections with excellent people from all over the world who matter to me a lot. These connections have truly enriched my life. Because of all this, I am truly a wealthy man. I have an overflowing travel bank account, and I can live off the interest for the rest of my days. To me, the world out there is no longer mysterious and foreign; it's just, well, the world.

It was a privilege and honor to travel the world with Remote Year, the company. Their systems and people were top-notch. They pioneered the digital nomad lifestyle and created a community out of thin air. Much respect to them! In my travels, it was never about how many places I got to see or how many adventures I got to check off my bucket list. It was, above all, about the journey, not the destination. What I saw with my own eyes has forever made me a humbler man. I am humbled because it is only by chance I was raised not in the Wildflower Home in Thailand by a single mother, but by a prosperous immigrant family in America. My birth karma could have me confined to a wheelchair with my arms and head strapped down, like I saw at the Mother Theresa orphanage in Cusco, Peru. Giving back this year was more than just writing a check at some black-tie charity event. The value was in the *doing* and in the *seeing*. I only wish I had done more to help others, but I have joy knowing that I can do more going forward. The smallest give-back felt better than making any amount of money. One of the ways of giving back was sharing the vegan message in some far-flung places. But it was never about me: it was, and still is, about helping people help themselves. Moreover, I think humanity will best be served when we stop trying to change others, but instead endeavor to change ourselves. My dream is that when a vegan walks into a room, even without him or her saying a word ... everyone turns vegan! Truly, I am a vegan in a not-yet-vegan world.

And although this story of my travels ends here, my life journey continues. Life *should* be an adventure. And I hope that this book has inspired you to make *your* life adventurous and extraordinary.

Have laptop? Go travel!

Acknowledgments

That this memoir is now a reality is nothing short of a milestone for me. From the outset, though, I wanted nothing to do with adding my name to the list of biographies that were self-serving or focused on so-called accomplishments. With my story, I have sought to inspire others to embark on their own voyage of self-discovery through travel. I hope I have done just that.

I have learned that life is not only an adventure, but it's also a team sport. Words won't capture my feelings here, but I'll try anyway by acknowledging and giving gratitude to some very special souls who helped birth this book.

LAUREN DEWITT, MY MEMOIR PROJECT MANAGER: I am grateful for all your hard work and dedication. Thank you for sticking with me on this project to completion. I am so grateful for you, my Mangata sister.

ABBY LODMER, THE CONSCIOUS COMEDIAN: Thank you, vegan sister, for coaching me along and always being so helpful and inspiring.

LOUIS AND HELEN NICOZISIS: Thank you, my dear parents, for always being parents!

LEXY AVERSA: Your motherly love and strategic guidance were crucial. Thank you so much.

BEST SELLER PUBLISHING: Thank you for believing in my project and getting it into the hands of many.

CARISSA KRANTZ: Thank you for your legal contributions, your informed opinion, and for giving the world BevVeg!

DEL STAECKER, BEST SELLING AUTHOR: Your initial words of advice became my strategic guidance throughout. Much gratitude!

MY MANGATA BROTHERS AND SISTERS: Vince, Addison, Josh, Curtis, Money Matt, Movie Matt, Trevor, and Dillon, Kristiana, Lauren, Christina, to name a few. To all the Mango nomads, including each one of my roommates during the Remote Year journey: *I love you all!*

REMOTE YEAR: Laura and Jolanda, you are the greatest Remote Year program leaders. Thanks for putting up with us at **mangatasupport@ remoteyear.com**. And Travis King at Remote Year Corporate—thanks for inspiring me to hang in there for 12 months and teaching us valuable lessons from the get-go.

CINDY AND LIZ: My secretaries who cheerfully made my remote life possible.

WILL AND MADELEINE TUTTLE: For me to be a small part of the international vegan movement that you lead is the privilege of a lifetime.

BRIAN AND ANNA MARIA CLEMENT, PAM BLUE: Your work at Hippocrates inspires me and countless others. Thank you for your life's work and leading us in this Army of Love.

ALL OF THE VEGAN ACTIVISTS I MET AND CAME TO LOVE LIKE FAMILY (IN NO PARTICULAR ORDER): Animal Friends Croatia, Lucas, Giselle, Aniket, Shankar, Dr. Vythi, Dr. Kamal, David and Rima, Saori, Nadia, Ian and Bibi, Maria and Santi, Dr. Henry, Yin Yin, Susan, Shara, Dr. Jayanthy, Dr. Nandita, and many others.

FRIENDS AND FAMILY WHO KEPT THE HOME FIRES BURNING: Alicia, Naveen, Karen and Brett, Sammy, Stuey, Jim, Rothy and Irina, Adam, Geoff, Jeannie and Kenny, Jonathan, Jeff, Doug, Amelia, Angela, Katherine, Leonard, just to name a few. Keeping in touch gave me great comfort and made the journey seem less distant.

NEW FRIENDS I MADE ALONG THE WAY: Even if we met only for a day, you proved that there are nice people everywhere!

Giving Back

*10% of the gross proceeds from this book will directly go to the Wildflower
Home in in Chiang Mai, Thailand (www.wildflowerhomeshop.com)*

About the Author

Philip Nicozisis is a public speaker, American vegan activist, traveler, and health educator from Hippocrates Health Institute. He is also a World Peace Diet facilitator, experienced businessman, real estate investor, PADI Divemaster, published songwriter, and musician based in West Palm Beach, FL.

Nicozisis changed his health and his heart with a switch to a plant-based diet. Since then, he has become an international speaker on veganism and has given presentations in several countries in South and North America, Europe, South Asia, and East Asia.

Itty-Bitty Glossary

COINSTEIN AND COINBERG: Nicknames I gave to my two Remote Year brothers. Both were early bitcoin investors but they also traded in alternative cryptocurrency coins.

DIGITAL NOMAD: A location-independent professional who can work from anywhere in the world so long as there is access to WI-FI.

GLOWTROTTER: An intrepid traveler who traverses the globe often and with ease.

MACHU PICCHU: The locale shown on the cover of this book, from where I simulated the digital nomad lifestyle, is a UNESCO World Heritage site. It is an ancient Incan citadel set high in the Andes Mountains in Peru, above the Urubamba River valley. Built in the 15th century and later abandoned, it's renowned for its sophisticated dry-stone walls that fuse huge blocks without the use of mortar—intriguing buildings that play on astronomical alignments and panoramic views. Besides all that, it boasts one the best views this side of heaven!

MANGATA: The name given to our Remote Year group of digital nomad travelers. It's a Swedish word for the road-like reflection that the moon makes over a body of water.

Mangos: The nickname given to the digital nomads of Mangata

Track: Curated, authentic, local experiences designed to immerse the Mangos in the unique aspects of each of the international homes throughout the year. They are like field trips, but not the kind a tourist would even know about.

Tramily: The traveling family of the Mangata digital nomads. We started out as 49 strangers on day one, and at the end of 12 months, we were down to 30.

Sparky, Sparkies: The nickname I give to all foreign currency that is not a U.S. dollar.

Remote Year (RY): I proudly traveled with Remote Year. They are a company that curates work and travel programs for location-independent professionals to work remotely from cities around the world without having to quit their jobs. Digital nomads join a year-long program and follow an itinerary with a group of like-minded participants from a variety of backgrounds, forming lifelong and borderless relationships along the way.

Coming soon from Phil:

To keep in touch with Phil about the forthcoming release of *The Vegan Manifesto*, or to request him as a speaker, contact: **pnicozisis@gmail.com** or visit **www.theveganmanifesto.co**